54

EVERYMAN'S LIBRARY

491

POETRY & DRAMA

Everyman, I will go with thee, and be thy guide,
In thy most need to go by thy side

MINOR ELIZABETHAN DRAMA

IN TWO VOLUMES: VOLUME ONE

PRE-SHAKESPEAREAN TRAGEDIES

INTRODUCTION BY
ASHLEY THORNDIKE

LONDON J. M. DENT & SONS LTD
NEW YORK E. P. DUTTON & CO INC

© Introduction, J. M. Dent & Sons Ltd, 1958
All rights reserved
Made in Great Britain
at the
Aldine Press · Letchworth · Herts
for
J. M. DENT & SONS LTD
Aldine House · Bedford Street · London
First published in this edition 1910
Last reprinted 1960

INTRODUCTION

THE dramas written during the first thirty years of Elizabeth's reign are not easily arranged in categories. They deal with many kinds of subjects, and they recall many different models. Any single play, in fact, is sure to reveal in some measure the conflicting influences of the two great traditions that were then struggling for mastery. The mediæval religious drama, with its miracles and moralities, had been for centuries virtually the only dramatic tradition existing; but by 1559, in England, as elsewhere in Europe, the new learning had brought to men's knowledge the tragedies and comedies of Greece and Rome. Although miracle plays had nearly ceased, their chief characteristics long survived: their epic structure, their adherence to the method of translation, their mixture of the terrible and the ludicrous, their medley of persons from all walks in life, and their readiness to exhibit anything whatever on the stage. And, although moralities were already losing their pre-eminence, abstractions figuring as characters in a symbolic presentation of life continued to be common until Shakespeare's time. The classical models, on the other hand, were winning imitators as well as admirers. By translations, by neo-Latin or vernacular imitations, by adaptations of biblical story to Terentian or Senecan form, by dramatisation of classical story or myth, and by many other processes, they were becoming familiar to actors and play-goers at court, school, and even in public theatres. While, as Sir Philip Sidney complained, there were very few "right comedies" or "right tragedies," there were an increasing number which showed that their authors had studied classical theory and practice.

The classical models adopted for tragedy were not, however, the Greek plays, but those of the Roman philosopher Seneca. These are but inferior rhetorical imitations of the Athenian masterpieces, but they won the unstinted admiration of the Renaissance. In England, as in every other nation of Western Europe, they were read in school and college, translated into the vernacular, and became the common property of all educated men. Moreover, although they were probably never acted in Rome, they were accepted by the Elizabethans as stage plays, and all their characteristics were applied to stage performance. Their stories, drawn from the most bloody and revolting of the Greek myths and tracing crimes to their final horrible retribution, as well as their brilliant and elaborate poetic diction, delighted both scholars and public. Cultured men of letters strove to create an English drama modelled in all respects upon Seneca, retaining his structure, chorus, unities of time and place, along with his sensational themes and showy style. Fortunately, however, the public theatres had created a popular demand which could not endure such solecisms, and they soon attracted poets of independent genius who preferred the licence of the public taste to the narrow laws of the scholars. Meanwhile, however, Seneca served as a standard to define tragedy. If the popular dramatist did not produce "right tragedy," he was nevertheless conscious of his model. He wrote of adultery, lust, lawless ambition, murder, and revenge, and he gave these themes all the poetical embellishments he could devise. Even popular tragedies were generally confined to the affairs of princes or persons of high rank, and dealt with a reversal of fortune, the downfall of a prince, the ruin of a kingdom, or the punishment of some monstrous crime.

"Gorboduc" (1565, acted 1562), the first English tragedy, was a definite attempt to follow the examples of Italy and France and to initiate English tragedy in strict conformity to the Senecan model. It was written by two gentlemen of standing, both at court and in letters, Thomas Norton and Thomas Sackville, afterwards Lord Buckhurst; and it was performed by the gentlemen of the Inner Temple as a part of their elaborate Christmas entertainment for the queen in 1561-2. The story of a fratricide and the resulting murders and wars was selected from English legend because of its likeness to Seneca's "Thebais;" and the long declamations, the chorus, the division into five acts, the messengers, and the narration of events, all follow Senecan practice. But even in "Gorboduc" the

Introduction vii

unities of time and place are violated, and the interminable debates are like those in the moralities rather than those in Seneca. The structure, too, is really narrative and not dramatic, and the dumb-shows between the acts introduce spectacles foreign to the classical drama. "Gorboduc" was followed by several other English Senecan plays, "Jocasta," "Tancred and Gismunda," and "The Misfortunes of Arthur," all written for special occasions and performed by amateurs before the queen. These, along with some lost university plays, represent the attempt and the failure to bind English tragedy to Seneca. Sidney praised "Gorboduc," and Bacon assisted in "The Misfortunes of Arthur;" but the Senecan devotees won hardly a nod from Poetry and Imagination. These awaited the call of the public playhouses.

By the time that Shakespeare began his career, nearly twenty years after the performance of "Gorboduc," the companies of professional actors were securely established in London. They had built playhouses, won the favour of the court and the patronage of a large public, and were beginning to attract brilliant young men from the universities as playwrights. Tragedy by this time was well initiated as a species of the popular drama. To be sure, the species was not closely defined, and it existed without support of criticism or theory, but it already comprised a number of plays that were written in ambitious verse and dealt with momentous and direful events, heroic and extraordinary persons, and atrocious crimes. Sensational and bloody, they appealed to an audience which was familiar with cruelty and brutality in its daily life, and which read history in the light of the career of Mary Stuart and the Massacre of St. Bartholomew. Intent mainly on exhibiting the striking incidents of a story, careless of structure, eager for incongruity, they appealed to an audience which came to the theatre craving a startling story and which liked to have its emotions mixed. Grandiose in theme and style, audacious in their extravagant romanticism, they satisfied the desire for novelty, adventure, and fantasy which was shared by illiterate apprentice and aspiring poet. The audience welcomed verbal fireworks as well as gruesome murder; and while it required an exciting story, it was willing enough that the poet should give this splendid verse and imaginative idealism.

The chief creator of this popular tragedy was Christopher Marlowe. His plays are contained in another volume of Everyman's Library, and need not be considered here; but any account of the pre-Shakespearean drama must be at pains to emphasise his importance. His plays deal with prodigious desires and the failures which inevitably result, and their dramatic interest centres upon the volitional struggles of their mighty protagonists. Marlowe freed himself from all allegiance to Senecan technique or diction, and devoted himself valiantly to the public theatres, providing his actors with great parts, his audience with sensation, spectacle, and rant, and the drama with genuine passion and exuberant poetry. His tragedies formed a type and set a fashion; and for several years all blank verse echoed his cadences, and the London stages witnessed ranting conquerors like Tamburlaine, monstrous villains like Barabbas, and death scenes like those of Faustus and Edward II. Shakespeare was his pupil, and in "Richard III." adopted his methods, and in "Richard II." and "The Merchant of Venice" wrote in emulation if no longer in imitation.

Only second to Marlowe in influence upon the pre-Shakespearian writers of tragedy was Thomas Kyd; and his influence is in most respects readily distinguishable from that of his greater rival. He was a "Senecal man." He translated the "Cornelia" of the French Senecan, Garnier; and in the one play on which his fame securely rests, "The Spanish Tragedy" (1592, acted 1588), he adapted a Senecan theme, and to some extent Senecan technique, to the popular stage. The main theme of revenge, the ghost, what there is left of the chorus, the philosophising, the introspection, the rhetorical antitheses and repetitions, are all Senecan. But Kyd was a born playwright, and he knew his theatre. In the main, the play was a crude, cumbrous, but powerful melodrama, so effective in its startling situations that it won an instantaneous, enormous, and long-continued popularity. Even the reader of to-day may find in its absurdities and bombast a not wholly powerless presentation of the struggle of the human will against evil and destiny.

Introduction

Imitations of "The Spanish Tragedy" were many. Shrieking ghosts, soliloquising avengers, and Machiavellian villains became hardly less common than Tamburlaine-like protagonists. "Titus Andronicus," whatever may have been Shakespeare's share in its composition, belongs to Kyd's school, as does "Soliman and Perseda," somewhat doubtfully attributed to Kyd himself. Another play attributed to Kyd is the original "Hamlet," not extant but certainly acted by 1589, a dozen years before Shakespeare wrote his "Hamlet," and almost certainly used by Shakespeare as the basis of his play. In "The Spanish Tragedy" Kyd had dealt with the revenge of a father for a murdered son; in "Hamlet" he dealt, probably in a similar fashion, with the revenge of a son for a father. These two plays made the beginning of a long series of revenge tragedies, distinguished, like "The Spanish Tragedy," by the presentation of ghosts, insanity, diabolic intrigue, physical horrors, much philosophising, and copious slaughter. Ben Jonson, in his "Additions" to Kyd's play, Chapman, Webster, Shirley, and others, endowed the species with far greater poetry and more searching psychology than Kyd could muster. But his was the conception of the avenger hesitating and irresolute in the face of overpowering evil—a conception which Shakespeare transformed into the eternally puzzling moods of Hamlet.

Most of the tragedies written between the dates of "The Spanish Tragedy" and Shakespeare's "Hamlet" exhibit a large indebtedness to Marlowe or Kyd, or to both; but there were various departures from their methods. One of these is exemplified by Peele's "David and Bethsabe" (1599, acted c. 1590); another by the realistic "Arden of Feversham" (1592, acted c. 1590), often attributed in part to Shakespeare, but without any evidence.

George Peele was a versatile and facile poet who began his dramatic career at Oxford, where he made a version of one of the "Iphigenias" of Euripides, and who was later in London the friend of Nash, Greene, and Marlowe, and the author of a number of plays of various modes. "David and Bethsabe" is unique among extant tragedies of its time in its use of a biblical story, but otherwise it offers little that was novel in dramatic art. In structure and characterisation it offers no advance on the average play of the period. Its most notable characteristic is undoubtedly its poetic style. This is generally monotonous and often absurd, as in the notorious passages where Absalom plays with conceits for many lines while hanging by his hair, and again for many lines after he has been stabbed. But Peele was famous as "primus verborum artifex," and he let no chance for poetry go by. No matter what the situation of his characters, he made them sing sweetly, and no matter what subjects were proposed, he could turn them to melodious and graceful fancy. And his play is not without charm and loveliness. It does not give us reality or wisdom or truth; it carries us into a world of verbal felicity, of music and fancy—a world that the Elizabethans loved, where the author of "Romeo and Juliet" was king.

"Arden of Feversham" represents tendencies in the drama opposite to those of "David and Bethsabe," and in the main counter to those prevailing in Elizabethan tragedy. It relates the history of a nearly contemporaneous murder, and is the earliest domestic tragedy extant. There had probably been earlier dramatisations of notorious criminal cases, and "Arden" makes the most of the public's morbid curiosity. But its author seems also to have designed a protest against current dramatic fashions. The tragedies of the day were concerned with kings and courts and state affairs; he would write of private men and domestic affairs. They were concerned with past events and remote scenes; he would write of English events of his own time. They sought to render their stories impressive by all the graces of imagery and ornament; he would tell the true story of an actual crime and let it point its own moral. He opposed the romanticism of the day with the creed of the realist.

> Gentlemen, we hope youle pardon this naked tragedy,
> Wherein no filed points are foisted in
> To make it gratious to the eare or eye;
> For simple truth is gratious enough,
> And needes no other points of glosing stuffe.

"Arden of Feversham" was followed by a number of criminal plays in the Elizabethan period, and in the eighteenth century it was revived by Lillo and perhaps influenced him in his "George Barnwell." None of its successors has surpassed it in its vivid presentation of facts, but the play does not merit half the laudation it has received. It borrows from Marlowe and Kyd, and its realism is tedious and over-detailed. Its unquestioned triumph lies in its portraiture of Alice Arden. No other evil woman in the drama before Lady Macbeth is comparable to her in verisimilitude.

"Arden of Feversham" might also be instanced as an example of plays based on the chronicles, for it follows Holinshed closely. Most of the chronicle plays, however, dealt with English history in a larger way, and they make up a loosely defined group. A considerable number of these have tragic themes and resemblances to some of the tragedies already discussed. Perhaps the most typical examples are the three parts of "Henry VI." In these Shakespeare had a share, but Marlowe's influence, if not his hand, is dominant. They form a panorama of Henry's long reign arranged to emphasise the "falls of princes;" and Shakespeare in "Richard III." carried on the tale to the downfall of the arch-villain and the triumph of the Tudor dynasty. Outside of the Shakespeare Folio the best tragic chronicle play is Marlowe's "Edward II."

With additions from these chronicle histories and the all-important work of Marlowe, the four plays in this volume illustrate the various essays and the most important tendencies in the beginnings of English tragedy. They indicate the way in which the field was prepared for Shakespeare; and their chief interest for us to-day is doubtless in their illustration of the conditions which he faced. They reveal themes, characters, stories, motives, stage effects, and traits of style which were examples and incentives for him. Under their tutelage he served his apprenticeship in dramatic art.

Naturally they suffer in comparison with his far more successful achievement. No one of the four plays is admirable as a whole. Only here and there, for a situation, a conception, a character, or a line—in the depiction of Alice Arden, in a verse here and there of Peele's, or a dramatic conception of Kyd's—can our praise become unreserved. But if we judge not by our own standards, and still less in comparison with Shakespeare, if we read these plays as the work of early pioneers of a new art and a new poetry, as novel experiments of literature to express the life and passion of a great national epoch, then there must be admiration as well as gratitude for these pioneers and pursuivants of an imperial triumph.

ASHLEY THORNDIKE.

COLUMBIA UNIVERSITY,
   NEW YORK.

NOTE TO 1933 EDITION

IN his Introduction, Professor Thorndike has already called attention to the failure of the attempt to bind English tragedy to Seneca, and of the movement which followed plays like *Gorboduc* to make tragedy a species of the popular drama; but the other three plays in the previous editions all belong to the period when that object was definitely achieved—*The Spanish Tragedy* is the earliest, and was acted in 1588, which was some thirty years after the production of *Gorboduc*. In view of the continued popularity of this volume the publishers have therefore decided to supplement the collection by adding a play belonging to this intermediary period, i.e. between *Gorboduc* and Kyd.

Cambyses was selected because it is being increasingly recognized as having great significance for English tragedy, and because it has remained almost inaccessible for the ordinary reader. The defects of the play are very obvious —its crude dramatic effects and awkward writing, and the bombast which Shakespeare parodied in Falstaff; but for all that it reveals in some measure all the characteristics of English drama of the later and greater Elizabethan period, and lacks only style and genius.

The text of the play has been modernized to a great extent, following the example set by the other plays, but every edition—including the original quarto—has been consulted, and it is hoped that the result is a satisfactory one for the ordinary reader and student. The Glossary at the end of the volume has been revised for this edition.

Select Bibliography

NOTE TO 1958 EDITION

A FEW statements in the Introduction now need correction or modification: " Richard II " may have slightly preceded " Edward II "; " The Spanish Tragedy " was probably first performed late in 1587; Thomas Dekker, rather than Ben Jonson, seems to be the author of the extant additions to this play; Shakespeare is widely regarded as the sole author of the three parts of " Henry VI."

R. G. HOWARTH.

SELECT BIBLIOGRAPHY

NORTON AND SACKVILLE. *Gorboduc*, first acted 1560–1, by the Gentlemen of the Inner Temple; 4to, 1565; later authorized version, *The Tragidie of Feerex and Porrex*, 1570; reprint, 1590; reprinted in R. Dodsley's *Old Plays*, 1744, 1780; in T. Hawkins's *Origin of the English Drama*, vol. i, 1773; in Sir W. Scott's *Ancient British Drama*, 1810; ed. W. D. Cooper (Shakespearean Society), 1847; ed. L. Toulmin Smith (Vollmoeller, *Englische Sprache-ü Literatur Denkmale*), 1883; in J. S. Farmer's *Early English Dramatists*, 1906; in J. S. Farmer's *Tudor Facsimile Texts*, 1908; and in A. K. McIlwraith's *Five Elizabethan Tragedies*, 1938.

SACKVILLE's *Works*. Reprinted in 1820; ed. R. W. Sackville-West, 1859.

THOMAS KYD. *The Spanish Tragedie, containing the lamentable end of Don Horatio and Bel-imperia, with the pitiful death of olde Hieronymo*, 4to, undated (? 1594); 4to, 1594; 4to, 1599; 1602 and later issues included new additions of the Painter's part and others; two entries in Henslowe's *Diary* speak of money advanced to Ben Jonson for these additions, but a doubt is nevertheless thrown on his authorship, the credit of five passages having been given to Webster, Dekker, or even Shakespeare; reprinted in R. Dodsley's *Old Plays*, ed. W. C. Hazlitt, vol. iii, 1874; ed. J. Shick (Temple Dramatists), 1898; W. W. Greg (1602 text, Malone Society), 1925; in A. K. McIlwraith's *Five Elizabethan Tragedies*, 1938; ed. W. W. Greg and D. Nichol Smith (Malone Society), 1949.

Works. Ed. F. S. Boas, 1901, 1955 (with supplement).

GEORGE PEELE. *Old Wives' Tale*, 4to, 1595; ed. F. B. Gummere (C. M. Gayley's *Representative English Comedies*, vol. 1), 1903; ed. W. W. Greg (Malone Society), 1908; *The Love of King David and Fair Bethsabe, with the Tragedie of Absalon*, 4to, 1599; in T. Hawkins's *Origin of the English Drama*, 1773; in J. M. Manly's *Specimens of Pre-Shakespearean Drama*, 1897; in A. K. McIlwraith's *Five Elizabethan Comedies*, 1934; and ed. W. W. Greg (Malone Society), 1912.

Works. Ed. A. Dyce, 1828, 1829–39; and with Greene's works, 1861; *Plays and Poems*, with Introduction by H. Morley (Morley's Universal Library), vol. lii, 1887; ed. A. H. Bullen, 1888; *Life and Minor Works*, ed. D. H. Horne, 1952.

The lamentable and true tragedie of Master Arden of Feversham in

Kent, doubtfully ascribed to Shakespeare, 4to, 1592, 1599, 1633; reprint, 1770; with Introduction by A. H. Britten, 1887; ed. R. Bayne (Temple Dramatists), 1897; with Introduction by A. F. Hopkinson (*Shakespeare's Doubtful Plays*), 1907; in C. F. T. Brooks's *Shakespeare Apocrypha*, 1908; in A. K. McIlwraith's *Five Elizabethan Tragedies*, 1938; ed. H. Macdonald (Malone Society), 1947.

NICHOLAS UDALL. *Ralph Roister Doister*, ?1577; reprinted, 1818, 1821; published in T. White's *Old English Drmaa*, 1830; by Shakespeare Society, 184); in *Arber's English Reprints*, 1869, 1895; and in Hazlitt's edition of R. Dodsley's *Old Plays*, vol. iii, 1874; ed. W. H. Williams and P. A. Robins (Temple Dramatists), 1901; ed. E. Flügel (Representative English Comedies), 1903; ed. C. G. Child, 1913; in F. S. Boas's *Five Pre-Shakespearean Comedies*, 1934; ed. W. W. Greg (Malone Society), 1935.

Works. J. S. Farmer (Early English Dramatists), 1906 (Museum Dramatists), 1907.

JOHN LYLY. *Endimion, The Man in the Moone*, 4to, 1591; in R. Dodsley's *Old Plays*, vol. i, 1814; ed. G. P. Baker, 1894.

Works. Ed. F. W. Fairholt, 1858; ed. R. W. Bond, 3 vols., 1902.

ROBERT GREENE. *The Honorable Historie of frier Bacon and frier Bongay*, 4to, 1594, 1630, 1655; in R. Dodsley's *Old Plays*, ed. J. P. Collier, vol. viii, 1826; in Sir A. W. Ward's *Old English Drama*, 1878; in C. M. Gayley's *Representative English Comedies*, vol. i, 1903; ed. W. W. Greg (Malone Society), 1926; in A. K. McIlwraith's *Five Elizabethan Comedies*, 1934; and ed. B. Cellini (with *John of Bordeaux, or the Second Part of Friar Bacon*), 1953; *The Scottish Historie of James the fourth, slaine at Flodden, entermixed with a pleasant Comedie presented by Oboram, King of Fayeries*, 4to, 1598; in J. M. Manly's *Specimens of Pre-Shakespearean Drama*, 1897; ed. A. E. Swaen and W. W. Greg (Malone Society), 1921.

Works. Plays, ed. A. Dyce, 1831; revised edition (Dramatic and Poetical), with Peele's works, 1861; complete works, 15 vols., ed. Dr Grosart, 1881–6; *Plays and Poems*, ed. J. Churton Collins, 1905; T. H. Dickinson (Mermaid Series), 1909.

THOMAS PRESTON. *A lam ntable Tragedie, mixed full of plesant mirth, containing the life of Cambises, king of Persia*, 4to, ?1569, ?1585; in T. Hawkins's *Origin of the English Drama*, vol. i, 1773; in Hazlitt's edition of R. Dodsley's *Old Plays*, vol. iv, and ed. J. M. Manly (*Specimens of Pre-Shakespearean Drama*), 1897.

CONTENTS

	PAGE
INTRODUCTION: by Ashley Thorndike	v
GORBODUC: by Thomas Norton and Thomas Sackville (Lord Buckhurst)	1
ARDEN OF FEVERSHAM	55
DAVID AND BETHSABE: by George Peele	125
THE SPANISH TRAGEDY: by Thomas Kyd	183
CAMBYSES, KING OF PERSIA: by Thomas Preston	273
GLOSSARY	319

GORBODUC

THE ARGUMENT

GORBODUC, King of Britain, divided his realm in his life time to his sons, Ferrex and Porrex. The sons fell to dissension. The younger killed the elder. The mother, that more dearly loved the elder, for revenge killed the younger. The people, moved with the cruelty of the fact, rose in rebellion, and slew both father and mother. The nobility assembled, and most terribly destroyed the rebels; and afterwards, for want of issue of the Prince, whereby the succession of the crown became uncertain, they fell to civil war, in which both they and many of their issues were slain, and the land for a long time almost desolate and miserably wasted.

DRAMATIS PERSONÆ

GORBODUC, *King of Great Britain.*
VIDENA, *Queen, and wife to King Gorboduc.*
FERREX, *Elder son to King Gorboduc.*
PORREX, *Younger son to King Gorboduc.*
CLOTYN, *Duke of Cornwall.*
FERGUS, *Duke of Albany.*
MANDUD, *Duke of Loegris.*
GWENARD, *Duke of Cumberland.*
EUBULUS, *Secretary to the King.*
AROSTUS, *a Counsellor to the King.*
DORDAN, *a Counsellor assigned by the King to his eldest son, Ferrex.*
PHILANDER, *a Counsellor assigned by the King to his youngest son, Porrex.*
Both being of the old king's council before.
HERMON, *a Parasite remaining with Ferrex.*
TYNDAR, *a Parasite remaining with Porrex.*
NUNTIUS, *a Messenger of the elder brother's death.*
NUNTIUS, *a Messenger of Duke Fergus rising in arms.*
MARCELLA, *a Lady of the Queen's privy-chamber.*
CHORUS, *four ancient and sage men of Britain.*

GORBODUC

THE ORDER OF THE DUMB SHOW BEFORE THE FIRST ACT, AND THE SIGNIFICATION THEREOF.

First, the music of violins began to play, during which came in upon the stage six wild men, clothed in leaves. Of whom the first bare on his neck a fagot of small sticks, which they all, both severally and together, assayed with all their strength to break; but it could not be broken by them. At the length, one of them pulled out one of the sticks, and brake it: and the rest plucking out all the other sticks, one after another, did easily break them, the same being severed; which being conjoined, they had before attempted in vain. After they had this done, they departed the stage, and the music ceased. Hereby was signified, that a state knit in unity doth continue strong against all force, but being divided, is easily destroyed; as befell upon Duke Gorboduc dividing his land to his two sons, which he before held in monarchy; and upon the dissension of the brethren, to whom it was divided.

ACT I

SCENE I

VIDENA. FERREX.

Vid. The silent night that brings the quiet pause,
    From painful travails of the weary day,
    Prolongs my careful thoughts, and makes me blame
    The slow Aurore, that so for love or shame
    Doth long delay to show her blushing face,
    And now the day renews my griefful plaint.
Fer. My gracious lady, and my mother dear,
    Pardon my grief for your so grieved mind
    To ask what cause tormenteth so your heart.

Vid. So great a wrong and so unjust despite,
    Without all cause against all course of kind![1]
Fer. Such causeless wrong, and so unjust despite,
    May have redress, or, at the least, revenge.
Vid. Neither, my son; such is the froward will,
    The person such, such my mishap and thine.
Fer. Mine know I none, but grief for your distress.
Vid. Yes; mine for thine, my son. A father? no:
    In kind a father, not in kindliness.
Fer. My Father? why, I know nothing at all,
    Wherein I have misdone unto his grace.
Vid. Therefore, the more unkind to thee and me.
    For, knowing well, my son, the tender love
    That I have ever borne, and bear to thee;
    He grieved thereat, is not content alone,
    To spoil thee of my sight, my chiefest joy,
    But thee, of thy birth-right and heritage,
    Causeless, unkindly, and in wrongful wise,
    Against all law and right, he will bereave:
    Half of his kingdom he will give away.
Fer. To whom?
Vid.   Even to Porrex, his younger son;
    Whose growing pride I do so sore suspect,
    That, being rais'd to equal rule with thee,
    Methinks I see his envious heart to swell,
    Fill'd with disdain and with ambitious hope.
    The end the gods do know, whose altars I
    Full oft have made in vain of cattle slain
    To send the sacred smoke to Heaven's throne,
    For thee, my son, if things do so succeed,
    As now my jealous mind misdeemeth sore.
Fer. Madam, leave care and careful plaint for me.
    Just hath my father been to every wight:
    His first injustice he will not extend
    To me, I trust, that give no cause thereof;
    My brother's pride shall hurt himself, not me.
Vid. So grant the gods! But yet, thy father so
    Hath firmly fixed his unmoved mind,
    That plaints and prayers can no whit avail;
    For those have I assay'd, but even this day
    He will endeavour to procure assent

[1] Nature.

      Of all his council to his fond devise. 50
Fer. Their ancestors from race to race have borne
      True faith to my forefathers and their seed:
      I trust they eke [1] will bear the like to me.
Vid. There resteth all. But if they fail thereof,
      And if the end bring forth an ill success,
      On them and theirs the mischief shall befall,
      And so I pray the gods requite it them;
      And so they will, for so is wont to be,
      When lords and trusted rulers under kings,
      To please the present fancy of the prince, 60
      With wrong transpose the course of governance,
      Murders, mischief, and civil sword at length,
      Or mutual treason, or a just revenge,
      When right succeeding line returns again,
      By Jove's just judgment and deserved wrath,
      Brings them to cruel and reproachful death,
      And roots their names and kindreds from the earth.
Fer. Mother, content you, you shall see the end.
Vid. The end! thy end I fear: Jove end me first!

SCENE II

GORBODUC. AROSTUS. PHILANDER. EUBULUS.

Gor. My lords, whose grave advice and faithful aid 70
      Have long upheld my honour and my realm,
      And brought me to this age from tender years,
      Guiding so great estate with great renown:
      Now more importeth me, than erst [2] to use
      Your faith and wisdom, whereby yet I reign;
      That when by death my life and rule shall cease,
      The kingdom yet may with unbroken course
      Have certain prince, by whose undoubted right
      Your wealth and peace may stand in quiet stay;
      And eke that they, whom nature hath prepared, 80
      In time to take my place in princely seat,
      While in their father's time their pliant youth
      Yields to the frame of skilful governance,
      May so be taught and trained in noble arts,

---

[1] Also.   [2] Formerly.

As what their fathers, which have reigned before,
Have with great fame derived down to them,
With honour they may leave unto their seed;
And not be thought, for their unworthy life,
And for their lawless swerving out of kind,
Worthy to lose what law and kind them gave; 90
But that they may preserve the common peace,
The cause that first began and still maintains
The lineal course of kings' inheritance,
For me, for mine, for you, and for the state
Whereof both I and you have charge and care.
Thus do I mean to use your wonted faith
To me and mine, and to your native land.
My lords, be plain without all wry respect,
Or poisonous craft to speak in pleasing wise,
Lest as the blame of ill-succeeding things 100
Shall light on you, so light the harms also.
Aros. Your good acceptance so, most noble king,
Of such our faithfulness, as heretofore
We have employed in duties to your grace,
And to this realm, whose worthy head you are,
Well proves, that neither you mistrust at all,
Nor we shall need in boasting wise to show
Our truth to you, nor yet our wakeful care
For you, for yours, and for our native land.
Wherefore, O king, I speak as one for all, 110
Sith all as one do bear you equal faith:
Doubt not to use our counsels and our aids,
Whose honours, goods, and lives are whole avow'd,
To serve, to aid, and to defend your grace.
Gor. My lords, I thank you all. This is the case:
Ye know, the gods, who have the sovereign care
For kings, for kingdoms, and for common weals,
Gave me two sons in my more lusty age,
Who now, in my decaying years, are grown
Well towards riper state of mind and strength, 120
To take in hand some greater princely charge.
As yet they live and spend their hopeful days
With me, and with their mother, here in court.
Their age now asketh other place and trade,
And mine also doth ask another change,
Theirs to more travail, mine to greater ease.

When fatal death shall end my mortal life,
My purpose is to leave unto them twain,
The realm divided in two sundry parts:
The one, Ferrex, mine elder son, shall have, 130
The other, shall the younger, Porrex, rule.
That both my purpose may more firmly stand,
And eke that they may better rule their charge,
I mean forthwith to place them in the same;
That in my life they may both learn to rule,
And I may joy to see their ruling well.
This is, in sum, what I would have you weigh:
First, whether ye allow my whole devise,
And think it good for me, for them, for you,
And for our country, mother of us all: 140
And if ye like it and allow it well,
Then, for their guiding and their governance,
Show forth such means of circumstance,
As ye think meet to be both known and kept.
Lo, this is all; now tell me your advice.
Aros. And this is much, and asketh great advice:
But for my part, my sovereign lord and king,
This do I think: Your majesty doth know,
How under you, in justice and in peace,
Great wealth and honour long we have enjoy'd: 150
So as we cannot seem with greedy minds
To wish for change of prince or governance:
But if we like your purpose and devise,
Our liking must be deemed to proceed
Of rightful reason, and of heedful care,
Not for ourselves, but for the common state,
Sith our own state doth need no better change.
I think in all as erst your grace hath said:
First, when you shall unload your aged mind
Of heavy care and troubles manifold, 160
And lay the same upon my lords, your sons,
Whose growing years may bear the burden long,
(And long I pray the gods to grant it so)
And in your life, while you shall so behold
Their rule, their virtues, and their noble deeds,
Such as their kind behighteth [1] to us all,
Great be the profits that shall grow thereof;

---

[1] To promise.

Your age in quiet shall the longer last,
Your lasting age shall be their longer stay.
For cares of kings, that rule as you have rul'd,   170
For public wealth, and not for private joy,
Do waste man's life and hasten crooked age,
With furrowed face, and with enfeebled limbs,
To draw on creeping death a swifter pace.
They two, yet young, shall bear the parted reign
With greater ease than one, now old, alone
Can wield the whole, for whom much harder is
With lessened strength the double weight to bear.
Your eye, your counsel, and the grave regard
Of father, yea, of such a father's name,   180
Now at beginning of their sundred reign,
When is the hazard of their whole success,
Shall bridle so their force of youthful heats,
And so restrain the rage of insolence,
Which most assails the young and noble minds,
And so shall guide and train in temper'd stay
Their yet green bending wits with reverend awe,
As now inur'd with virtues at the first,
Custom, O king, shall bring delightfulness,
By use of virtue, vice shall grow in hate.   190
But if you so dispose it, that the day
Which ends your life, shall first begin their reign,
Great is the peril, what will be the end,
When such beginning of such liberties,
Void of such stays as in your life do lie,
Shall leave them free to random of their will,
An open prey to traitorous flattery,
The greatest pestilence of noble youth:
Which peril shall be past, if in your life,
Their temper'd youth with aged father's awe   200
Be brought in ure [1] of skilful stayedness;
And in your life, their lives disposed so
Shall length your noble life in joyfulness.
Thus think I that your grace hath wisely thought,
And that your tender care of common weal
Hath bred this thought, so to divide your land,
And plant your sons to bear the present rule,
While you yet live to see their ruling well,

[1] Use, practice.

That you may longer live by joy therein.
What further means behooveful are and meet,   210
At greater leisure may your grace devise,
When all have said, and when we be agreed
If this be best, to part the realm in twain,
And place your sons in present government:
Whereof, as I have plainly said my mind,
So would I hear the rest of all my lords.
Phil. In part I think as hath been said before;
In part, again, my mind is otherwise.
As for dividing of this realm in twain,
And lotting out the same in equal parts   220
To either of my lords, your grace's sons,
That think I best for this your realm's behoof,
For profit and advancement of your sons,
And for your comfort and your honour eke:
But so to place them while your life do last,
To yield to them your royal governance,
To be above them only in the name
Of father, not in kingly state also,
I think not good for you, for them, nor us.
This kingdom, since the bloody civil field   230
Where Morgan slain did yield his conquer'd part
Unto his cousin's sword in Camberland,[1]
Containeth all that whilom did suffice
Three noble sons of your forefather Brute;
So your two sons it may suffice also,
The more the stronger, if they 'gree in one.
The smaller compass that the realm doth hold,
The easier is the sway thereof to wield,
The nearer justice to the wronged poor,
The smaller charge, and yet enough for one.   240
And when the region is divided so
That brethren be the lords of either part,
Such strength doth nature knit between them both,
In sundry bodies by conjoined love,
That, not as two, but one of doubled force,
Each is to other as a sure defence:

[1] The event here alluded to is recorded in the History of Geoffrey of Monmouth, b. ii. c. 15. Morgan and Cunedagius, who were cousins, and nephews of Cordeilla Queen of Britain, having forcibly taken possession of the kingdom, divided it between themselves. Morgan, in his attempt afterwards to obtain the sole government, was slain by Cunedagius.

The nobleness and glory of the one
Doth sharp the courage of the other's mind,
With virtuous envy to contend for praise.
And such an equalness hath nature made   250
Between the brethren of one father's seed,
As an unkindly wrong it seems to be,
To throw the brother subject under feet
Of him, whose peer he is by course of kind;
And Nature, that did make this equalness,
Oft so repineth at so great a wrong,
That oft she raiseth up a grudging grief
In younger brethren at the elder's state:
Whereby both towns and kingdoms have been rased,
And famous stocks of royal blood destroyed: 260
The brother, that should be the brother's aid,
And have a wakeful care for his defence,
Gapes for his death, and blames the lingering years
That draw not forth his end with faster course;
And, oft impatient of so long delays,
With hateful slaughter he prevents the fates,
And heaps a just reward for brother's blood,
With endless vengeance on his stock for aye.
Such mischiefs here are wisely met withal;
If equal state may nourish equal love,   270
Where none hath cause to grudge at other's good.
But now the head to stoop beneath them both,
Ne kind, ne reason, ne good order bears.
And oft it hath been seen, where nature's course
Hath been perverted in disordered wise,
When fathers cease to know that they should rule,
The children cease to know they should obey;
And often over kindly tenderness
Is mother of unkindly stubbornness.
I speak not this in envy or reproach,   280
As if I grudg'd the glory of your sons,
Whose honour I beseech the gods increase:
Nor yet as if I thought there did remain
So filthy cankers in their noble breasts,
Whom I esteem (which is their greatest praise)
Undoubted children of so good a king.
Only I mean to show by certain rules,
Which kind hath graft within the mind of man,

That Nature hath her order and her course,
Which (being broken) doth corrupt the state 290
Of minds and things, ev'n in the best of all.
My lords, your sons, may learn to rule of you,
Your own example in your noble court
Is fittest guider of their youthful years.
If you desire to see some present joy
By sight of their well ruling in your life,
See them obey, so shall you see them rule:
Who so obeyeth not with humbleness
Will rule with outrage and with insolence.
Long may they rule, I do beseech the gods, 300
Long [1] may they learn, ere they begin to rule.
If kind and fates would suffer, I would wish
Them aged princes, and immortal kings.
Wherefore, most noble king, I well assent
Between your sons that you divide your realm,
And as in kind, so match them in degree.
But while the gods prolong your royal life,
Prolong your reign; for thereto live you here,
And therefore have the gods so long forborne 310
To join you to themselves, that still you might
Be prince and father of our common weal.
They, when they see your children ripe to rule,
Will make them room, and will remove you hence,
That yours, in right ensuing of your life,
May rightly honour your immortal name.

Eub. Your wonted true regard of faithful hearts
Makes me, O king, the bolder to presume
To speak what I conceive within my breast;
Although the same do not agree at all 320
With that which other here my lords have said,
Nor which yourself have seemed best to like.
Pardon I crave, and that my words be deem'd
To flow from hearty zeal unto your grace,
And to the safety of your common weal.
To part your realm unto my lords, your sons,
I think not good for you, ne yet for them,
But worst of all for this our native land.
Within one land, one single rule is best:
Divided reigns do make divided hearts; 330

---

[1] But long.—*Edit.* 1570.

But peace preserves the country and the prince.
Such is in man the greedy mind to reign,
So great is his desire to climb aloft,
In worldly stage the stateliest parts to bear,
That faith and justice, and all kindly love,
Do yield unto desire of sovereignty,
Where equal state doth raise an equal hope
To win the thing that either would attain.
Your grace remembereth how in passed years,
The mighty Brute, first prince of all this land,[1] 340
Possess'd the same, and rul'd it well in one:
He, thinking that the compass did suffice
For his three sons three kingdoms eke to make,
Cut it in three, as you would now in twain.
But how much British blood hath since been spilt,
To join again the sunder'd unity!
What princes slain before their timely hour!
What waste of towns and people in the land!
What treasons heap'd on murders and on spoils!
Whose just revenge ev'n yet is scarcely ceas'd, 350
Ruthful remembrance is yet raw in mind.
The gods forbid the like to chance again:
And you, O king, give not the cause thereof.
My lord Ferrex, your elder son, perhaps
(Whom kind and custom gives a rightful hope
To be your heir, and to succeed your reign)
Shall think that he doth suffer greater wrong
Than he perchance will bear, if power serve.
Porrex, the younger, so uprais'd in state,
Perhaps in courage will be rais'd also. 360
If flattery then, which fails not to assail
The tender minds of yet unskilful youth,
In one shall kindle and increase disdain,
And envy in the other's heart inflame,
This fire shall waste their love, their lives, their land,
And ruthful ruin shall destroy them both.
I wish not this, O king, so to befall,
But fear the thing, that I do most abhor.
Give no beginning to so dreadful end,
Keep them in order and obedience, 370
And let them both by now obeying you,

[1] See Geoffrey of Monmouth, book i.

Learn such behaviour as beseems their state;
The elder, mildness in his governance,
The younger, a yielding contentedness.
And keep them near unto your presence still,
That they, restrained by the awe of you,
May live in compass of well temper'd stay,
And pass the perils of their youthful years.
Your aged life draws on to feebler time,
Wherein you shall less able be to bear 380
The travails that in youth you have sustain'd,
Both in your person's and your realm's defence.
If planting now your sons in further parts,
You send them further from your present reach,
Less shall you know how they themselves demean:
Traitorous corrupters of their pliant youth
Shall have unspied a much more free access;
And if ambition and inflam'd disdain
Shall arm the one, the other, or them both,
To civil war, or to usurping pride, 390
Late shall you rue that you ne reck'd[1] before.
Good is I grant of all to hope the best,
But not to live still dreadless of the worst.
So trust the one that th' other be foreseen.
Arm not unskilfulness with princely power.
But you that long have wisely rul'd the reins
Of royalty within your noble realm,
So hold them, while the gods, for our avails,
Shall stretch the thread of your prolonged days.
Too soon he clomb into the flaming car, 400
Whose want of skill did set the earth on fire.
Time, and example of your noble Grace,
Shall teach your sons both to obey and rule.
When time hath taught them, time shall make them place,
The place that now is full: and so I pray
Long it remain, to comfort of us all.
Gor. I take your faithful hearts in thankful part:
But sith I see no cause to draw my mind,
To fear the nature of my loving sons,
Or to misdeem that envy or disdain 410
Can there work hate, where nature planteth love;
In one self purpose do I still abide.

[1] To heed, to care for.

My love extendeth equally to both,
My land sufficeth for them both also.
Humber shall part the marches of their realms:
The southern part the elder shall possess,
The northern shall Porrex, the younger, rule.
In quiet I will pass mine aged days,
Free from the travail, and the painful cares,
That hasten age upon the worthiest kings.   420
But lest the fraud, that ye do seem to fear,
Of flattering tongues, corrupt their tender youth,
And writhe them to the ways of youthful lust,
To climbing pride, or to revenging hate,
Or to neglecting of their careful charge
Lewdly to live in wanton recklessness,
Or to oppressing of the rightful cause,
Or not to wreak the wrongs done to the poor,
To tread down truth, or favour false deceit;
I mean to join to either of my sons   430
Some one of those, whose long approved faith
And wisdom tried, may well assure my heart,
That mining fraud shall find no way to creep
Into their fenced ears with grave advice.
This is the end; and so I pray you all
To bear my sons the love and loyalty
That I have found within your faithful breasts.
Aros. You, nor your sons, my sovereign lord, shall want
    Our faith and service, while our hearts do last.   [*Exeunt.*

CHORUS.

When settled stay doth hold the royal throne   440
    In steadfast place, by known and doubtless right,
And chiefly when descent on one alone
    Makes single and unparted reign to light;
Each change of course unjoints the whole estate,
And yields it thrall to ruin by debate.

The strength that knit by fast accord in one,
    Against all foreign power of mighty foes,
Could of itself defend itself alone,
    Disjoined once, the former force doth lose.

The sticks, that sunder'd brake so soon in twain,   450
In fagot bound attempted were in vain.

Oft tender mind that leads the partial eye
  Of erring parents in their children's love,
Destroys the wrongly loved child thereby.
  This doth the proud son of Apollo prove,
Who, rashly set in chariot of his sire,
Inflam'd the parched earth with heaven's fire.

And this great king that doth divide his land,
  And change the course of his descending crown,
And yields the reign into his children's hand,   460
  From blissful state of joy and great renown,
A mirror shall become to princes all,
To learn to shun the cause of such a fall.

THE ORDER AND SIGNIFICATION OF THE DUMB SHOW BEFORE THE SECOND ACT.

First, the music of cornets began to play, during which came in upon the stage a king accompanied with a number of his nobility and gentlemen. And after he had placed himself in a chair of estate prepared for him, there came and kneeled before him a grave and aged gentleman, and offered up unto him a cup of wine in a glass, which the king refused. After him comes a brave and lusty young gentleman, and presents the king with a cup of gold filled with poison, which the king accepted, and drinking the same, immediately fell down dead upon the stage, and so was carried thence away by his lords and gentlemen, and then the music ceased. Hereby was signified, that as glass by nature holdeth no poison, but is clear and may easily be seen through, ne boweth by any art; so a faithful counsellor holdeth no treason, but is plain and open, ne yieldeth to any indiscreet affection, but giveth wholesome counsel, which the ill advised prince refuseth. The delightful gold filled with poison betokeneth flattery, which under fair seeming of pleasant words beareth deadly poison, which destroyeth the prince that receiveth it. As befel in the two brethren, Ferrex and Porrex, who, refusing the wholesome advice of grave counsellors, credited these young parasites, and brought to themselves death and destruction thereby.

ACT II

SCENE I

FERREX. HERMON. DORDAN.

Fer. I marvel much what reason led the king,
My father, thus, without all my desert,
To reave me half the kingdom, which by course
Of law and nature should remain to me.
Her. If you with stubborn and untamed pride
Had stood against him in rebelling wise;
Or if, with grudging mind, you had envied

So slow a sliding of his aged years;
Or sought before your time to haste the course
Of fatal death upon his royal head;
Or stain'd your stock with murder of your kin;
Some face of reason might perhaps have seem'd
To yield some likely cause to spoil ye thus.

Fer. The wreakful gods pour on my cursed head
Eternal plagues and never-dying woes,
The hellish prince adjudge my damned ghost
To Tantale's thirst, or proud Ixion's wheel,
Or cruel Gripe [1] to gnaw my growing heart,
To during torments and unquenched flames,
If ever I conceiv'd so foul a thought,
To wish his end of life, or yet of reign.

Dor. Ne yet your father, O most noble prince,
Did ever think so foul a thing of you;
For he, with more than father's tender love,
While yet the fates do lend him life to rule,
(Who long might live to see your ruling well)
To you, my lord, and to his other son,
Lo, he resigns his realm and royalty;
Which never would so wise a prince have done,
If he had once misdeem'd that in your heart
There ever lodged so unkind a thought.
But tender love, my lord, and settled trust
Of your good nature, and your noble mind,
Made him to place you thus in royal throne,
And now to give you half this realm to guide;
Yea, and that half which, in abounding store
Of things that serve to make a wealthy realm,
In stately cities, and in fruitful soil,
In temperate breathing of the milder heaven,
In things of needful use, which friendly sea
Transports by traffic from the foreign parts,
In flowing wealth, in honour, and in force,
Doth pass the double value of the part
That Porrex hath allotted to his reign.
Such is your case, such is your father's love.

Fer. Ah love, my friends! Love wrongs not whom he loves.

Dor. Ne yet he wrongeth you, that giveth you
So large a reign, ere that the course of time

[1] Griffin.

   Bring you to kingdom by descended right,
   Which time perhaps might end your time before. 50
Fer. Is this no wrong, say you, to reave from me
   My native right of half so great a realm,
   And thus to match his younger son with me
   In equal pow'r, and in as great degree?
   Yea, and what son? The son whose swelling pride
   Would never yield one point of reverence,
   When I the elder and apparent heir
   Stood in the likelihood to possess the whole;
   Yea, and that son which from his childish age
   Envieth mine honour, and doth hate my life. 60
   What will he now do, when his pride, his rage,
   The mindful malice of his grudging heart
   Is arm'd with force, with wealth, and kingly state?
Her. Was this not wrong? yea, ill advised wrong,
   To give so mad a man so sharp a sword,
   To so great peril of so great mishap,
   Wide open thus to set so large a way?
Dor. Alas, my lord, what griefful thing is this,
   That of your brother you can think so ill?
   I never saw him utter likely sign, 70
   Whereby a man might see or once misdeem
   Such hate of you, ne such unyielding pride.
   Ill is their counsel, shameful be their end,
   That raising such mistrustful fear in you,
   Sowing the seed of such unkindly hate,
   Travail by treason to destroy you both.
   Wise is your brother, and of noble hope,
   Worthy to wield a large and mighty realm.
   So much a stronger friend have you thereby,
   Whose strength is your strength if you 'gree in one. 80
Her. If Nature and the Gods had pinched so
   Their flowing bounty, and their noble gifts
   Of princely qualities, from you, my lord,
   And pour'd them all at once in wasteful wise
   Upon your father's younger son alone;
   Perhaps there be, that in your prejudice
   Would say that birth should yield to worthiness.
   But sith in each good gift and princely art
   Ye are his match, and in the chief of all
   In mildness and in sober governance 90

Ye far surmount; and sith there is in you
Sufficing skill and hopeful towardness
To wield the whole, and match your elder's praise;
I see no cause why ye should lose the half,
Ne would I wish you yield to such a loss:
Lest your mild sufferance of so great a wrong,
Be deemed cowardice and simple dread,
Which shall give courage to the fiery head
Of your young brother to invade the whole.
While yet therefore sticks in the people's mind   100
The loathed wrong of your disheritance;
And ere your brother have, by settled power,
By guileful cloak of an alluring show,
Got him some force and favour in the realm;
And while the noble queen, your mother, lives,
To work and practise all for your avail;
Attempt redress by arms, and wreak yourself
Upon his life that gaineth by your loss,
Who now to shame of you, and grief of us,
In your own kingdom triumphs over you.   110
Show now your courage meet for kingly state,
That they which have avow'd to spend their goods,
Their lands, their lives and honours in your cause,
May be the bolder to maintain your part,
When they do see that coward fear in you
Shall not betray, ne fail their faithful hearts.
If once the death of Porrex end the strife,
And pay the price of his usurped reign,
Your mother shall persuade the angry king,
The lords, your friends, eke shall appease his rage.   120
For they be wise, and well they can foresee,
That ere long time your aged father's death
Will bring a time when you shall well requite
Their friendly favour, or their hateful spite,
Yea, or their slackness to advance your cause.
" Wise men do not so hang on passing state
Of present princes, chiefly in their age,
But they will further cast their reaching eye,
To view and weigh the times and reigns to come."
Ne is it likely, though the king be wroth,   130
That he yet will, or that the realm will bear,
Extreme revenge upon his only son:

>   Or, if he would, what one is he that dare
>   Be minister to such an enterprise?
>   And here you be now placed in your own,
>   Amid your friends, your vassals, and your strength:
>   We shall defend and keep your person safe,
>   Till either counsel turn his tender mind,
>   Or age or sorrow end his weary days.
>   But if the fear of gods, and secret grudge   140
>   Of nature's law, repining at the fact,
>   Withhold your courage from so great attempt,
>   Know ye, that lust of kingdoms hath no law.
>   The gods do bear, and well allow in kings,
>   The things that they abhor [1] in rascal routs.
>   " When kings on slender quarrels run to wars,
>   And then in cruel and unkindly wise,
>   Command thefts, rapes, murders of innocents,
>   The spoil of towns, ruins of mighty realms;
>   Think you such princes do suppose themselves   150
>   Subject to laws of kind, and fear of gods?"
>   Murders and violent thefts in private men
>   Are heinous crimes, and full of foul reproach;
>   Yet none offence, but decked with glorious name
>   Of noble conquests in the hands of kings.
>   But if you like not yet so hot devise,
>   Ne list to take such vantage of the time,
>   But, though with peril of your own estate,
>   You will not be the first that shall invade;
>   Assemble yet your force for your defence,   160
>   And for your safety stand upon your guard.
> *Dor.* O heaven! was there ever heard or known,
>   So wicked counsel to a noble prince?
>   Let me, my lord, disclose unto your grace
>   This heinous tale, what mischief it contains;
>   Your father's death, your brother's, and your own,
>   Your present murder, and eternal shame.
>   Hear me, O king, and suffer not to sink
>   So high a treason in your princely breast.
> *Fer.* The mighty gods forbid that ever I   170
>   Should once conceive such mischief in my heart.
>   Although my brother hath bereft my realm,
>   And bear, perhaps, to me an hateful mind,

---

[1] The thinges they abhor.—*Edit.* 1570.

> Shall I revenge it with his death therefore?
> Or shall I so destroy my father's life
> That gave me life? The gods forbid, I say:
> Cease you to speak so any more to me;
> Ne you, my friend, with answer once repeat
> So foul a tale. In silence let it die.
> What lord or subject shall have hope at all, 180
> That under me they safely shall enjoy
> Their goods, their honours, lands, and liberties,
> With whom, neither one only brother dear,
> Ne father dearer, could enjoy their lives?
> But, sith I fear my younger brother's rage,
> And sith, perhaps, some other man may give
> Some like advice, to move his grudging head
> At mine estate; which counsel may perchance
> Take greater force with him, than this with me;
> I will in secret so prepare myself, 190
> As, if his malice or his lust to reign
> Break forth in arms or sudden violence,
> I may withstand his rage and keep mine own.
> > *[Exeunt Ferrex and Hermon.*
>
> *Dor.* I fear the fatal time now draweth on,
> When civil hate shall end the noble line
> Of famous Brute, and of his royal seed.
> Great Jove, defend the mischiefs now at hand!
> O that the secretary's wise advice
> Had erst been heard, when he besought the king
> Not to divide his land, nor send his sons 200
> To further parts, from presence of his court,
> Ne yet to yield to them his governance.
> Lo, such are they now in the royal throne
> As was rash Phaeton in Phœbus' car;
> Ne then the fiery steeds did draw the flame
> With wilder random through the kindled skies,
> Than traitorous counsel now will whirl about
> The youthful heads of these unskilful kings.
> But I hereof their father will inform;
> The reverence of him perhaps shall stay 210
> The growing mischiefs, while they yet are green.
> If this help not, then woe unto themselves,
> The prince, the people, the divided land! *[Exit.*

SCENE II

Porrex. Tyndar. Philander.

Por. And is it thus? and doth he so prepare
    Against his brother as his mortal foe?
    And now, while yet his aged father lives?
    Neither regards he him? nor fears he me?
    War would he have? and he shall have it so.
Tyn. I saw, myself, the great prepared store
    Of horse, of armour, and of weapons there: 220
    Ne bring I to my lord reported tales,
    Without the ground of seen and searched truth.
    Lo, secret quarrels run about his court,
    To bring the name of you, my lord, in hate.
    Each man, almost, can now debate the cause,
    And ask a reason of so great a wrong,
    Why he, so noble and so wise a prince,
    Is, as unworthy, reft his heritage?
    And why the king, misled by crafty means,
    Divided thus his land from course of right? 230
    The wiser sort hold down their griefful heads;
    Each man withdraws from talk and company
    Of those that have been known to favour you:
    To hide the mischief of their meaning there,
    Rumours are spread of your preparing here.
    The rascal numbers of unskilful sort
    Are filled with monstrous tales of you and yours.
    In secret, I was counsell'd by my friends
    To haste me thence, and brought you, as you know,
    Letters from those that both can truly tell, 240
    And would not write unless they knew it well.
Phil. My lord, yet ere you move unkindly war,
    Send to your brother, to demand the cause.
    Perhaps some traitorous tales have filled his ears
    With false reports against your noble grace;
    Which, once disclos'd, shall end the growing strife,
    That else, not stay'd with wise foresight in time,
    Shall hazard both your kingdoms and your lives.
    Send to your father eke, he shall appease

  Your kindled minds, and rid you of this fear.   250
Por. Rid me of fear! I fear him not at all;
 Ne will to him, ne to my father send.
 If danger were for one to tarry there,
 Think ye it safety to return again?
 In mischiefs, such as Ferrex now intends,
 The wonted courteous laws to messengers
 Are not observ'd, which in just war they use.
 Shall I so hazard any one of mine?
 Shall I betray my trusty friends to him,
 That have disclosed his treason unto me?   260
 Let him entreat that fears; I fear him not.
 Or shall I to the king, my father, send?
 Yea, and send now, while such a mother lives,
 That loves my brother, and that hateth me?
 Shall I give leisure, by my fond delays,
 To Ferrex to oppress me all unware?
 I will not; but I will invade his realm,
 And seek the traitor prince within his court.
 Mischief for mischief is a due reward.
 His wretched head shall pay the worthy price   270
 Of this his treason and his hate to me.
 Shall I abide, and treat, and send, and pray,
 And hold my yielding throat to traitor's knife,
 While I, with valiant mind and conquering force,
 Might rid myself of foes, and win a realm?
 Yet rather, when I have the wretch's head,
 Then to the king, my father, will I send.
 The bootless case may yet appease his wrath:
 If not, I will defend me as I may.
          [Exeunt Porrex and Tyndar.
Phil. Lo, here the end of these two youthful kings!   280
 The father's death! the ruin of their realms!
 " O most unhappy state of counsellors,
 That light on so unhappy lords and times,
 That neither can their good advice be heard,
 Yet must they bear the blames of ill success."
 But I will to the king, their father, haste,
 Ere this mischief come to the likely end;
 That, if the mindful wrath of wreakful gods
 (Since mighty Ilion's fall not yet appeas'd
  With these poor remnants of the Trojan name)   290

Have not determin'd by unmoved fate,
Out of this realm to raze the British line,
By good advice, by awe of father's name,
By force of wiser lords, this kindled hate
May yet be quench'd ere it consume us all. [*Exit.*

CHORUS

When youth, not bridled with a guiding stay,
　Is left to random of their own delight,
And wields whole realms by force of sovereign sway,
　Great is the danger of unmaster'd might,
Lest skilless rage throw down, with headlong fall, 300
Their lands, their states, their lives, themselves and all.

When growing pride doth fill the swelling breast,
　And greedy lust doth raise the climbing mind,
Oh, hardly may the peril be repress'd.
　Ne fear of angry gods, ne lawes kind,
Ne country's care can fired hearts restrain,
When force hath armed envy and disdain.

When kings of foresight will neglect the rede [1]
　Of best advice, and yield to pleasing tales
That do their fancies' noisome humour feed, 310
　Ne reason nor regard of right avails.
Succeeding heaps of plagues shall teach, too late,
To learn the mischiefs of misguided state.

Foul fall the traitor false, that undermines
　The love of brethren, to destroy them both.
Woe to the prince, that pliant ear inclines,
　And yields his mind to poisonous tale that floweth
From flattering mouth! And woe to wretched land,
That wastes itself with civil sword in hand!
　Lo thus it is, poison in gold to take, 320
　And wholesome drink in homely cup forsake.

[1] Counsel.

THE ORDER AND SIGNIFICATION OF THE DUMB SHOW BEFORE THE THIRD ACT.

First, the music of flutes began to play, during which came in upon the stage, a company of mourners, all clad in black, betokening death and sorrow to ensue upon the ill-advised misgovernment and dissension of brethren, as befel upon the murder of Ferrex by his younger brother. After the mourners had passed thrice about the stage, they departed, and then the music ceased.

ACT III

SCENE I

GORBODUC. EUBULUS. AROSTUS.

Gor. O cruel fates, O mindful wrath of gods,
Whose vengeance, neither Simois' stained streams
Flowing with blood of Trojan princes slain,
Nor Phrygian fields made rank with corpses dead
Of Asian kings and lords, can yet appease;
Ne slaughter of unhappy Priam's race,
Nor Ilion's fall, made level with the soil,
Can yet suffice: but still continued rage
Pursues our lives, and from the farthest seas
Doth chase the issues of destroyed Troy.   10
" Oh, no man happy till his end be seen."
If any flowing wealth and seeming joy
In present years might make a happy wight,
Happy was Hecuba, the woefull'st wretch
That ever lived to make a mirror of;
And happy Priam, with his noble sons;
And happy I, till now, alas! I see
And feel my most unhappy wretchedness.
Behold, my lords, read ye this letter here;
Lo, it contains the ruin of our realm,   20
If timely speed provide not hasty help.

> Yet, O ye gods, if ever woeful king
> Might move ye, kings of kings, wreak it on me
> And on my sons, not on this guiltless realm:
> Send down your wasting flames from wrathful skies,
> To reave me and my sons the hateful breath.
> Read, read, my lords; this is the matter why
> I call'd ye now, to have your good advice.

The letter from DORDAN, *the Counsellor of the elder Prince.*

EUBULUS *readeth the letter.*

> My sovereign lord, what I am loath to write,
> But loathest am to see, that I am forc'd   30
> By letters now to make you understand.
> My lord Ferrex, your eldest son, misled
> By traitorous fraud of young untemper'd wits,
> Assembleth force against your younger son,
> Ne can my counsel yet withdraw the heat
> And furious pangs of his inflamed head.
> Disdain, saith he, of his disheritance
> Arms him to wreak the great pretended wrong,
> With civil sword upon his brother's life.
> If present help do not restrain this rage,   40
> This flame will waste your sons, your land, and you.
> > *Your Majesty's faithful,*
> > > *and most humble subject,*
> > > > DORDAN.

Aros. O king, appease your grief, and stay your plaint;
> Great is the matter, and a woeful case:
> But timely knowledge may bring timely help.
> Send for them both unto your presence here:
> The reverence of your honour, age, and state,
> Your grave advice, the awe of father's name,   50
> Shall quickly knit again this broken peace.
> And if in either of my lords, your sons,
> Be such untamed and unyielding pride,
> As will not bend unto your noble hests;[1]
> If Ferrex, the elder son, can bear no peer,
> Or Porrex, not content, aspires to more
> Than you him gave above his native right;

[1] Commands.

    Join with the juster side, so shall you force
    Them to agree, and hold the land in stay.
Eub. What meaneth this? Lo, yonder comes in haste 60
    Philander from my lord, your younger son.

Enter PHILANDER.

Gor. The gods send joyful news!
Phil.   The mighty Jove
    Preserve your majesty, O noble king.
Gor. Philander, welcome: but how doth my son?
Phil. Your son, sir, lives, and healthy I him left.
    But yet, O king, the want of lustful health
    Could not be half so griefful to your grace,
    As these most wretched tidings that I bring.
Gor. O heavens, yet more? no end of woes to me?
Phil. Tyndar, O king, came lately from the court 70
    Of Ferrex, to my lord your younger son,
    And made report of great prepared store
    For war, and saith that it is wholly meant
    Against Porrex, for high disdain that he
    Lives now a king, and equal in degree
    With him that claimeth to succeed the whole,
    As by due title of descending right.
    Porrex is now so set on flaming fire,
    Partly with kindled rage of cruel wrath,
    Partly with hope to gain a realm thereby, 80
    That he in haste prepareth to invade
    His brother's land, and with unkindly war
    Threatens the murder of your elder son;
    Ne could I him persuade, that first he should
    Send to his brother to demand the cause;
    Nor yet to you to stay this hateful strife.
    Wherefore sith there no more I can be heard,
    I come myself now to inform your grace,
    And to beseech you, as you love the life
    And safety of your children and your realm, 90
    Now to employ your wisdom and your force
    To stay this mischief ere it be too late.
Gor. Are they in arms? would he not send to me?
    Is this the honour of a father's name?
    In vain we travail to assuage their minds,

  As if their hearts, whom neither brother's love,
Nor father's awe, nor kingdom's cares, can move,
Our counsels could withdraw from raging heat.
Jove slay them both, and end the cursed line.
For though perhaps fear of such mighty force 100
As I, my lords, joined with your noble aids,
May yet raise, shall repress their present heat,
The secret grudge and malice will remain,
The fire not quench'd, but kept in close restraint,
Fed still within, breaks forth with double flame.
Their death and mine must 'pease the angry gods.
Phil. Yield not, O king, so much to weak despair:
Your sons yet live, and long, I trust, they shall.
If fates had taken you from earthly life,
Before beginning of this civil strife, 110
Perhaps your sons in their unmaster'd youth,
Loose from regard of any living wight,
Would run on headlong, with unbridled race,
To their own death, and ruin of this realm.
But sith the gods, that have the care for kings,
Of things and times dispose the order so,
That in your life this kindled flame breaks forth,
While yet your life, your wisdom, and your power,
May stay the growing mischief, and repress
The fiery blaze of their enkindled heat; 120
It seems, and so ye ought to deem thereof,
That loving Jove hath temper'd so the time
Of this debate to happen in your days,
That you yet living may the same appease,
And add it to the glory of your age,
And they your sons may learn to live in peace
Beware, O king, the greatest harm of all,
Lest, by your wailful plaints, your hastened death
Yield larger room unto their growing rage.
Preserve your life, the only hope of stay. 130
And if your highness herein list to use
Wisdom or force, counsel or knightly aid,
Lo we, our persons, powers, and lives are yours;
Use us till death, O king, we are your own.
Eub. Lo, here the peril that was erst foreseen,
When you, O king, did first divide your land,
And yield your present reign unto your sons.

But now, O noble prince, now is no time
To wail and plain, and waste your woeful life;
Now is the time for present good advice.   140
Sorrow doth dark the judgment of the wit.
"The heart unbroken, and the courage free
From feeble faintness of bootless despair,
Doth either rise to safety or renown
By noble valour of unvanquish'd mind,
Or yet doth perish in more happy sort."
Your grace may send to either of your sons
Some one both wise and noble personage,
Which with good counsel, and with weighty name
Of father, shall present before their eyes   150
Your hest, your life, your safety, and their own,
The present mischief of their deadly strife.
And in the while, assemble you the force
Which your commandment and the speedy haste
Of all my lords here present can prepare.
The terror of your mighty power shall stay
The rage of both, or yet of one at least.

Enter NUNTIUS.

Nun. O king, the greatest grief that ever prince did hear,
  That ever woeful messenger did tell,
  That ever wretched land hath seen before,   160
  I bring to you: Porrex your younger son
  With sudden force invaded hath the land
  That you to Ferrex did allot to rule;
  And with his own most bloody hand he hath
  His brother slain, and doth possess his realm.
Gor. O heavens, send down the flames of your revenge!
  Destroy, I say, with flash of wreakful fire
  The traitor son, and then the wretched sire!
  But let us go, that yet perhaps I may
  Die with revenge, and 'pease the hateful gods.   [*Exeunt.*

CHORUS.

  The lust of kingdom knows no sacred faith,   171
    No rule of reason, no regard of right,
  No kindly love, no fear of heaven's wrath;
    But with contempt of gods, and man's despite,

Through bloody slaughter doth prepare the ways
  To fatal sceptre and accursed reign.
The son so loathes the father's lingering days,
  Ne dreads his hand in brother's blood to stain.
O wretched prince, ne dost thou yet record
  The yet fresh murders done within the land   180
Of thy forefathers, when the cruel sword
  Bereft Morgan his life with cousin's hand?
Thus fatal plagues pursue the guilty race,
  Whose murderous hand, imbru'd with guiltless blood,
Asks vengeance still before the heaven's face,
  With endless mischiefs on the cursed brood.
The wicked child thus brings to woeful sire
  The mournful plaints to waste his very life.
Thus do the cruel flames of civil fire
  Destroy the parted reign with hateful strife.   190
And hence doth spring the well from which doth flow
The dead black streams of mourning, plaints, and woe.

THE ORDER AND SIGNIFICATION OF THE DUMB SHOW BEFORE THE FOURTH ACT

First, the music of hautboys began to play, during which there came forth from under the stage, as though out of hell, three furies, Alecto, Megæra, and Tisiphone, clad in black garments sprinkled with blood and flames, their bodies girt with snakes, their heads spread with serpents instead of hair, the one bearing in her hand a snake, the other a whip, and the third a burning firebrand : each driving before them a king and a queen ; which, moved by furies, unnaturally had slain their own children. The names of the kings and queens were these, Tantalus, Medea, Athamas, Ino, Cambyses, Althea ; after that the furies and these had passed about the stage thrice, they departed, and then the music ceased. Hereby was signified the unnatural murders to follow ; that is to say, Porrex slain by his own mother, and of king Gorboduc and queen Videna, killed by their own subjects.

ACT IV

SCENE I

VIDENA *sola.*

Why should I live, and linger forth my time
In longer life to double my distress?
O me, most woeful wight, whom no mishap
Long ere this day could have bereaved hence.
Might not these hands, by fortune or by fate,
Have pierc'd this breast, and life with iron reft?
Or in this palace here, where I so long
Have spent my days, could not that happy hour
Once, once have happ'd, in which these hugy frames
With death by fall might have oppressed me? 10
Or should not this most hard and cruel soil,
So oft where I have press'd my wretched steps,

Sometime had ruth of mine accursed life
To rend in twain, and swallow me therein?
So had my bones possessed now in peace
Their happy grave within the closed ground,
And greedy worms had gnawn this pined heart
Without my feeling pain: so should not now
This living breast remain the ruthful tomb,
Wherein my heart yielden to death is graved; 20
Nor dreary thoughts, with pangs of pining grief,
My doleful mind had not afflicted thus.
O my beloved son! O my sweet child!
My dear Ferrex, my joy, my life's delight!
Is my beloved son, is my sweet child,
My dear Ferrex, my joy, my life's delight,
Murder'd with cruel death? O hateful wretch!
O heinous traitor both to heaven and earth!
Thou, Porrex, thou this damned deed hast wrought;
Thou, Porrex, thou shalt dearly bye [1] the same. 30
Traitor to kin and kind, to sire and me,
To thine own flesh, and traitor to thyself:
The gods on thee in hell shall wreak their wrath,
And here in earth this hand shall take revenge
On thee, Porrex, thou false and caitiff wight.
If after blood so eager were thy thirst,
And murd'rous mind had so possessed thee,
If such hard heart of rock and stony flint
Liv'd in thy breast, that nothing else could like
Thy cruel tyrant's thought but death and blood: 40
Wild savage beasts, might not their slaughter serve
To feed thy greedy will, and in the midst
Of their entrails to stain thy deadly hands
With blood deserv'd, and drink thereof thy fill?
Or if nought else but death and blood of man
Might please thy lust, could none in Britain land,
Whose heart betorn out of his panting breast
With thine own hand, or work what death thou would'st,
Suffice to make a sacrifice to 'pease
That deadly mind and murderous thought in thee, 50
But he who in the selfsame womb was wrapp'd,
Where thou in dismal hour receivedst life?
Or if needs, needs thy hand must slaughter make,

[1] Abye. To abide, to suffer for.

Mightest thou not have reach'd a mortal wound,
And with thy sword have pierc'd this cursed womb
That the accursed Porrex brought to light,
And given me a just reward therefore?
So Ferrex yet sweet life might have enjoyed,
And to his aged father comfort brought,
With some young son in whom they both might live.   60
But whereunto waste I this ruthful speech,
To thee that hast thy brother's blood thus shed?
Shall I still think that from this womb thou sprung?
That I thee bare? or take thee for my son?
No, traitor, no; I thee refuse for mine:
Murderer, I thee renounce; thou art not mine.
Never, O wretch, this womb conceived thee;
Nor never bode I painful throws for thee.
Changeling to me thou art, and not my child,
Nor to no wight that spark of pity knew.   70
Ruthless, unkind, monster of nature's work,
Thou never suck'd the milk of woman's breast;
But, from thy birth, the cruel tiger's teats
Have nursed thee; nor yet of flesh and blood
Form'd is thy heart, but of hard iron wrought;
And wild and desert woods bred thee to life.
But canst thou hope to 'scape my just revenge?
Or that these hands will not be wroke on thee?
Dost thou not know that Ferrex' mother lives,
That loved him more dearly than herself?   80
And doth she live, and is not veng'd on thee?

SCENE II

Gorboduc. Arostus.

Gor. We marvel much, whereto this ling'ring stay
    Falls out so long: Porrex unto our court,
    By order of our letters, is return'd;
    And Eubulus receiv'd from us behest,
    At his arrival here, to give him charge
    Before our presence straight to make repair,
    And yet we have no word whereof he stays.
Aros. Lo where he comes, and Eubulus with him.

Enter Eubulus *and* Porrex.

Eub. According to your highness' hest to me, 90
  Here have I Porrex brought, even in such sort
  As from his wearied horse he did alight,
  For that your grace did will such haste therein.
Gor. We like and praise this speedy will in you,
  To work the thing that to your charge we gave.
  Porrex, if we so far should swerve from kind,
  And from those bounds which law of nature sets,
  As thou hast done by vile and wretched deed,
  In cruel murder of thy brother's life;
  Our present hand could stay no longer time, 100
  But straight should bathe this blade in blood of thee,
  As just revenge of thy detested crime.
  No; we should not offend the law of kind,
  If now this sword of ours did slay thee here:
  For thou hast murder'd him, whose heinous death
  Even nature's force doth move us to revenge
  By blood again; and justice forceth us
  To measure death for death, thy due desert.
  Yet since thou art our child, and sith as yet
  In this hard case what word thou canst allege 110
  For thy defence, by us hath not been heard,
  We are content to stay our will for that
  Which justice bids us presently to work,
  And give thee leave to use thy speech at full,
  If ought thou have to lay for thine excuse.
Por. Neither, O king, I can or will deny
  But that this hand from Ferrex life hath reft:
  Which fact how much my doleful heart doth wail,
  Oh! would it might as full appear to sight,
  As inward grief doth pour it forth to me. 120
  So yet, perhaps, if ever ruthful heart
  Melting in tears within a manly breast,
  Through deep repentance of his bloody fact;
  If ever grief, if ever woeful man
  Might move regret with sorrow of his fault,
  I think the torment of my mournful case,
  Known to your grace, as I do feel the same,
  Would force even Wrath herself to pity me.

But as the water, troubled with the mud,
Shows not the face which else the eye should see;
Even so your ireful mind with stirred thought
Cannot so perfectly discern my cause.
But this unhap, amongst so many haps,
I must content me with, most wretched man,
That to myself I must reserve my woe,
In pining thoughts of mine accursed fact;
Since I may not show here my smallest grief,
Such as it is, and as my breast endures,
Which I esteem the greatest misery
Of all mishaps that fortune now can send.
Not that I rest in hope with plaint and tears
To purchase life; for to the gods I clepe[1]
For true record of this my faithful speech;
Never this heart shall have the thoughtful dread
To die the death that by your grace's doom,
By just desert, shall be pronounced to me:
Nor never shall this tongue once spend the speech,
Pardon to crave, or seek by suit to live.
I mean not this as though I were not touch'd
With care of dreadful death, or that I held
Life in contempt: but that I know the mind
Stoops to no dread, although the flesh be frail.
And for my guilt, I yield the same so great
As in myself I find a fear to sue
For grant of life.

Gor.   In vain, O wretch, thou showest
A woeful heart: Ferrex now lies in grave,
Slain by thy hand.

Por.   Yet this, O father, hear;
And then I end. Your majesty well knows,
That when my brother Ferrex and myself
By your own hest were join'd in governance
Of this your grace's realm of Britain land,
I never sought nor travail'd for the same;
Nor by myself, nor by no friend I wrought,
But from your highness' will alone it sprung,
Of your most gracious goodness bent to me.
But how my brother's heart even then repin'd
With swollen disdain against mine equal rule,

[1] To call.

Seeing that realm, which by descent should grow
Wholly to him, allotted half to me;
Even in your highness' court he now remains,   170
And with my brother then in nearest place,
Who can record what proof thereof was show'd,
And how my brother's envious heart appear'd.
Yet I that judged it my part to seek
His favour and good will, and loath to make
Your highness know the thing which should have brought
Grief to your grace, and your offence to him;
Hoping my earnest suit should soon have won
A loving heart within a brother's breast,
Wrought in that sort, that, for a pledge of love   180
And faithful heart, he gave to me his hand.
This made me think that he had banish'd quite
All rancour from his thought, and bare to me
Such hearty love as I did owe to him.
But after once we left your grace's court,
And from your highness' presence liv'd apart,
This equal rule still, still did grudge him so,
That now those envious sparks which erst lay rak'd
In living cinders of dissembling breast,
Kindled so far within his heart disdain,   190
That longer could he not refrain from proof
Of secret practice to deprive me life
By poison's force; and had bereft me so,
If mine own servant hired to this fact,
And mov'd by truth with hate to work the same,
In time had not bewray'd it unto me.
When thus I saw the knot of love unknit,
All honest league and faithful promise broke,
The law of kind and truth thus rent in twain,
His heart on mischief set, and in his breast   200
Black treason hid; then, then did I despair
That ever time could win him friend to me;
Then saw I how he smiled with slaying knife
Wrapp'd under cloak, then saw I deep deceit
Lurk in his face and death prepar'd for me:
Even nature moved me then to hold my life
More dear to me than his, and bade this hand,
Since by his life my death must needs ensue,
And by his death my life to be preserved,

   To shed his blood, and seek my safety so.   210
   And wisdom willed me without protract
   In speedy wise to put the same in ure.
   Thus have I told the cause that moved me
   To work my brother's death; and so I yield
   My life, my death, to judgment of your grace.
Gor. Oh cruel wight, should any cause prevail
   To make thee stain thy hands with brother's blood?
   But what of thee we will resolve to do
   Shall yet remain unknown. Thou in the mean
   Shalt from our royal presence banish'd be,   220
   Until our princely pleasure further shall
   To thee be show'd. Depart therefore our sight,
   Accursed child! [*Exit Porrex.*] What cruel destiny,
   What froward fate hath sorted us this chance,
   That even in those, where we should comfort find,
   Where our delight now in our aged days
   Should rest and be, even there our only grief
   And deepest sorrows to abridge our life,
   Most pining cares and deadly thoughts do grow.
Aros. Your grace should now, in these grave years of yours, 230
   Have found ere this the price of mortal joys;
   How short they be, how fading here in earth,
   How full of change, how brittle our estate,
   Of nothing sure, save only of the death,
   To whom both man and all the world doth owe
   Their end at last; neither shall nature's power
   In other sort against your heart prevail,
   Than as the naked hand whose stroke assays
   The armed breast where force doth light in vain.
Gor. Many can yield right sage and grave advice   240
   Of patient spirit to others wrapp'd in woe,
   And can in speech both rule and conquer kind;
   Who, if by proof they might feel nature's force,
   Would show themselves men as they are indeed,
   Which now will needs be gods. But what doth mean
   The sorry cheer of her that here doth come?

       Enter MARCELLA.

Mar. Oh where is ruth? or where is pity now?
   Whither is gentle heart and mercy fled?

Are they exil'd out of our stony breasts,
Never to make return? is all the world 250
Drowned in blood, and sunk in cruelty?
If not in women mercy may be found,
If not, alas, within the mother's breast,
To her own child, to her own flesh and blood;
If ruth be banish'd thence, if pity there
May have no place, if there no gentle heart
Do live and dwell, where should we seek it then?
Gor. Madam, alas, what means your woeful tale?
Mar. O silly woman I! why to this hour
Have kind and fortune thus deferr'd my breath, 260
That I should live to see this doleful day?
Will ever wight believe that such hard heart
Could rest within the cruel mother's breast,
With her own hand to slay her only son?
But out, alas! these eyes beheld the same:
They saw the dreary sight, and are become
Most ruthful records of the bloody fact.
Porrex, alas, is by his mother slain,
And with her hand, a woeful thing to tell,
While slumbering on his careful bed he rests, 270
His heart stabb'd in with knife is reft of life.
Gor. O Eubulus, oh draw this sword of ours,
And pierce this heart with speed! O hateful light,
O loathsome life, O sweet and welcome death!
Dear Eubulus, work this we thee beseech!
Eub. Patient your grace; perhaps he liveth yet,
With wound receiv'd, but not of certain death.
Gor. O let us then repair unto the place,
And see if Porrex live, or thus be slain.
  [*Exeunt Gorboduc and Eubulus.*
Mar. Alas, he liveth not! it is too true, 280
That with these eyes, of him a peerless prince,
Son to a king, and in the flower of youth,
Even with a twink a senseless stock I saw.
Aros. O damned deed!
Mar.   But hear his ruthful end:
The noble prince, pierc'd with the sudden wound,
Out of his wretched slumber hastely start,
Whose strength now failing straight he overthrew,
When in the fall his eyes, ev'n new unclos'd,

Beheld the queen, and cried to her for help.
We then, alas, the ladies which that time
Did there attend, seeing that heinous deed,
And hearing him oft call the wretched name
Of mother, and to cry to her for aid,
Whose direful hand gave him the mortal wound,
Pitying, alas, (for nought else could we do)
His ruthful end, ran to the woeful bed,
Despoiled straight his breast, and all we might
Wiped in vain with napkins next at hand,
The sudden streams of blood that flushed fast
Out of the gaping wound. O what a look,
O what a ruthful steadfast eye methought
He fix'd upon my face, which to my death
Will never part from me, when with a braid [1]
A deep-fetch'd sigh he gave, and therewithal
Clasping his hands, to heaven he cast his sight;
And straight pale death pressing within his face,
The flying ghost his mortal corpse forsook.
Aros. Never did age bring forth so vile a fact.
Mar. O hard and cruel hap, that thus assign'd
Unto so worthy a wight so wretched end:
But most hard cruel heart that could consent
To lend the hateful destinies that hand,
By which, alas, so heinous crime was wrought.
O queen of adamant! O marble breast!
If not the favour of his comely face,
If not his princely cheer and countenance,
His valiant active arms, his manly breast,
If not his fair and seemly personage,
His noble limbs in such proportion cast
As would have wrapt a silly woman's thought;
If this might not have mov'd thy bloody heart,
And that most cruel hand the wretched weapon
Ev'n to let fall, and kiss'd him in the face,
With tears for ruth to reave such one by death;
Should nature yet consent to slay her son?
O mother, thou to murder thus thy child!
Even Jove with justice must with lightening flames
From heaven send down some strange revenge on thee.
Ah, noble prince, how oft have I beheld

---

[1] A start.

Thee mounted on thy fierce and trampling steed, 330
Shining in armour bright before the tilt,
And with thy mistress' sleeve tied on thy helm,
And charge thy staff, to please thy lady's eye,
That bow'd the head-piece of thy friendly foe!
How oft in arms on horse to bend the mace,
How oft in arms on foot to break the sword,
Which never now these eyes may see again!

Aros. Madam, alas, in vain these plaints are shed;
Rather with me depart, and help to 'swage
The thoughtful griefs that in the aged king 340
Must needs by nature grow by death of this
His only son, whom he did hold so dear.

Mar. What wight is that which saw that I did see,
And could refrain to wail with plaint and tears?
Not I, alas! that heart is not in me:
But let us go, for I am griev'd anew,
To call to mind the wretched father's woe.   [*Exeunt.*

CHORUS.

When greedy lust in royal seat to reign
   Hath reft all care of gods and eke of men;
And cruel heart, wrath, treason, and disdain, 350
   Within ambitious breast are lodged, then
Behold how mischief wide herself displays,
And with the brother's hand the brother slays.

When blood thus shed doth stain the heaven's face,
   Crying to Jove for vengeance of the deed,
The mighty god ev'n moveth from his place,
   With wrath to wreak: then sends he forth with speed
The dreadful Furies, daughters of the night,
   With serpents girt, carrying the whip of ire,
With hair of stinging snakes, and shining bright 360
   With flames and blood, and with a brand of fire.
These, for revenge of wretched murder done,
Do make the mother kill her only son.

Blood asketh blood, and death must death requite:
   Jove, by his just and everlasting doom,

Justly hath ever so requited it.
The times before record. and times to come
Shall find it true, and so doth present proof
Present before our eyes for our behoof.

O happy wight, that suffers not the snare
  Of murderous mind to tangle him in blood;
And happy he, that can in time beware
  By other's harms, and turn it to his good.
But woe to him that, fearing not to offend,
Doth serve his lust, and will not see the end.

THE ORDER AND SIGNIFICATION OF THE DUMB SHOW BEFORE THE FIFTH ACT.

First, the drums and flutes began to sound, during which there came forth upon the stage a company of harquebussiers, and of armed men, all in order of battle. These, after their pieces discharged, and that the armed men had three times marched about the stage, departed, and then the drums and flutes did cease. Hereby was signified tumults, rebellions, arms, and civil wars to follow, as fell in the realm of Great Britain, which, by the space of fifty years and more, continued in civil war between the nobility after the death af king Gorboduc and of his issues, for want of certain limitation in the succession of the crown, till the time of Dunwallo Molmutius, who reduced the land to monarchy.

ACT V

SCENE I

CLOTYN. MANDUD. GWENARD. FERGUS. EUBULUS.

Clot. Did ever age bring forth such tyrant hearts?
    The brother hath bereft the brother's life,
    The mother, she hath dyed her cruel hands
    In blood of her own son; and now at last
    The people, lo, forgetting truth and love,
    Contemning quite both law and loyal heart,
    Ev'n they have slain their sovereign lord and queen.
Man. Shall this their traitorous crime unpunish'd rest?
    Ev'n yet they cease not, carried on with rage,
    In their rebellious routs, to threaten still   10
    A new bloodshed unto the prince's kin,
    To slay them all, and to uproot the race
    Both of the king and queen; so are they mov'd
    With Porrex' death, wherein they falsely charge
    The guiltless king, without desert at all;

Act V. Scene I.

And traitorously have murder'd him therefore,
And eke the queen.
Gwen.   Shall subjects dare with force
  To work revenge upon their prince's fact?
  Admit the worst that may, as sure in this
  The deed was foul, the queen to slay her son,
  Shall yet the subject seek to take the sword,
  Arise against his lord, and slay his king?
  O wretched state, where those rebellious hearts
  Are not rent out ev'n from their living breasts.
  And with the body thrown unto the fowls,
  As carrion food, for terrour of the rest.
Ferg. There can no punishment be thought too great
  For this so grievous crime: let speed therefore
  Be used therein, for it behooveth so.
Eub. Ye all, my lords, I see, consent in one,
  And I as one consent with ye in all.
  I hold it more than need, with sharpest law
  To punish this tumultuous bloody rage.
  For nothing more may shake the common state,
  Than sufferance of uproars without redress;
  Whereby how some kingdoms of mighty power,
  After great conquests made, and flourishing
  In fame and wealth, have been to ruin brought:
  I pray to Jove, that we may rather wail
  Such hap in them than witness in ourselves.
  Eke fully with the duke my mind agrees,[1]
  Though kings forget to govern as they ought,
  Yet subjects must obey as they are bound.

[1] The following lines are in the unauthorised edition of 1565:—

> "That no cause serves, whereby the subject may
> Call to account the doings of his prince,
> Much less in blood by sword to work revenge,
> No more than may the hand cut off the head;
> In act nor speech, no not in secret thought
> The subject may rebel against his lord,
> Or judge of him that sits in Cæsar's seat,
> With grudging mind to damn those he mislikes."

Warton, vol. iii. p. 370, attributes the suppression of these lines to Thomas Norton. He says, " It is well known that the Calvinists carried their ideas of reformation and refinement into government as well as religion; and it seems probable, that these eight verses were suppressed by Thomas Norton, Sackville's supposed assistant in the play, who was not only an active and, I believe, a sensible Puritan, but a licencer of the publication of books under the commission of the Bishop of London."

But now, my lords, before ye farther wade,
Or spend your speech, what sharp revenge shall fall
By justice' plague on these rebellious wights;
Methinks ye rather should first search the way,
By which in time the rage of this uproar
Might be repress'd, and these great tumults ceas'd.
Even yet the life of Britain land doth hang   50
In traitors' balance of unequal weight.
Think not, my lords, the death of Gorboduc,
Nor yet Videna's blood, will cease their rage:
Ev'n our own lives, our wives, and children dear,
Our country, dear'st of all, in danger stands,
Now to be spoil'd, now, now made desolate,
And by ourselves a conquest to ensue.
For, give once sway unto the people's lusts,
To rush forth on, and stay them not in time,
And as the stream that rolleth down the hill,   60
So will they headlong run with raging thoughts
From blood to blood, from mischief unto more,
To ruin of the realm, themselves, and all:
So giddy are the common people's minds,
So glad of change, more wavering than the sea.
Ye see, my lords, what strength these rebels have,
What hugy number is assembled still:
For though the traitorous fact, for which they rose,
Be wrought and done, yet lodge they still in field;
So that, how far their furies yet will stretch,   70
Great cause we have to dread. That we may seek
By present battle to repress their power,
Speed must we use to levy force therefore;
For either they forthwith will mischief work,
Or their rebellious roars forthwith will cease.
These violent things may have no lasting long.
Let us, therefore, use this for present help;
Persuade by gentle speech, and offer grace
With gift of pardon, save unto the chief;
And that upon condition that forthwith   80
They yield the captains of their enterprise,
To bear such guerdon [1] of their traitorous fact
As may be both due vengeance to themselves,
And wholesome terrour to posterity.

[1] Reward, recompense.

This shall, I think, scatter the greatest part
That now are holden with desire of home,
Wearied in field with cold of winter's nights,
And some, no doubt, stricken with dread of law.
When this is once proclaimed, it shall make
The captains to mistrust the multitude, 90
Whose safety bids them to betray their heads;
And so much more, because the rascal routs,
In things of great and perilous attempts,
Are never trusty to the noble race.
And while we treat, and stand on terms of grace,
We shall both stay their furious rage the while,
And eke gain time, whose only help sufficeth
Withouten war to vanquish rebels' power.
In the meanwhile, make you in readiness
Such band of horsemen as ye may prepare. 100
Horsemen, you know, are not the commons' strength,
But are the force and store of noble men;
Whereby the unchosen and unarmèd sort
Of skilless rebels, whom none other power
But number makes to be of dreadful force,
With sudden brunt may quickly be oppress'd.
And if this gentle mean of proffer'd grace
With stubborn hearts cannot so far avail,
As to assuage their desp'rate courages;
Then do I wish such slaughter to be made, 110
As present age, and eke posterity,
May be adrad [1] with horrour of revenge
That justly then shall on these rebels fall.
This is, my lords, the sum of mine advice.
Clot. Neither this case admits debate at large;
And though it did, this speech that hath been said,
Hath well abridged the tale I would have told.
Fully with Eubulus do I consent
In all that he hath said: and if the same
To you, my lords, may seem for best advice, 120
I wish that it should straight be put in ure.
Man. My lords, then let us presently depart,
And follow this that liketh us so well.
          [*Exeunt Clotyn, Mandud, Gwenard, and Eubulus.*
Ferg. If ever time to gain a kingdom here

[1] Afraid.

Were offer'd man, now it is offer'd me.
The realm is reft both of their king and queen,
The offspring of the prince is slain and dead,
No issue now remains, the heir unknown,
The people are in arms and mutinies,
The nobles, they are busied how to cease 130
These great rebellious tumults and uproars;
And Britain land, now desert left alone
Amid these broils uncertain where to rest,
Offers herself unto that noble heart
That will or dare pursue to bear her crown.
Shall I, that am the Duke of Albany,
Descended from that line of noble blood,
Which hath so long flourish'd in worthy fame
Of valiant hearts, such as in noble breasts
Of right should rest above the baser sort, 140
Refuse to venture life to win a crown?
Whom shall I find enemies that will withstand
My fact herein, if I attempt by arms
To seek the same now in these times of broil?
These dukes' power can hardly well appease
The people that already are in arms.
But if, perhaps, my force be once in field,
Is not my strength in power above the best
Of all these lords now left in Britain land?
And though they should match me with power of men, 150
Yet doubtful is the chance of battles joined.
If victors of the field we may depart,
Ours is the sceptre then of Great Britain;
If slain amid the plain this body lie,
Mine enemies yet shall not deny me this,
But that I died giving the noble charge
To hazard life for conquest of a crown.
Forthwith, therefore, will I in post depart
To Albany, and raise in armour there
All power I can: and here my secret friends, 160
By secret practice shall solicit still,
To seek to win to me the people's hearts. [*Exit.*

SCENE II

Eubulus *solus*.

Eub. O Jove, how are these people's hearts abus'd!
What blind fury thus headlong carries them?
That though so many books, so many rolls
Of ancient time, record what grievous plagues
Light on these rebels aye, and though so oft
Their ears have heard their aged fathers tell
What just reward these traitors still receive;
Yea, though themselves have seen deep death and blood, 170
By strangling cord, and slaughter of the sword,
To such assign'd, yet can they not beware,
Yet cannot stay their lewd rebellious hands;
But suffering, lo, foul treason to distain
Their wretched minds, forget their loyal heart,
Reject all truth, and rise against their prince.
A ruthful case, that those, whom duty's bond,
Whom grafted law, by nature, truth, and faith,
Bound to preserve their country and their king,
Born to defend their commonwealth and prince, 180
Ev'n they should give consent thus to subvert
Thee, Britain land, and from thy womb should spring,
O native soil, those that will needs destroy
And ruin thee, and eke themselves in fine.
For lo, when once the dukes had offer'd grace
Of pardon sweet, the multitude, misled
By traitorous fraud of their ungracious heads,
One sort that saw the dangerous success
Of stubborn standing in rebellious war,
And knew the difference of prince's power 190
From headless number of tumultuous routs,
Whom common country's care, and private fear
Taught to repent the error of their rage,
Laid hands upon the captains of their band,
And brought them bound unto the mighty dukes:
And other sort, not trusting yet so well
The truth of pardon, or mistrusting more
Their own offence than that they could conceive
Such hope of pardon for so foul misdeed,

Or for that they their captains could not yield, 200
Who, fearing to be yielded, fled before,
Stole home by silence of the secret night:
The third unhappy and enraged sort
Of desp'rate hearts, who, stain'd in princes' blood,
From traitorous furour could not be withdrawn
By love, by law, by grace, ne yet by fear,
By proffer'd life, ne yet by threaten'd death,
With minds hopeless of life, dreadless of death,
Careless of country, and aweless of God,
Stood bent to fight, as furies did them move, 210
With violent death to close their traitorous life.
These all by power of horsemen were oppress'd,
And with revenging sword slain in the field,
Or with the strangling cord hang'd on the trees,
Where yet their carrion carcases do preach
The fruits that rebels reap of their uproars,
And of the murder of their sacred prince.
But lo, where do approach the noble dukes
By whom these tumults have been thus appeas'd.

Enter CLOTYN, MANDUD, GWENARD, *and* AROSTUS.

Clot. I think the world will now at length beware 220
And fear to put on arms against their prince.
Man. If not, those traitorous hearts that dare rebel,
Let them behold the wide and hugy fields
With blood and bodies spread of rebels slain;
The lofty trees cloth'd with the corpses dead,
That, strangled with the cord, do hang thereon.
Aros. A just reward; such as all times before
Have ever lotted to those wretched folks.
Gwen. But what means he that cometh here so fast?

Enter NUNTIUS.

Nun. My lords, as duty and my troth doth move, 230
And of my country work a care in me,
That, if the spending of my breath avail'd
To do the service that my heart desires,
I would not shun to embrace a present death;
So have I now, in that wherein I thought
My travail might perform some good effect,
Ventur'd my life to bring these tidings here.

> Fergus, the mighty duke of Albany,
> Is now in arms, and lodgeth in the field
> With twenty thousand men: hither he bends
> His speedy march, and minds to invade the crown.
> Daily he gathereth strength, and spreads abroad,
> That to this realm no certain heir remains,
> That Britain land is left without a guide,
> That he the sceptre seeks, for nothing else
> But to preserve the people and the land,
> Which now remain as ship without a stern.
> Lo, this is that which I have here to say.

Clot. Is this his faith? and shall he falsely thus
> Abuse the vantage of unhappy times?
> O wretched land, if his outrageous pride,
> His cruel and untemper'd wilfulness,
> His deep dissembling shows of false pretence,
> Should once attain the crown of Britain land!
> Let us, my lords, with timely force resist
> The new attempt of this our common foe,
> As we would quench the flames of common fire.

Man. Though we remain without a certain prince,
> To wield the realm, or guide the wand'ring rule,
> Yet now the common mother of us all,
> Our native land, our country, that contains
> Our wives, children, kindred, ourselves, and all
> That ever is or may be dear to man,
> Cries unto us to help ourselves and her.
> Let us advance our powers to repress
> This growing foe of all our liberties.

Gwen. Yea, let us so, my lords, with hasty speed.
> And ye, O gods, send us the welcome death,
> To shed our blood in field, and leave us not
> In loathsome life to linger out our days,
> To see the hugy heaps of these unhaps,
> That now roll down upon the wretched land,
> Where empty place of princely governance,
> No certain stay now left of doubtless heir,
> Thus leave this guideless realm an open prey
> To endless storms and waste of civil war.

Aros. That ye, my lords, do so agree in one,
> To save your country from the violent reign
> And wrongfully usurped tyranny

Of him that threatens conquest of you all,
To save your realm, and in this realm yourselves,
From foreign thraldom of so proud a prince,
Much do I praise; and I beseech the gods,
With happy honour to requite it you.
But, O my lords, sith now the heaven's wrath
Hath reft this land the issue of their prince;
Sith of the body of our late sovereign lord
Remains no more, since the young kings be slain,
And of the title of descended crown
Uncertainly the divers minds do think
Even of the learned sort, and more uncertainly
Will partial fancy and affection deem;
But most uncertainly will climbing pride
And hope of reign withdraw to sundry parts
The doubtful right and hopeful lust to reign.
When once this noble service is achiev'd
For Britain land, the mother of ye all,
When once ye have with armed force repress'd
The proud attempts of this Albanian prince,
That threatens thraldom to your native land,
When ye shall vanquishers return from field,
And find the princely state an open prey
To greedy lust and to usurping power,
Then, then, my lords, if ever kindly care
Of antient honour of your ancestors,
Of present wealth and nobless of your stocks,
Yea of the lives and safety yet to come
Of your dear wives, your children, and yourselves,
Might move your noble hearts with gentle ruth,
Then, then, have pity on the torn estate;
Then help to salve the well-near hopeless sore;
Which ye shall do, if ye yourselves withhold
The slaying knife from your own mother's throat.
Her shall you save, and you, and yours in her,
If ye shall all with one assent forbear
Once to lay hand or take unto yourselves
The crown, by colour of pretended right,
Or by what other means soe'er it be,
Till first by common counsel of you all
In parliament, the regal diadem
Be set in certain place of governance;

     In which your parliament, and in your choice,
     Prefer the right, my lords, without respect
     Of strength or friends, or whatsoever cause
     That may set forward any other's part.
     For right will last, and wrong cannot endure.
     Right mean I his or hers, upon whose name
     The people rest by mean of native line.
     Or by the virtue of some former law,
     Already made their title to advance.   330
     Such one, my lords, let be your chosen king,
     Such one so born within your native land;
     Such one prefer, and in no wise admit
     The heavy yoke of foreign governance:
     Let foreign titles yield to public wealth.
     And with that heart wherewith ye now prepare
     Thus to withstand the proud invading foe,
     With that same heart, my lords, keep out also
     Unnatural thraldom of stranger's reign;
     Ne suffer you, against the rules of kind,   340
     Your mother land to serve a foreign prince.
Eub. Lo, here the end of Brutus' royal line,
     And lo, the entry to the woeful wreck
     And utter ruin of this noble realm.
     The royal king and eke his sons are slain;
     No ruler rests within the regal seat;
     The heir, to whom the sceptre 'longs, unknown;
     That to each force of foreign princes' power,
     Whom vantage of our wretched state may move
     By sudden arms to gain so rich a realm,   350
     And to the proud and greedy mind at home,
     Whom blinded lust to reign leads to aspire,
     Lo, Britain realm is left an open prey,
     A present spoil by conquest to ensue.
     Who seeth not now how many rising minds
     Do feed their thoughts with hope to reach a realm?
     And who will not by force attempt to win
     So great a gain, that hope persuades to have?
     A simple colour shall for title serve.
     Who wins the royal crown will want no right,   360
     Nor such as shall display by long descent
     A lineal race to prove him lawful king.
     In the meanwhile these civil arms shall rage,

And thus a thousand mischiefs shall unfold,
And far and near spread thee, O Britain land;
All right and law shall cease, and he that had
Nothing to-day, to-morrow shall enjoy
Great heaps of gold, and he that flow'd in wealth,
Lo, he shall be bereft of life and all;
And happiest he that then possesseth least. 370
The wives shall suffer rape, the maids deflour'd,
And children fatherless shall weep and wail;
With fire and sword thy native folk shall perish,
One kinsman shall bereave another's life,
The father shall unwitting slay the son,
The son shall slay the sire and know it not.
Women and maids the cruel soldier's sword
Shall pierce to death, and silly children lo,
That playing [1] in the streets and fields are found,
By violent hands shall close their latter day. 380
Whom shall the fierce and bloody soldier
Reserve to life? whom shall he spare from death?
Ev'n thou, O wretched mother, half alive,
Thou shalt behold thy dear and only child
Slain with the sword while he yet sucks thy breast.
Lo, guiltless blood shall thus each where be shed.
Thus shall the wasted soil yield forth no fruit,
But dearth and famine shall possess the land.
The towns shall be consum'd and burnt with fire,
The peopled cities shall wax desolate; 390
And thou, O Britain, whilom in renown,
Whilom in wealth and fame, shalt thus be torn,
Dismember'd thus, and thus be rent in twain,
Thus wasted and defac'd, spoil'd and destroy'd.
These be the fruits your civil wars will bring.
Hereto it comes when kings will not consent
To grave advice, but follow wilful will.
This is the end, when in fond princes' hearts
Flattery prevails, and sage rede hath no place:
These are the plagues, when murder is the mean 400
To make new heirs unto the royal crown.
Thus wreak the gods, when that the mother's wrath
Nought but the blood of her own child may swage;
These mischiefs spring when rebels will arise

[1] Play.—*Edit.* 1570.

To work revenge and judge their prince's fact.
This, this ensues, when noble men do fail
In loyal truth, and subjects will be kings.
And this doth grow, when lo, unto the prince,
Whom death or sudden hap of life bereaves,
No certain heir remains, such certain heir,
As not all only is the rightful heir,
But to the realm is so made known to be;
And troth thereby vested in subjects' hearts,
To owe faith there where right is known to rest.
Alas, in parliament what hope can be,
When is of parliament no hope at all,
Which, though it be assembled by consent,
Yet is not likely with consent to end;
While each one for himself, or for his friend,
Against his foe, shall travail what he may;
While now the state, left open to the man
That shall with greatest force invade the same,
Shall fill ambitious minds with gaping hope;
When will they once with yielding hearts agree?
Or in the while, how shall the realm be used?
No, no: then parliament should have been holden,
And certain heirs appointed to the crown,
To stay the title of established right,
And in the people plant obedience,
While yet the prince did live, whose name and power
By lawful summons and authority
Might make a parliament to be of force,
And might have set the state in quiet stay.
But now, O happy man, whom speedy death
Deprives of life, ne is enforc'd to see
These hugy mischiefs, and these miseries,
These civil wars, these murders, and these wrongs.
Of justice, yet must God in fine restore
This noble crown unto the lawful heir:
For right will always live, and rise at length,
But wrong can never take deep root to last.

ARDEN OF FEVERSHAM

DRAMATIS PERSONÆ

THOMAS ARDEN, *Gentleman, of Feversham.*
FRANKLIN, *his Friend.*
MOSBIE.
CLARKE, *a Painter.*
ADAM FOWLE, *Landlord of the Flower-de-Luce.*
BRADSHAW, *a Goldsmith.*
MICHAEL, *Arden's Servant.*
GREENE.

RICHARD REEDE, *a Sailor.*
BLACK WILL } *Murderers.*
SHAKEBAG }
A PRENTICE.
A FERRYMAN.
LORD CHEINY, *and his Men.*
MAYOR OF FEVERSHAM, *and Watch.*

ALICE, *Arden's Wife.*
SUSAN, *Mosbie's Sister.*

ARDEN OF FEVERSHAM

ACT I

A Room in Arden's House.

Enter ARDEN *and* FRANKLIN.

Franklin. Arden, cheer up thy spirits, and droop no more!
    My gracious Lord, the Duke of Somerset,
    Hath freely given to thee and to thy heirs,
    By letters patents from his Majesty,
    All the lands of the Abbey of Feversham.
    Here are the deeds,   [*He hands them.*
    Sealed and subscribed with his name and the king's:
    Read them, and leave this melancholy mood.
Arden. Franklin, thy love prolongs my weary life;   10
    And but for thee how odious were this life,
    That shows me nothing but torments my soul,
    And those foul objects that offend mine eyes!
    Which makes me wish that for this veil of heaven
    The earth hung over my head and covered me.
    Love-letters pass 'twixt Mosbie and my wife,
    And they have privy meetings in the town:
    Nay, on his finger did I spy the ring
    Which at our marriage-day the priest put on.
    Can any grief be half so great as this?
Franklin. Comfort thyself, sweet friend; it is not strange   20
    That women will be false and wavering.
Arden. Ay, but to dote on such a one as he
    Is monstrous, Franklin, and intolerable.
Franklin. Why, what is he?
Arden. A botcher, and no better at the first;
    Who, by base brokage getting some small stock,
    Crept into service of a nobleman,
    And by his servile flattery and fawning
    Is now become the steward of his house,

   And bravely jets it in his silken gown.   30
Franklin. No nobleman will countenance such a peasant.
Arden. Yes, the Lord Clifford, he that loves not me.
   But through his favour let him not grow proud;
   For were he by the Lord Protector backed,
   He should not make me to be pointed at.
   I am by birth a gentleman of blood,
   And that injurious ribald, that attempts
   To violate my dear wife's chastity
   (For dear I hold her love, as dear as heaven)
   Shall on the bed which he thinks to defile 40
   See his dissevered joints and sinews torn,
   Whilst on the planchers pants his weary body,
   Smeared in the channels of his lustful blood.
Franklin. Be patient, gentle friend, and learn of me
   To ease thy grief and save her chastity:
   Intreat her fair; sweet words are fittest engines
   To race the flint walls of a woman's breast.
   In any case be not too jealous,
   Nor make no question of her love to thee;
   But, as securely, presently take horse, 50
   And lie with me at London all this term;
   For women, when they may, will not,
   But, being kept back, straight grow outrageous.
Arden. Though this abhors from reason, yet I'll try it,
   And call her forth and presently take leave.
   How! Alice!

      Here enters ALICE.

Alice. Husband, what mean you to get up so early?
   Summer nights are short, and yet you rise ere day.
   Had I been wake, you had not risen so soon.
Arden. Sweet love, thou knowest that we two, Ovid-like, 60
   Have often chid the morning when it 'gan to peep,
   And often wished that dark night's purblind steeds
   Would pull her by the purple mantle back,
   And cast her in the ocean to her love.
   But this night, sweet Alice, thou hast killed my heart:
   I heard thee call on Mosbie in thy sleep.
Alice. 'Tis like I was asleep when I named him,
   For being awake he comes not in my thoughts.

Arden. Ay, but you started up and suddenly,
   Instead of him, caught me about the neck. 70
Alice. Instead of him? why, who was there but you?
   And where but one is, how can I mistake?
Franklin. Arden, leave to urge her over-far.
Arden. Nay, love, there is no credit in a dream;
   Let it suffice I know thou lovest me well.
Alice. Now I remember whereupon it came:
   Had we no talk of Mosbie yesternight?
Franklin. Mistress Alice, I heard you name him once or twice.
Alice. And thereof came it, and therefore blame not me.
Arden. I know it did, and therefore let it pass. 80
   I must to London, sweet Alice, presently.
Alice. But tell me, do you mean to stay there long?
Arden. No longer there till my affairs be done.
Franklin. He will not stay above a month at most.
Alice. A month? ay me! Sweet Arden, come again
   Within a day or two, or else I die.
Arden. I cannot long be from thee, gentle Alice.
   Whilst Michael fetch our horses from the field,
   Franklin and I will down unto the quay;
   For I have certain goods there to unload. 90
   Meanwhile prepare our breakfast, gentle Alice;
   For yet ere noon we'll take horse and away.
      [*Exeunt Arden and Franklin.*
Alice. Ere noon he means to take horse and away!
   Sweet news is this. O that some airy spirit
   Would in the shape and likeness of a horse
   Gallop with Arden 'cross the Ocean,
   And throw him from his back into the waves!
   Sweet Mosbie is the man that hath my heart:
   And he usurps it, having nought but this,
   That I am tied to him by marriage. 100
   Love is a God, and marriage is but words;
   And therefore Mosbie's title is the best.
   Tush! whether it be or no, he shall be mine,
   In spite of him, of Hymen, and of rites.

Here enters ADAM *of the Flower-de-luce.*

   And here comes Adam of the Flower-de-luce;
   I hope he brings me tidings of my love.

—How now, Adam, what is the news with you?
Be not afraid; my husband is now from home.
Adam. He whom you wot of, Mosbie, Mistress Alice,
Is come to town, and sends you word by me 110
In any case you may not visit him.
Alice. Not visit him?
Adam. No, nor take no knowledge of his being here.
Alice. But tell me, is he angry or displeased?
Adam. It should seem so, for he is wondrous sad.
Alice. Were he as mad as raving Hercules,
I'll see him, I; and were thy house of force,
These hands of mine should race it to the ground,
Unless that thou wouldst bring me to my love.
Adam. Nay, and you be so impatient, I'll be gone. 120
Alice. Stay, Adam, stay; thou wert wont to be my friend.
Ask Mosbie how I have incurred his wrath;
Bear him from me these pair of silver dice,
With which we played for kisses many a time,
And when I lost, I won, and so did he;—
Such winning and such losing Jove send me!
And bid him, if his love do not decline,
To come this morning but along my door,
And as a stranger but salute me there:
This may he do without suspect or fear. 130
Adam. I'll tell him what you say, and so farewell. [*Exit Adam.*
Alice. Do, and one day I'll make amends for all.—
I know he loves me well, but dares not come,
Because my husband is so jealous,
And these my narrow-prying neighbours blab,
Hinder our meetings when we would confer.
But, if I live, that block shall be removed,
And, Mosbie, thou that comes to me by stealth,
Shalt neither fear the biting speech of men,
Nor Arden's looks; as surely shall he die 140
As I abhor him and love only thee.

Here enters MICHAEL.

How now, Michael, whither are you going?
Michael. To fetch my master's nag.
I hope you'll think on me.
Alice. Ay; but, Michael, see you keep your oath,

*And be as secret as you are resolute.
Michael. I'll see he shall not live above a week.
Alice. On that condition, Michael, here's my hand:
 None shall have Mosbie's sister but thyself.
Michael. I understand the painter here hard by
 Hath made report that he and Sue is sure.
Alice. There's no such matter, Michael; believe it not.
Michael. But he hath sent a dagger sticking in a heart,
 With a verse or two stolen from a painted cloth,
 The which I hear the wench keeps in her chest.
 Well, let her keep it! I shall find a fellow
 That can both write and read and make rhyme too.
 And if I do—well, I say no more:
 I'll send from London such a taunting letter
 As she shall eat the heart he sent with salt
 And fling the dagger at the painter's head.
Alice. What needs all this? I say that Susan's thine.
Michael. Why, then I say that I will kill my master,
 Or anything that you will have me do.
Alice. But, Michael, see you do it cunningly.
Michael. Why, say I should be took, I'll ne'er confess
 That you know anything; and Susan, being a maid,
 May beg me from the gallows of the sheriff.
Alice. Trust not to that, Michael.
Michael. You cannot tell me, I have seen it, I.
 But, mistress, tell her, whether I live or die,
 I'll make her more worth than twenty painters can;
 For I will rid mine elder brother away,
 And then the farm of Bolton is mine own.
 Who would not venture upon house and land,
 When he may have it for a right down blow?

Here enters MOSBIE.

Alice. Yonder comes Mosbie. Michael, get thee gone,
 And let not him nor any know thy drifts. [*Exit Michael.*
 Mosbie, my love!
Mosbie. Away, I say, and talk not to me now.
Alice. A word or two, sweet heart, and then I will.
 'Tis yet but early days, thou needst not fear.
Mosbie. Where is your husband?
Alice. 'Tis now high water, and he is at the quay.

Mosbie. There let him be; henceforward know me not.
Alice. Is this the end of all thy solemn oaths?
    Is this the fruit thy reconcilement buds?
    Have I for this given thee so many favours,
    Incurred my husband's hate, and, out alas!
    Made shipwreck of mine honour for thy sake?   190
    And dost thou say "henceforward know me not"?
    Remember, when I lock'd thee in my closet,
    What were thy words and mine; did we not both
    Decree to murder Arden in the night?
    The heavens can witness, and the world can tell,
    Before I saw that falsehood look of thine,
    'Fore I was tangled with thy 'ticing speech,
    Arden to me was dearer than my soul,—
    And shall be still: base peasant, get thee gone,
    And boast not of thy conquest over me,   200
    Gotten by witchcraft and mere sorcery!
    For what hast thou to countenance my love,
    Being descended of a noble house,
    And matched already with a gentleman
    Whose servant thou may'st be!—and so farewell.
Mosbie. Ungentle and unkind Alice, now I see
    That which I ever feared, and find too true:
    A woman's love is as the lightning-flame,
    Which even in bursting forth consumes itself.
    To try thy constancy have I been strange;   210
    Would I had never tried, but lived in hope!
Alice. What need'st thou try me whom thou ne'er found false?
Mosbie. Yet pardon me, for love is jealous.
Alice. So lists the sailor to the mermaid's song,
    So looks the traveller to the basilisk:
    I am content for to be reconciled,
    And that, I know, will be mine overthrow.
Mosbie. Thine overthrow? first let the world dissolve.
Alice. Nay, Mosbie, let me still enjoy thy love,
    And happen what will, I am resolute.   220
    My saving husband hoards up bags of gold
    To make our children rich, and now is he
    Gone to unload the goods that shall be thine,
    And he and Franklin will to London straight.
Mosbie. To London, Alice? if thou'lt be ruled by me,
    We'll make him sure enough for coming there.

Alice. Ah, would we could!
Mosbie. I happened on a painter yesternight,
    The only cunning man of Christendom;
    For he can temper poison with his oil, 230
    That whoso looks upon the work he draws
    Shall, with the beams that issue from his sight,
    Suck venom to his breast and slay himself.
    Sweet Alice, he shall draw thy counterfeit,
    That Arden may, by gazing on it, perish.
Alice. Ay, but Mosbie, that is dangerous,
    For thou, or I, or any other else,
    Coming into the chamber where it hangs, may die.
Mosbie. Ay, but we'll have it covered with a cloth
    And hung up in the study for himself. 240
Alice. It may not be, for when the picture's drawn,
    Arden, I know, will come and show it me.
Mosbie. Fear not; we'll have that shall serve the turn.
    This is the painter's house; I'll call him forth.
Alice. But, Mosbie, I'll have no such picture, I.
Mosbie. I pray thee leave it to my discretion.
    How! Clarke!

Here enters CLARKE.

Oh, you are an honest man of your word! you served me well.
Clarke. Why, sir, I'll do it for you at any time,
    Provided, as you have given your word, 250
    I may have Susan Mosbie to my wife.
    For, as sharp-witted poets, whose sweet verse
    Make heavenly gods break off their nectar draughts
    And lay their ears down to the lowly earth,
    Use humble promise to their sacred Muse,
    So we that are the poets' favourites
    Must have a love: ay, Love is the painter's muse,
    That makes him frame a speaking countenance,
    A weeping eye that witnesses heart's grief.
    Then tell me, Master Mosbie, shall I have her? 260
Alice. 'Tis pity but he should; he'll use her well.
Mosbie. Clarke, here's my hand: my sister shall be thine.
Clarke. Then, brother, to requite this courtesy,
    You shall command my life, my skill, and all.

Alice. Ah, that thou couldst be secret.
Mosbie. Fear him not; leave; I have talked sufficient.
Clarke. You know not me that ask such questions.
  Let it suffice I know you love him well,
  And fain would have your husband made away:
  Wherein, trust me, you show a noble mind, 270
  That rather than you'll live with him you hate,
  You'll venture life, and die with him you love.
  The like will I do for my Susan's sake.
Alice. Yet nothing could inforce me to the deed
  But Mosbie's love. Might I without control
  Enjoy thee still, then Arden should not die:
  But seeing I cannot, therefore let him die.
Mosbie. Enough, sweet Alice; thy kind words makes me melt.
  Your trick of poisoned pictures we dislike;
  Some other poison would do better far. 280
Alice. Ay, such as might be put into his broth,
  And yet in taste not to be found at all.
Clarke. I know your mind, and here I have it for you.
  Put but a dram of this into his drink,
  Or any kind of broth that he shall eat,
  And he shall die within an hour after.
Alice. As I am a gentlewoman, Clarke, next day
  Thou and Susan shall be married.
Mosbie. And I'll make her dowry more than I'll talk of, Clarke.
Clarke. Yonder's your husband. Mosbie, I'll be gone. 290

Here enters ARDEN *and* FRANKLIN.

Alice. In good time see where my husband comes.
  Master Mosbie, ask him the question yourself. [*Exit Clarke.*
Mosbie. Master Arden, being at London yesternight,
  The Abbey lands, whereof you are now possessed,
  Were offered me on some occasion
  By Greene, one of Sir Antony Ager's men:
  I pray you, sir, tell me, are not the lands yours?
  Hath any other interest herein?
Arden. Mosbie, that question we'll decide anon.
  Alice, make ready my breakfast, I must hence. 300
      [*Exit Alice.*
  As for the lands, Mosbie, they are mine
  By letters patents from his Majesty.

But I must have a mandate for my wife;
They say you seek to rob me of her love:
Villain, what makes thou in her company?
She's no companion for so base a groom.

Mosbie. Arden, I thought not on her, I came to thee;
But rather than I pocket up this wrong——

Franklin. What will you do, sir?

Mosbie. Revenge it on the proudest of you both. 310
    [*Then Arden draws forth Mosbie's sword.*

Arden. So, sirrah; you may not wear a sword,
The statute makes against artificers;
I warrant that I do. Now use your bodkin,
Your Spanish needle, and your pressing iron,
For this shall go with me; and mark my words,
You goodman botcher, 'tis to you I speak:
The next time that I take thee near my house,
Instead of legs I'll make thee crawl on stumps.

Mosbie. Ah, Master Arden, you have injured me:
I do appeal to God and to the world. 320

Franklin. Why, canst thou deny thou wert a botcher once?

Mosbie. Measure me what I am, not what I was.

Arden. Why, what art thou now but a velvet drudge,
A cheating steward, and base-minded peasant?

Mosbie. Arden, now thou hast belched and vomited
The rancorous venom of thy mis-swoll'n heart,
Hear me but speak: as I intend to live
With God and his elected saints in heaven,
I never meant more to solicit her;
And that she knows, and all the world shall see. 330
I loved her once;—sweet Arden, pardon me,
I could not choose, her beauty fired my heart!
But time hath quenched these over-raging coals;
And, Arden, though I now frequent thy house,
'Tis for my sister's sake, her waiting-maid,
And not for hers. Mayest thou enjoy her long:
Hell-fire and wrathful vengeance light on me,
If I dishonour her or injure thee.

Arden. Mosbie, with these thy protestations
The deadly hatred of my heart's appeased, 340
And thou and I'll be friends, if this prove true.
As for the base terms I gave thee late,
Forget them, Mosbie: I had cause to speak,

            When all the knights and gentlemen of Kent
            Make common table-talk of her and thee.
Mosbie. Who lives that is not touched with slanderous tongues?
Franklin. Then, Mosbie, to eschew the speech of men,
            Upon whose general bruit all honour hangs,
            Forbear his house.
Arden. Forbear it! nay, rather frequent it more: 350
            The world shall see that I distrust her not.
            To warn him on the sudden from my house
            Were to confirm the rumour that is grown.
Mosbie. By my faith, sir, you say true,
            And therefore will I sojourn here a while,
            Until our enemies have talked their fill;
            And then, I hope, they'll cease, and at last confess
            How causeless they have injured her and me.
Arden. And I will lie at London all this term
            To let them see how light I weigh their words.   360

Here enters ALICE.

Alice. Husband, sit down; your breakfast will be cold.
Arden. Come, Master Mosbie, will you sit with us?
Mosbie. I cannot eat, but I'll sit for company.
Arden. Sirrah Michael, see our horse be ready.
Alice. Husband, why pause ye? why eat you not?
Arden. I am not well; there's something in this broth
            That is not wholesome: didst thou make it, Alice?
Alice. I did, and that's the cause it likes not you.
            [*Then she throws down the broth on the ground.*
            There's nothing that I do can please your taste;
            You were best to say I would have poisoned you.   370
            I cannot speak or cast aside my eye,
            But he imagines I have stepped awry.
            Here's he that you cast in my teeth so oft:
            Now will I be convinced or purge myself.
            I charge thee speak to this mistrustful man,
            Thou that wouldst see me hang, thou, Mosbie, thou:
            What favour hast thou had more than a kiss
            At coming or departing from the town?
Mosbie. You wrong yourself and me to cast these doubts:
            Your loving husband is not jealous.   380
Arden. Why, gentle Mistress Alice, cannot I be ill

But you'll accuse yourself?
Franklin, thou hast a box of mithridate;
I'll take a little to prevent the worst.
Franklin. Do so, and let us presently take horse;
My life for yours, ye shall do well enough.
Alice. Give me a spoon, I'll eat of it myself;
Would it were full of poison to the brim,
Then should my cares and troubles have an end.
Was ever silly woman so tormented? 390
Arden. Be patient, sweet love; I mistrust not thee.
Alice. God will revenge it, Arden, if thou dost;
For never woman loved her husband better
Than I do thee.
Arden. I know it, sweet Alice; cease to complain,
Lest that in tears I answer thee again.
Franklin. Come, leave this dallying, and let us away.
Alice. Forbear to wound me with that bitter word;
Arden shall go to London in my arms.
Arden. Loth am I to depart, yet I must go. 400
Alice. Wilt thou to London, then, and leave me here?
Ah, if thou love me, gentle Arden, stay.
Yet, if thy business be of great import
Go, if thou wilt, I'll bear it as I may;
But write from London to me every week,
Nay, every day, and stay no longer there
Than thou must needs, lest that I die for sorrow.
Arden. I'll write unto thee every other tide,
And so farewell, sweet Alice, till we meet next.
Alice. Farewell, husband, seeing you'll have it so; 410
And, Master Franklin, seeing you take him hence,
In hope you'll hasten him home, I'll give you this.
                    [*And then she kisseth him.*
Franklin. And if he stay, the fault shall not be mine.
Mosbie, farewell, and see you keep your oath.
Mosbie. I hope he is not jealous of me now.
Arden. No, Mosbie, no; hereafter think of me
As of your dearest friend, and so farewell.
                    [*Exeunt Arden, Franklin, and Michael.*
Alice. I am glad he is gone; he was about to stay,
But did you mark me then how I brake off?
Mosbie. Ay, Alice, and it was cunningly performed. 420
But what a villain is that painter Clarke!

Alice. Was it not a goodly poison that he gave?
  Why, he's as well now as he was before.
  It should have been some fine confection
  That might have given the broth some dainty taste:
  This powder was too gross and populous.
Mosbie. But had he eaten but three spoonfuls more,
  Then had he died and our love continued.
Alice. Why, so it shall, Mosbie, albeit he live.
Mosbie. It is unpossible, for I have sworn   430
  Never hereafter to solicit thee,
  Or, whilst he lives, once more importune thee.
Alice. Thou shalt not need, I will importune thee.
  What? shall an oath make thee forsake my love?
  As if I have not sworn as much myself
  And given my hand unto him in the church!
  Tush, Mosbie; oaths are words, and words is wind,
  And wind is mutable: then, I conclude,
  'Tis childishness to stand upon an oath.
Mosbie. Well proved, Mistress Alice; yet by your leave   440
  I'll keep mine unbroken whilst he lives.
Alice. Ay, do, and spare not, his time is but short;
  For if thou beest as resolute as I,
  We'll have him murdered as he walks the streets.
  In London many alehouse ruffians keep,
  Which, as I hear, will murder men for gold.
  They shall be soundly fee'd to pay him home.

Here enters GREENE.

Mosbie. Alice, what's he that comes yonder? knowest thou him?
Alice. Mosbie, be gone: I hope 'tis one that comes
  To put in practice our intended drifts.   [*Exit Mosbie.*
Greene. Mistress Arden, you are well met.   451
  I am sorry that your husband is from home,
  When as my purposed journey was to him:
  Yet all my labour is not spent in vain,
  For I suppose that you can full discourse
  And flat resolve me of the thing I seek.
Alice. What is it, Master Greene? If that I may
  Or can with safety, I will answer you.
Greene. I heard your husband hath the grant of late,
  Confirmed by letters patents from the king,   460

>   Of all the lands of the Abbey of Feversham,
>   Generally intitled, so that all former grants
>   Are cut off; whereof I myself had one;
>   But now my interest by that is void.
>   This is all, Mistress Arden; is it true or no?
> *Alice.* True, Master Greene; the lands are his in state,
>   And whatsoever leases were before
>   Are void for term of Master Arden's life;
>   He hath the grant under the Chancery seal.
> *Greene.* Pardon me, Mistress Arden, I must speak, 470
>   For I am touched. Your husband doth me wrong
>   To wring me from the little land I have.
>   My living is my life, and only that
>   Resteth remainder of my portion.
>   Desire of wealth is endless in his mind,
>   And he is greedy-gaping still for gain;
>   Nor cares he though young gentlemen do beg,
>   So he may scrape and hoard up in his pouch.
>   But, seeing he hath ta'en my lands, I'll value life
>   As careless as he is careful for to get: 480
>   And tell him this from me, I'll be revenged,
>   And so as he shall wish the Abbey lands
>   Had rested still within their former state.
> *Alice.* Alas, poor gentleman, I pity you,
>   And woe is me that any man should want!
>   God knows 'tis not my fault; but wonder not
>   Though he be hard to others, when to me,—
>   Ah, Master Greene, God knows how I am used.
> *Greene.* Why, Mistress Arden, can the crabbed churl
>   Use you unkindly? respects he not your birth, 490
>   Your honourable friends, nor what you brought?
>   Why, all Kent knows your parentage and what you are.
> *Alice.* Ah, Master Greene, be it spoken in secret here,
>   I never live good day with him alone:
>   When he's at home, then have I froward looks,
>   Hard words and blows to mend the match withal;
>   And though I might content as good a man,
>   Yet doth he keep in every corner trulls;
>   And when he's weary with his trugs at home,
>   Then rides he straight to London; there, forsooth, 500
>   He revels it among such filthy ones
>   As counsels him to make away his wife.

Thus live I daily in continual fear,
In sorrow; so despairing of redress
As every day I wish with hearty prayer
That he or I were taken forth the world.
Greene. Now trust me, Mistress Alice, it grieveth me
So fair a creature should be so abused.
Why, who would have thought the civil sir so sullen?
He looks so smoothly. Now, fie upon him, churl! 510
And if he live a day, he lives too long.
But frolic, woman! I shall be the man
Shall set you free from all this discontent;
And if the churl deny my interest
And will not yield my lease into my hand,
I'll pay him home, whatever hap to me.
Alice. But speak you as you think?
Greene. Ay, God's my witness, I mean plain dealing,
For I had rather die than lose my land.
Alice. Then, Master Greene, be counsellèd by me: 520
Indanger not yourself for such a churl,
But hire some cutter for to cut him short,
And here's ten pound to wager them withal;
When he is dead, you shall have twenty more,
And the lands whereof my husband is possess'd
Shall be intitled as they were before.
Greene. Will you keep promise with me?
Alice. Or count me false and perjured whilst I live.
Greene. Then here's my hand, I'll have him so dispatched.
I'll up to London straight, I'll thither post, 530
And never rest till I have compassed it.
Till then farewell.
Alice. Good fortune follow all your forward thoughts.

[*Exit Greene.*

And whosoever doth attempt the deed,
A happy hand I wish, and so farewell.—
All this goes well: Mosbie, I long for thee
To let thee know all that I have contrived.

Here enters MOSBIE *and* CLARKE.

Mosbie. How, now, Alice, what's the news?
Alice. Such as will content thee well, sweetheart.
Mosbie. Well, let them pass a while, and tell me, Alice, 540

How have you dealt and tempered with my sister?
What, will she have my neighbour Clarke, or no?
Alice. What, Master Mosbie! let him woo himself!
Think you that maids look not for fair words?
Go to her, Clarke; she's all alone within;
Michael my man is clean out of her books.
Clarke. I thank you, Mistress Arden, I will in;
And if fair Susan and I can make a gree,
You shall command me to the uttermost,
As far as either goods or life may stretch.   [*Exit Clarke.*
Mosbie. Now, Alice, let's hear thy news.   551
Alice. They be so good that I must laugh for joy,
Before I can begin to tell my tale.
Mosbie. Let's hear them, that I may laugh for company.
Alice. This morning, Master Greene, Dick Greene I mean,
From whom my husband had the Abbey land,
Came hither, railing, for to know the truth
Whether my husband had the lands by grant.
I told him all, whereat he stormed amain
And swore he would cry quittance with the churl,   560
And, if he did deny his interest,
Stab him, whatsoever did befall himself.
Whenas I saw his choler thus to rise,
I whetted on the gentleman with words;
And, to conclude, Mosbie, at last we grew
To composition for my husband's death.
I gave him ten pound for to hire knaves,
By some device to make away the churl;
When he is dead, he should have twenty more
And repossess his former lands again.   570
On this we 'greed, and he is ridden straight
To London, for to bring his death about.
Mosbie. But call you this good news?
Alice. Ay, sweetheart, be they not?
Mosbie. 'Twere cheerful news to hear the churl were dead;
But trust me, Alice, I take it passing ill
You would be so forgetful of our state
To make recount of it to every groom.
What! to acquaint each stranger with our drifts,
Chiefly in case of murder, why, 'tis the way   580
To make it open unto Arden's self
And bring thyself and me to ruin both.

Forewarned, forearmed; who threats his enemy,
Lends him a sword to guard himself withal.
Alice. I did it for the best.
Mosbie. Well, seeing 'tis done, cheerly let it pass.
You know this Greene; is he not religious?
A man, I guess, of great devotion?
Alice. He is.
Mosbie. Then, sweet Alice, let it pass: I have a drift   590
Will quiet all, whatever is amiss.

Here enters CLARKE *and* SUSAN.

Alice. How now, Clarke? have you found me false?
Did I not plead the matter hard for you?
Clarke. You did.
Mosbie. And what? wilt be a match?
Clarke. A match, i' faith, sir: ay, the day is mine.
The painter lays his colours to the life,
His pencil draws no shadows in his love.
Susan is mine.
Alice. You make her blush.   600
Mosbie. What, sister, is it Clarke must be the man?
Susan. It resteth in your grant; some words are past,
And haply we be grown unto a match,
If you be willing that it shall be so.
Mosbie. Ah, Master Clarke, it resteth at my grant:
You see my sister's yet at my dispose,
But, so you'll grant me one thing I shall ask,
I am content my sister shall be yours.
Clarke. What is it, Master Mosbie?
Mosbie. I do remember once in secret talk   610
You told me how you could compound by art
A crucifix impoisoned,
That whoso look upon it should wax blind
And with the scent be stifled, that ere long
He should die poisoned that did view it well.
I would have you make me such a crucifix,
And then I'll grant my sister shall be yours.
Clarke. Though I am loth, because it toucheth life,
Yet, rather or I'll leave sweet Susan's love,
I'll do it, and with all the haste I may.   620
But for whom is it?

Alice. Leave that to us. Why, Clarke, is it possible
　That you should paint and draw it out yourself,
　The colours being baleful and impoisoned,
　And no ways prejudice yourself withal?
Mosbie. Well questioned, Alice; Clarke, how answer you that?
Clarke. Very easily: I'll tell you straight
　How I do work of these impoisoned drugs.
　I fasten on my spectacles so close
　As nothing can any way offend my sight;　　　　　　630
　Then, as I put a leaf within my nose,
　So put I rhubarb to avoid the smell,
　And softly as another work I paint.
Mosbie. 'Tis very well; but against when shall I have it?
Clarke. Within this ten days.
Mosbie.　　　　　　　　　　'Twill serve the turn.
　Now, Alice, let's in and see what cheer you keep.
　I hope, now Master Arden is from home,
　You'll give me leave to play your husband's part.
Alice. Mosbie, you know, who's master of my heart,
　He well may be the master of the house.　　　　　　640
　　　　　　　　　　　　　　　　　　　[*Exeunt.*

ACT II

SCENE I.—*Country between Feversham and London.*

Enter GREENE *and* BRADSHAW.

Bradshaw. See you them that comes yonder, Master Greene?
Greene. Ay, very well: do you know them?

Here enters BLACK WILL *and* SHAKEBAG.

Bradshaw. The one I know not, but he seems a knave
  Chiefly for bearing the other company;
  For such a slave, so vile a rogue as he,
  Lives not again upon the earth.
  Black Will is his name. I tell you, Master Greene,
  At Boulogne he and I were fellow-soldiers,
  Where he played such pranks
  As all the camp feared him for his villainy   10
  I warrant you he bears so bad a mind
  That for a crown he'll murder any man.
Greene. The fitter is he for my purpose, marry!
Will. How now, fellow Bradshaw? Whither away so early?
Bradshaw. O Will, times are changed: no fellows now,
  Though we were once together in the field;
  Yet thy friend to do thee any good I can.
Will. Why, Bradshaw, was not thou and I fellow-soldiers at
  Boulogne, where I was a corporal, and thou but a base
  mercenary groom? No fellows now! because you are a
  goldsmith and have a little plate in your shop! You were
  glad to call me "fellow Will," and with a curtsey to the
  earth, "One snatch, good corporal," when I stole the half
  ox from John the victualer, and domineer'd with it amongst
  good fellows in one night.   25
Bradshaw. Ay, Will, those days are past with me.
Will. Ay, but they be not past with me, for I keep that same
  honourable mind still. Good neighbour Bradshaw, you
  are too proud to be my fellow; but were it not that I see
  more company coming down the hill, I would be fellows
  with you once more, and share crowns with you too. But
  let that pass, and tell me whither you go.   32

Bradshaw. To London, Will, about a piece of service,
  Wherein haply thou mayest pleasure me.
Will. What is it?
Bradshaw. Of late Lord Cheiny lost some plate,
  Which one did bring and sold it at my shop,
  Saying he served Sir Antony Cooke.
  A search was made, the plate was found with me,
  And I am bound to answer at the 'size.   40
  Now, Lord Cheiny solemnly vows, if law
  Will serve him, he'll hang me for his plate.
  Now I am going to London upon hope
  To find the fellow. Now, Will, I know
  Thou art acquainted with such companions.
Will. What manner of man was he?
Bradshaw. A lean-faced writhen knave,
  Hawk-nosed and very hollow-eyed,
  With mighty furrows in his stormy brows;
  Long hair down his shoulders curled;   50
  His chin was bare, but on his upper lip
  A mutchado, which he wound about his ear.
Will. What apparel had he?
Bradshaw. A watchet satin doublet all-to torn,
  The inner side did bear the greater show;
  A pair of thread-bare velvet hose, seam rent,
  A worsted stocking rent above the shoe,
  A livery cloak, but all the lace was off;
  'Twas bad, but yet it served to hide the plate.
Will. Sirrah Shakebag, canst thou remember since we trolled the
  bowl at Sittingburgh, where I broke the tapster's head of
  the Lion with a cudgel stick?   62
Shakebag. Ay, very well, Will.
Will. Why, it was with the money that the plate was sold for.
  Sirrah Bradshaw, what wilt thou give him that can tell
  thee who sold thy plate?
Bradshaw. Who, I pray thee, good Will?
Will. Why, 'twas one Jack Fitten. He's now in Newgate for
  stealing a horse, and shall be arraigned the next 'size.
Bradshaw. Why, then let Lord Cheiny seek Jack Fitten forth,
  For I'll back and tell him who robbed him of his plate.   71
  This cheers my heart; Master Greene, I'll leave you,
  For I must to the Isle of Sheppy with speed.
Greene. Before you go, let me intreat you

To carry this letter to Mistress Arden of Feversham
And humbly recommend me to herself.
Bradshaw. That will I, Master Greene, and so farewell.
Here, Will, there's a crown for thy good news.
            [*Exit Bradshaw.*
Will. Farewell, Bradshaw; I'll drink no water for thy sake
whilst this lasts.—Now, gentleman, shall we have your
company to London?   81
Greene. Nay, stay, sirs:
A little more I needs must use your help,
And in a matter of great consequence,
Wherein if you'll be secret and profound,
I'll give you twenty angels for your pains.
Will. How? twenty angels? give my fellow George Shakebag
and me twenty angels? And if thou'lt have thy own father
slain, that thou may'st inherit his land, we'll kill him.
Shakebag. Ay, thy mother, thy sister, thy brother, or all thy
kin.   90
Greene. Well, this is it: Arden of Feversham
Hath highly wronged me about the Abbey land,
That no revenge but death will serve the turn.
Will you two kill him? here's the angels down,
And I will lay the platform of his death.
Will. Plat me no platforms; give me the money, and I'll stab
him as he stands pissing against a wall, but I'll kill him.
Shakebag. Where is he?
Greene. He is now at London, in Aldersgate Street.
Shakebag. He's dead as if he had been condemned by an Act of
Parliament, if once Black Will and I swear his death. 101
Greene. Here is ten pound, and when he is dead,
Ye shall have twenty more.
Will. My fingers itches to be at the peasant. Ah, that I might
be set a work thus through the year, and that murder would
grow to an occupation, that a man might follow without
danger of law:—zounds, I warrant I should be warden of
the company! Come, let us be going, and we'll bait at
Rochester, where I'll give thee a gallon of sack to handsel the
match withal.   110
                    [*Exeunt.*

SCENE II.—*London. A Street near St. Paul's.*

Enter MICHAEL.

Michael. I have gotten such a letter as will touch the painter:
And thus it is:

Here enters ARDEN *and* FRANKLIN *and hears* MICHAEL *read this letter.*

"My duty remembered, Mistress Susan, hoping in God you be in good health, as I Michael was at the making hereof. This is to certify you that as the turtle true, when she hath lost her mate, sitteth alone, so I, mourning for your absence, do walk up and down Paul's till one day I fell asleep and lost my master's pantofles. Ah, Mistress Susan, abolish that paltry painter, cut him off by the shins with a frowning look of your crabbed countenance, and think upon Michael, who, drunk with the dregs of your favour, will cleave as fast to your love as a plaster of pitch to a galled horse-back. Thus hoping you will let my passions penetrate, or rather impetrate mercy of your meek hands, I end
"Yours, Michael, or else not Michael."

Arden. Why, you paltry knave,
Stand you here loitering, knowing my affairs,
What haste my business craves to send to Kent?
Franklin. Faith, friend Michael, this is very ill,
Knowing your master hath no more but you, 130
And do ye slack his business for your own?
Arden. Where is the letter, sirrah? let me see it.
                    [*Then he gives him the letter.*
See, Master Franklin, here's proper stuff:
Susan my maid, the painter, and my man,
A crew of harlots, all in love, forsooth;
Sirrah, let me hear no more of this,
Nor for thy life once write to her a word.

Here enters GREENE, WILL, *and* SHAKEBAG.

Wilt thou be married to so base a trull?
'Tis Mosbie's sister: come I once at home,
I'll rouse her from remaining in my house. 140

Now, Master Franklin, let us go walk in Paul's;
Come but a turn or two, and then away. [*Exeunt.*
Greene. The first is Arden, and that's his man,
The other is Franklin, Arden's dearest friend.
Will. Zounds, I'll kill them all three.
Greene. Nay, sirs, touch not his man in any case;
But stand close, and take you fittest standing,
And at his coming forth speed him:
To the Nag's Head, there is this coward's haunt.
But now I'll leave you till the deed be done. [*Exit Greene.*
Shakebag. If he be not paid his own, ne'er trust Shakebag. 151
Will. Sirrah Shakebag, at his coming forth I'll run him through, and then to the Blackfriars, and there take water and away.
Shakebag. Why, that's the best; but see thou miss him not.
Will. How can I miss him, when I think on the forty angels I must have more?

Here enters PRENTICE.

Prentice. 'Tis very late; I were best shut up my stall, for here will be old filching, when the press comes forth of Paul's.
[*Then lets he down his window, and it breaks Black Will's head.*
Will. Zounds, draw, Shakebag, I am almost killed.
Prentice. We'll tame you, I warrant. 160
Will. Zounds, I am tame enough already.

Here enters ARDEN, FRANKLIN, *and* MICHAEL.

Arden. What troublesome fray or mutiny is this?
Franklin. 'Tis nothing but some brabling paltry fray,
Devised to pick men's pockets in the throng.
Arden. Is't nothing else? come, Franklin, let's away. [*Exeunt.*
Will. What 'mends shall I have for my broken head?
Prentice. Marry, this 'mends, that if you get you not away all the sooner, you shall be well beaten and sent to the Counter.
[*Exit Prentice.*
Will. Well, I'll be gone, but look to your signs, for I'll pull them down all. Shakebag, my broken head grieves me not so much as by this means Arden hath escaped. 171

Here enters GREENE.

I had a glimpse of him and his companion.
Greene. Why, sirs, Arden's as well as I; I met him and Franklin
  going merrily to the ordinary. What, dare you not do it?
Will. Yes, sir, we dare do it; but, were my consent to give
  again, we would not do it under ten pound more. I value
  every drop of my blood at a French crown. I have had
  ten pound to steal a dog, and we have no more here to kill
  a man; but that a bargain is a bargain, and so forth, you
  should do it yourself. 180
Greene. I pray thee, how came thy head broke?
Will. Why, thou seest it is broke, dost thou not?
Shakebag. Standing against a stall, watching Arden's coming,
  a boy let down his shop-window, and broke his head;
  whereupon arose a brawl, and in the tumult Arden escaped
  us and passed by unthought on. But forbearance is no
  acquittance; another time we'll do it, I warrant thee.
Greene. I pray thee, Will, make clean thy bloody brow,
  And let us bethink us on some other place
  Where Arden may be met with handsomely. 190
  Remember how devoutly thou hast sworn
  To kill the villain; think upon thine oath.
Will. Tush, I have broken five hundred oaths!
  But wouldst thou charm me to effect this deed,
  Tell me of gold, my resolution's fee;
  Say thou seest Mosbie kneeling at my knees,
  Offering me service for my high attempt,
  And sweet Alice Arden, with a lap of crowns,
  Comes with a lowly curtsey to the earth,
  Saying " Take this but for thy quarterage, 200
  Such yearly tribute will I answer thee."
  Why, this would steel soft-mettled cowardice,
  With which Black Will was never tainted yet.
  I tell thee, Greene, the forlorn traveller,
  Whose lips are glued with summer's parching heat,
  Ne'er longed so much to see a running brook
  As I to finish Arden's tragedy.
  Seest thou this gore that cleaveth to my face?
  From hence ne'er will I wash this bloody stain,
  Till Arden's heart be panting in my hand. 210

Greene. Why, that's well said; but what saith Shakebag?
Shakebag. I cannot paint my valour out with words:
    But, give me place and opportunity,
    Such mercy as the starven lioness,
    When she is dry sucked of her eager young,
    Shows to the prey that next encounters her,
    On Arden so much pity would I take.
Greene. So should it fare with men of firm resolve.
    And now, sirs, seeing that this accident
    Of meeting him in Paul's hath no success,   220
    Let us bethink us of some other place
    Whose earth may swallow up this Arden's blood.

                Here enters MICHAEL.

    See, yonder comes his man: and wot you what?
    The foolish knave's in love with Mosbie's sister,
    And for her sake, whose love he cannot get
    Unless Mosbie solicit his suit,
    The villain hath sworn the slaughter of his master.
    We'll question him, for he may stead us much,—
    How now, Michael, whether are you going?
Michael. My master hath new supped,   230
    And I am going to prepare his chamber.
Greene. Where supped Master Arden?
Michael. At the Nag's Head, at the eighteen pence ordinary.
    How now, Master Shakebag? what, Black Will! God's
    dear lady, how chance your face is so bloody?
Will. Go to, sirrah, there is a chance in it; this sauciness in
    you will make you be knocked.
Michael. Nay, an you be offended, I'll be gone.
Greene. Stay, Michael, you may not escape us so.
    Michael, I know you love your master well.   240
Michael. Why, so I do; but wherefore urge you that?
Greene. Because I think you love your mistress better.
Michael. So think not I; but say, i'faith, what, if I should?
Shakebag. Come to the purpose, Michael; we hear
    You have a pretty love in Feversham.
Michael. Why, have I two or three, what's that to thee!
Will. You deal too mildly with the peasant. Thus it is:
    'Tis known to us that you love Mosbie's sister;
    We know besides that you have ta'en your oath

> To further Mosbie to your mistress' bed, 250
> And kill your master for his sister's sake.
> Now, sir, a poorer coward than yourself
> Was never fostered in the coast of Kent:
> How comes it then that such a knave as you
> Dare swear a matter of such consequence?

Greene. Ah, Will——

Will. Tush, give me leave, there's no more but this:
> Sith thou hast sworn, we dare discover all;
> And hadst thou or should'st thou utter it,
> We have devised a complat under hand, 260
> Whatever shall betide to any of us,
> To send thee roundly to the devil of hell.
> And therefore thus: I am the very man,
> Marked in my birth-hour by the destinies,
> To give an end to Arden's life on earth;
> Thou but a member but to whet the knife
> Whose edge must search the closet of his breast:
> Thy office is but to appoint the place,
> And train thy master to his tragedy;
> Mine to perform it when occasion serves. 270
> Then be not nice, but here devise with us
> How and what way we may conclude his death.

Shakebag. So shalt thou purchase Mosbie for thy friend,
> And by his friendship gain his sister's love.

Greene. So shall thy mistress be thy favourer,
> And thou disburdened of the oath thou made.

Michael. Well, gentlemen, I cannot but confess,
> Sith you have urged me so apparently,
> That I have vowed my master Arden's death;
> And he whose kindly love and liberal hand 280
> Doth challenge nought but good deserts of me,
> I will deliver over to your hands.
> This night come to his house at Aldersgate:
> The doors I'll leave unlock'd against you come.
> No sooner shall ye enter through the latch,
> Over the threshold to the inner court,
> But on your left hand shall you see the stairs
> That leads directly to my master's chamber:
> There take him and dispose him as ye please.
> Now it were good we parted company; 290
> What I have promised, I will perform.

Will. Should you deceive us, 'twould go wrong with you.
Michael. I will accomplish all I have revealed.
Will. Come, let's go drink: choler makes me as dry as a dog.
            [*Exeunt Will, Greene, and Shakebag. Manet Michael.*
Michael. Thus feeds the lamb securely on the down,
    Whilst through the thicket of an arbour brake
    The hunger-bitten wolf o'erpries his haunt
    And takes advantage for to eat him up.
    Ah, harmless Arden, how hast thou misdone,
    That thus thy gentle life is levelled at? 300
    The many good turns that thou hast done to me.
    Now must I quittance with betraying thee.
    I that should take the weapon in my hand
    And buckler thee from ill-intending foes,
    Do lead thee with a wicked fraudful smile,
    As unsuspected, to the slaughter-house.
    So have I sworn to Mosbie and my mistress,
    So have I promised to the slaughtermen;
    And should I not deal currently with them,
    Their lawless rage would take revenge on me. 310
    Tush, I will spurn at mercy for this once:
    Let pity lodge where feeble women lie,
    I am resolved, and Arden needs must die.
                                    [*Exit Michael.*

ACT III

SCENE I.—*A Room in Franklin's House, at Aldersgate.*

Enter ARDEN *and* FRANKLIN.

Arden. No, Franklin, no: if fear or stormy threats,
  If love of me or care of womanhood,
  If fear of God or common speech of men,
  Who mangle credit with their wounding words,
  And couch dishonour as dishonour buds,
  Might join repentance in her wanton thoughts,
  No question then but she would turn the leaf
  And sorrow for her dissolution;
  But she is rooted in her wickedness,
  Perverse and stubborn, not to be reclaimed;   10
  Good counsel is to her as rain to weeds,
  And reprehension makes her vice to grow
  As Hydra's head that plenished by decay.
  Her faults, methink, are painted in my face,
  For every searching eye to overread;
  And Mosbie's name, a scandal unto mine,
  Is deeply trenchèd in my blushing brow.
  Ah, Franklin, Franklin, when I think on this,
  My heart's grief rends my other powers
  Worse than the conflict at the hour of death.   20
Franklin. Gentle Arden, leave this sad lament:
  She will amend, and so your griefs will cease;
  Or else she'll die, and so your sorrows end.
  If neither of these two do haply fall,
  Yet let your comfort be that others bear
  Your woes, twice doubled all, with patience.
Arden. My house is irksome; there I cannot rest.
Franklin. Then stay with me in London; go not home.
Arden. Then that base Mosbie doth usurp my room
  And makes his triumph of my being thence.   30
  At home or not at home, where'er I be,
  Here, here it lies, ah Franklin, here it lies
  That will not out till wretched Arden lies.

Here enters MICHAEL.

Franklin. Forget your griefs a while; here comes your man.
Arden. What a-clock is't, sirrah?
Michael. Almost ten.
Arden. See, see, how runs away the weary time!
  Come, Master Franklin, shall we go to bed?
        [*Exeunt Arden and Michael. Manet Franklin.*
Franklin. I pray you, go before: I'll follow you.
  —Ah, what a hell is fretful jealousy! 40
  What pity-moving words, what deep-fetched sighs,
  What grievous groans and overlading woes
  Accompanies this gentle gentleman!
  Now will he shake his care-oppressèd head,
  Then fix his sad eyes on the sullen earth,
  Ashamed to gaze upon the open world;
  Now will he cast his eyes up towards the heavens,
  Looking that ways for redress of wrong:
  Sometimes he seeketh to beguile his grief
  And tells a story with his careful tongue; 50
  Then comes his wife's dishonour in his thoughts
  And in the middle cutteth off his tale,
  Pouring fresh sorrow on his weary limbs.
  So woe-begone, so inly charged with woe,
  Was never any lived and bare it so.

Here enters MICHAEL.

Michael. My master would desire you come to bed.
Franklin. Is he himself already in his bed?
        [*Exit Franklin. Manet Michael.*
Michael. He is, and fain would have the light away.
  —Conflicting thoughts, encampèd in my breast,
  Awake me with the echo of their strokes, 60
  And I, a judge to censure either side,
  Can give to neither wishèd victory.
  My master's kindness pleads to me for life
  With just demand, and I must grant it him:
  My mistress she hath forced me with an oath,
  For Susan's sake, the which I may not break,
  For that is nearer than a master's love:

That grim-faced fellow, pitiless Black Will,
And Shakebag, stern in bloody stratagem,
—Two rougher ruffians never lived in Kent,—
Have sworn my death, if I infringe my vow,
A dreadful thing to be considered of.
Methinks I see them with their bolstered hair
Staring and grinning in thy gentle face,
And in their ruthless hands their daggers drawn,
Insulting o'er thee with a peck of oaths,
Whilst thou submissive, pleading for relief,
Art mangled by their ireful instruments.
Methinks I hear them ask where Michael is,
And pitiless Black Will cries: "Stab the slave!
The peasant will detect the tragedy!"
The wrinkles in his foul death-threat'ning face
Gapes open wide, like graves to swallow men.
My death to him is but a merriment,
And he will murder me to make him sport.
He comes, he comes! ah, Master Franklin, help!
Call on the neighbours, or we are but dead!

Here enters FRANKLIN *and* ARDEN.

Franklin. What dismal outcry calls me from my rest?
Arden. What hath occasioned such a fearful cry?
  Speak, Michael: hath any injured thee?
Michael. Nothing, sir; but as I fell asleep,
  Upon the threshold leaning to the stairs,
  I had a fearful dream that troubled me,
  And in my slumber thought I was beset
  With murderer thieves that came to rifle me.
  My trembling joints witness my inward fear:
  I crave your pardons for disturbing you.
Arden. So great a cry for nothing I ne'er heard.
  What? are the doors fast locked and all things safe?
Michael. I cannot tell; I think I locked the doors.
Arden. I like not this, but I'll go see myself.—
  Ne'er trust me but the doors were all unlocked:
  This negligence not half contenteth me.
  Get you to bed, and if you love my favour,
  Let me have no more such pranks as these.
  Come, Master Franklin, let us go to bed.

Franklin. Ay, by my faith; the air is very cold.
    Michael, farewell; I pray thee dream no more.   [*Exeunt.*

SCENE II.—*Outside Franklin's house.*

Here enters WILL, GREENE, *and* SHAKEBAG.

Shakebag. Black night hath hid the pleasures of the day,
    And sheeting darkness overhangs the earth,   110
    And with the black fold of her cloudy robe
    Obscures us from the eyesight of the world,
    In which sweet silence such as we triumph.
    The lazy minutes linger on their time,
    As loth to give due audit to the hour,
    Till in the watch our purpose be complete
    And Arden sent to everlasting night.
    Greene, get you gone, and linger here about,
    And at some hour hence come to us again,
    Where we will give you instance of his death.   120
Greene. Speed to my wish, whose will so e'er says no;
    And so I'll leave you for an hour or two.   [*Exit Greene.*
Will. I tell thee, Shakebag, would this thing were done:
    I am so heavy that I can scarce go;
    This drowsiness in me bodes little good.
Shakebag. How now, Will? become a precisian?
    Nay, then let's go sleep, when bugs and fears
    Shall kill our courages with their fancy's work.
Will. Why, Shakebag, thou mistakes me much,
    And wrongs me too in telling me of fear.   130
    Were't not a serious thing we go about,
    It should be slipt till I had fought with thee,
    To let thee know I am no coward, I.
    I tell thee, Shakebag, thou abusest me.
Shakebag. Why, thy speech bewrayed an inly kind of fear,
    And savoured of a weak relenting spirit.
    Go forward now in that we have begun,
    And afterwards attempt me when thou darest.
Will. And if I do not, heaven cut me off!
    But let that pass, and show me to this house,   140
    Where thou shalt see I'll do as much as Shakebag.
Shakebag. This is the door; but soft, methinks 'tis shut.

The villain Michael hath deceived us.
Will. Soft, let me see, Shakebag; 'tis shut indeed.
  Knock with thy sword, perhaps the slave will hear.
Shakebag. It will not be; the white-livered peasant
  Is gone to bed, and laughs us both to scorn.
Will. And he shall buy his merriment as dear
  As ever coistril bought so little sport:
  Ne'er let this sword assist me when I need,   150
  But rust and canker after I have sworn,
  If I, the next time that I meet the hind,
  Lop not away his leg, his arm, or both.
Shakebag. And let me never draw a sword again,
  Nor prosper in the twilight, cockshut light,
  When I would fleece the wealthy passenger,
  But lie and languish in a loathsome den,
  Hated and spit at by the goers-by,
  And in that death may die unpitied,
  If I, the next time that I meet the slave,   160
  Cut not the nose from off the coward's face
  And trample on it for this villainy.
Will. Come, let's go seek out Greene; I know he'll swear.
Shakebag. He were a villain, an he would not swear.
  'Twould make a peasant swear among his boys,
  That ne'er durst say before but "yea" and "no,"
  To be thus flouted of a coistril.
Will. Shakebag, let's seek out Greene, and in the morning
  At the alehouse butting Arden's house
  Watch the out-coming of that prick-eared cur,   170
  And then let me alone to handle him.   [*Exeunt.*

SCENE III.—*Room in Franklin's house as before.*

Here enters ARDEN, FRANKLIN, *and* MICHAEL.

Arden. Sirrah, get you back to Billingsgate
  And learn what time the tide will serve our turn;
  Come to us in Paul's. First go make the bed,
  And afterwards go hearken for the flood. [*Exit Michael.*
  Come, Master Franklin, you shall go with me.
  This night I dreamt that, being in a park,
  A toil was pitched to overthrow the deer,

    And I upon a little rising hill
    Stood whistly watching for the herd's approach.   180
    Even there, methoughts, a gentle slumber took me,
    And summoned all my parts to sweet repose;
    But in the pleasure of this golden rest
    An ill-thewed foster had removed the toil,
    And rounded me with that beguiling home
    Which late, methought, was pitched to cast the deer.
    With that he blew an evil-sounding horn,
    And at the noise another herdman came,
    With falchion drawn, and bent it at my breast,
    Crying aloud, "Thou art the game we seek!"   190
    With this I woke and trembled every joint,
    Like one obscured in a little bush,
    That sees a lion foraging about,
    And, when the dreadful forest-king is gone,
    He pries about with timorous suspect
    Throughout the thorny casements of the brake,
    And will not think his person dangerless,
    But quakes and shivers, though the cause be gone:
    So, trust me, Franklin, when I did awake,
    I stood in doubt whether I waked or no: 200
    Such great impression took this fond surprise.
    God grant this vision bedeem me any good.
Franklin. This fantasy doth rise from Michael's fear,
    Who being awaked with the noise he made,
    His troubled senses yet could take no rest;
    And this, I warrant you, procured your dream.
Arden. It may be so, God frame it to the best:
    But oftentimes my dreams presage too true.
Franklin. To such as note their nightly fantasies,
    Some one in twenty may incur belief;   210
    But use it not, 'tis but a mockery.
Arden. Come, Master Franklin; we'll now walk in Paul's
    And dine together at the ordinary,
    And by my man's direction draw to the quay,
    And with the tide go down to Feversham.
    Say, Master Franklin, shall it not be so?
Franklin. At your good pleasure, sir; I'll bear you company.
                                                    [Exeunt.

SCENE IV.—*Aldersgate.*

Here enters MICHAEL *at one door.*

Here enters GREENE, WILL, *and* SHAKEBAG *at another door.*

Will. Draw, Shakebag, for here's that villain Michael.
Greene. First, Will, let's hear what he can say.
Will. Speak, milksop slave, and never after speak. 220
Michael. For God's sake, sirs, let me excuse myself:
    For here I swear, by heaven and earth and all,
    I did perform the utmost of my task,
    And left the doors unbolted and unlocked.
    But see the chance: Franklin and my master
    Were very late conferring in the porch,
    And Franklin left his napkin where he sat
    With certain gold knit in it, as he said.
    Being in bed, he did bethink himself,
    And coming down he found the doors unshut: 230
    He locked the gates, and brought away the keys,
    For which offence my master rated me.
    But now I am going to see what flood it is,
    For with the tide my master will away;
    Where you may front him well on Rainham Down,
    A place well-fitting such a stratagem.
Will. Your excuse hath somewhat mollified my choler.
    Why now, Greene, 'tis better now nor e'er it was.
Greene. But, Michael, is this true?
Michael. As true as I report it to be true. 240
Shakebag. Then, Michael, this shall be your penance,
    To feast us all at the Salutation,
    Where we will plat our purpose thoroughly.
Greene. And, Michael, you shall bear no news of this tide,
    Because they two may be in Rainham Down
    Before your master.
Michael. Why, I'll agree to anything you'll have me,
    So you will except of my company. [*Exeunt.*

SCENE V.—*Arden's House at Feversham.*

Here enters MOSBIE.

Mosbie. Disturbèd thoughts drives me from company
    And dries my marrow with their watchfulness;   250
    Continual trouble of my moody brain
    Feebles my body by excess of drink,
    And nips me as the bitter north-east wind
    Doth check the tender blossoms in the spring.
    Well fares the man, howe'er his cates do taste,
    That tables not with foul suspicion;
    And he but pines amongst his delicates,
    Whose troubled mind is stuffed with discontent.
    My golden time was when I had no gold;
    Though then I wanted, yet I slept secure;   260
    My daily toil begat me night's repose,
    My night's repose made daylight fresh to me.
    But since I climbed the top-bough of the tree
    And sought to build my nest among the clouds,
    Each gentle stirry gale doth shake my bed,
    And makes me dread my downfall to the earth.
    But whither doth contemplation carry me?
    The way I seek to find, where pleasure dwells,
    Is hedged behind me that I cannot back,
    But needs must on, although to danger's gate.   270
    Then, Arden, perish thou by that decree;
    For Greene doth ear the land and weed thee up
    To make my harvest nothing but pure corn.
    And for his pains I'll hive him up a while,
    And after smother him to have his wax:
    Such bees as Greene must never live to sting.
    Then is there Michael and the painter too,
    Chief actors to Arden's overthrow;
    Who when they shall see me sit in Arden's seat,
    They will insult upon me for my meed,   280
    Or fright me by detecting of his end.
    I'll none of that, for I can cast a bone
    To make these curs pluck out each other's throat,
    And then am I sole ruler of mine own.

Yet Mistress Arden lives; but she's myself,
And holy Church rites makes us two but one.
But what for that? I may not trust you, Alice:
You have supplanted Arden for my sake,
And will extirpen me to plant another.
'Tis fearful sleeping in a serpent's bed,   290
And I will cleanly rid my hands of her.

Here enters ALICE.

But here she comes, and I must flatter her.
—How now, Alice? what, sad and passionate?
Make me partaker of thy pensiveness:
Fire divided burns with lesser force.
Alice. But I will dam that fire in my breast
Till by the force thereof my part consume.
Ah, Mosbie!
Mosbie. Such deep pathaires, like to a cannon's burst
Discharged against a ruinated wall,   300
Breaks my relenting heart in thousand pieces.
Ungentle Alice, thy sorrow is my sore;
Thou know'st it well, and 'tis thy policy
To forge distressful looks to wound a breast
Where lies a heart that dies when thou art sad.
It is not love that loves to anger love.
Alice. It is not love that loves to murder love.
Mosbie. How mean you that?
Alice. Thou knowest how dearly Arden loved me.
Mosbie. And then?   310
Alice. And then—conceal the rest, for 'tis too bad,
Lest that my words be carried with the wind,
And published in the world to both our shames.
I pray thee, Mosbie, let our springtime wither;
Our harvest else will yield but loathsome weeds.
Forget, I pray thee, what hath passed betwixt us,
For how I blush and tremble at the thoughts!
Mosbie. What? are you changed?
Alice. Ay, to my former happy life again,
From title of an odious strumpet's name   320
To honest Arden's wife, not Arden's honest wife.
Ha, Mosbie! 'tis thou has rifled me of that
And made me slanderous to all my kin;

   Even in my forehead is thy name ingraven,
   A mean artificer, that low-born name.
   I was bewitched: woe worth the hapless hour
   And all the causes that enchanted me!
Mosbie. Nay, if you ban, let me breathe curses forth,
   And if you stand so nicely at your fame,
   Let me repent the credit I have lost.   330
   I have neglected matters of import
   That would have stated me above thy state,
   Forslowed advantages, and spurned at time:
   Ay, Fortune's right hand Mosbie hath forsook
   To take a wanton giglot by the left.
   I left the marriage of an honest maid,
   Whose dowry would have weighed down all thy wealth,
   Whose beauty and demeanour far exceeded thee:
   This certain good I lost for changing bad,
   And wrapt my credit in thy company.   340
   I was bewitched,—that is no theme of thine,
   And thou unhallowed has enchanted me.
   But I will break thy spells and exorcisms,
   And put another sight upon these eyes
   That showed my heart a raven for a dove.
   Thou art not fair, I viewed thee not till now;
   Thou art not kind, till now I knew thee not;
   And now the rain hath beaten off thy gilt,
   Thy worthless copper shows thee counterfeit.
   It grieves me not to see how foul thou art,   350
   But mads me that ever I thought thee fair.
   Go, get thee gone, a copesmate for thy hinds;
   I am too good to be thy favourite.
Alice. Ay, now I see, and too soon find it true,
   Which often hath been told me by my friends,
   That Mosbie loves me not but for my wealth,
   Which too incredulous I ne'er believed.
   Nay, hear me speak, Mosbie, a word or two;
   I'll bite my tongue if it speak bitterly.
   Look on me, Mosbie, or I'll kill myself: 360
   Nothing shall hide me from thy stormy look.
   If thou cry war, there is no peace for me;
   I will do penance for offending thee,
   And burn this prayer-book, where I here use
   The holy word that had converted me.

See, Mosbie, I will tear away the leaves,
And all the leaves, and in this golden cover
Shall thy sweet phrases and thy letters dwell;
And thereon will I chiefly meditate,
And hold no other sect but such devotion. 370
Wilt thou not look? is all thy love o'erwhelmed?
Wilt thou not hear? what malice stops thine ears?
Why speaks thou not? what silence ties thy tongue?
Thou hast been sighted as the eagle is,
And heard as quickly as the fearful hare,
And spoke as smoothly as an orator,
When I have bid thee hear or see or speak,
And art thou sensible in none of these?
Weigh all thy good turns with this little fault,
And I deserve not Mosbie's muddy looks. 380
A fence of trouble is not thickened still:
Be clear again, I'll ne'er more trouble thee.
Mosbie. O no, I am a base artificer:
My wings are feathered for a lowly flight.
Mosbie? fie! no, not for a thousand pound.
Make love to you? why, 'tis unpardonable;
We beggars must not breathe where gentles are.
Alice. Sweet Mosbie is as gentle as a king,
And I too blind to judge him otherwise.
Flowers do sometimes spring in fallow lands, 390
Weeds in gardens, roses grow on thorns;
So, whatsoe'er my Mosbie's father was,
Himself is valued gentle by his worth.
Mosbie. Ah, how you women can insinuate,
And clear a trespass with your sweet-set tongue!
I will forget this quarrel, gentle Alice,
Provided I'll be tempted so no more.

Here enters BRADSHAW.

Alice. Then with thy lips seal up this new-made match.
Mosbie. Soft, Alice, here comes somebody.
Alice. How now, Bradshaw, what's the news with you? 400
Bradshaw. I have little news, but here's a letter
That Master Greene importuned me to give you.
Alice. Go in, Bradshaw; call for a cup of beer;
'Tis almost supper-time, thou shalt stay with us.
[*Exit Bradshaw.*

Then she reads the letter.

"We have missed of our purpose at London, but shall perform it by the way. We thank our neighbour Bradshaw.—Yours, Richard Greene."
    How likes my love the tenor of this letter?
Mosbie. Well, were his date completed and expired.
Alice. Ah, would it were! Then comes my happy hour: 410
    Till then my bliss is mixed with bitter gall.
    Come, let us in to shun suspicion.
Mosbie. Ay, to the gates of death to follow thee.   *[Exeunt.*

SCENE VI.—*Country near Rochester.*

Here enters GREENE, WILL, *and* SHAKEBAG.

Shakebag. Come, Will, see thy tools be in a readiness!
    Is not thy powder dank, or will thy flint strike fire?
Will. Then ask me if my nose be on my face,
    Or whether my tongue be frozen in my mouth.
    Zounds, here's a coil!
    You were best swear me on the interrogatories
    How many pistols I have took in hand,   420
    Or whether I love the smell of gunpowder,
    Or dare abide the noise the dag will make,
    Or will not wink at flashing of the fire.
    I pray thee, Shakebag, let this answer thee,
    That I have took more purses in this down
    Than e'er thou handledst pistols in thy life.
Shakebag. Ay, haply thou has picked more in a throng:
    But, should I brag what booties I have took,
    I think the overplus that's more than thine
    Would mount to a greater sum of money   430
    Then either thou or all thy kin are worth.
    Zounds, I hate them as I hate a toad
    That carry a muscado in their tongue,
    And scarce a hurting weapon in their hand.
Will. O Greene, intolerable!
    It is not for mine honour to bear this.
    Why, Shakebag, I did serve the king at Boulogne,
    And thou canst brag of nothing that thou hast done.

Shakebag. Why, so can Jack of Feversham,
    That sounded for a fillip of the nose, 440
    When he that gave it him holloed in his ear,
    And he supposed a cannon-bullet hit him.

Then they fight.

Greene. I pray you, sirs, list to Æsop's talk:
    Whilst two stout dogs were striving for a bone,
    There comes a cur and stole it from them both;
    So, while you stand striving on these terms of manhood,
    Arden escapes us, and deceives us all.
Shakebag. Why, he begun.
Will.   And thou shalt find I'll end;
    I do but slip it until better time: 450
    But, if I do forget——
    [*Then he kneels down and holds up his hands to heaven.*
Greene. Well, take your fittest standings, and once more
    Lime well your twigs to catch this wary bird.
    I'll leave you, and at your dag's discharge
    Make towards, like the longing water-dog
    That coucheth till the fowling-piece be off,
    Then seizeth on the prey with eager mood.
    Ah, might I see him stretching forth his limbs,
    As I have seen them beat their wings ere now!
Shakebag. Why, that thou shalt see, if he come this way.
Greene. Yes, that he doth, Shakebag, I warrant thee: 460
    But brawl not when I am gone in any case.
    But, sirs, be sure to speed him when he comes,
    And in that hope I'll leave you for an hour.

                                  [*Exit Greene.*

Here enters ARDEN, FRANKLIN, *and* MICHAEL.

Michael. 'Twere best that I went back to Rochester:
    The horse halts downright; it were not good
    He travelled in such pain to Feversham;
    Removing of a shoe may haply help it.
Arden. Well, get you back to Rochester; but, sirrah, see
    Ye o'ertake us ere we come to Rainham Down,
    For 't will be very late ere we get home. 470
Michael. Ay, God he knows, and so doth Will and Shakebag,

That thou shalt never go further than that down;
And therefore have I pricked the horse on purpose,
Because I would not view the massacre.   [*Exit Michael.*
Arden. Come, Master Franklin, onwards with your tale.
Franklin. I do assure you, sir, you task me much:
   A heavy blood is gathered at my heart,
   And on the sudden is my wind so short
   As hindereth the passage of my speech;
   So fierce a qualm yet ne'er assailed me.   480
Arden. Come, Master Franklin, let us go on softly:
   The annoyance of the dust or else some meat
   You ate at dinner cannot brook with you.
   I have been often so, and soon amended.
Franklin. Do you remember where my tale did leave?
Arden. Ay, where the gentleman did check his wife.
Franklin. She being reprehended for the fact,
   Witness produced that took her with the deed,
   Her glove brought in which there she left behind,
   And many other assured arguments,   490
   Her husband asked her whether it were not so.
Arden. Her answer then? I wonder how she looked,
   Having forsworn it with such vehement oaths,
   And at the instant so approved upon her.
Franklin. First did she cast her eyes down to the earth,
   Watching the drops that fell amain from thence;
   Then softly draws she forth her handkercher,
   And modestly she wipes her tear-stained face;
   Them hemmed she out, to clear her voice should seem,
   And with a majesty addressed herself   500
   To encounter all their accusations.—
   Pardon me, Master Arden, I can no more;
   This fighting at my heart makes short my wind.
Arden. Come, we are almost now at Rainham Down:
   Your pretty tale beguiles the weary way;
   I would you were in state to tell it out.
Shakebag. Stand close, Will, I hear them coming.

Here enters LORD CHEINY *with his men.*

Will. Stand to it, Shakebag, and be resolute.
L. Cheiny. Is it so near night as it seems,
   Or will this black-faced evening have a shower?   510

   —What, Master Arden? you are well met,
  I have longed this fortnight's day to speak with you:
  You are a stranger, man, in the Isle of Sheppy.
Arden. Your honour's always! bound to do you service.
L. Cheiny. Come you from London, and ne'er a man with
    you?
Arden. My man's coming after, but here's
  My honest friend that came along with me.
L. Cheiny. My Lord Protector's man I take you to be.
Franklin. Ay, my good lord, and highly bound to you.
L. Cheiny. You and your friend come home and sup with
    me.   520
Arden. I beseech your honour pardon me;
  I have made a promise to a gentleman,
  My honest friend, to meet him at my house;
  The occasion is great, or else would I wait on you.
L. Cheiny. Will you come to-morrow and dine with me,
  And bring your honest friend along with you?
  I have divers matters to talk with you about.
Arden. To-morrow we'll wait upon your honour.
L. Cheiny. One of you stay my horse at the top of the hill.
  —What! Black Will? for whose purse wait you? 530
  Thou wilt be hanged in Kent, when all is done.
Will. Not hanged, God save your honour;
  I am your bedesman, bound to pray for you.
L. Cheiny. I think thou ne'er said'st prayer in all thy life.—
  One of you give him a crown:—
  And, sirrah, leave this kind of life;
  If thou beest tainted for a penny-matter,
  And come in question, surely thou wilt truss.
  —Come, Master Arden, let us be going;
  Your way and mine lies four miles together.   540
      [*Exeunt. Manet Black Will and Shakebag.*
Will. The devil break all your necks at four miles' end!
  Zounds, I could kill myself for very anger!
  His lordship chops me in,
  Even when my dag was levelled at his heart.
  I would his crown were molten down his throat.
Shakebag. Arden, thou hast wondrous holy luck.
  Did ever man escape as thou hast done?
  Well, I'll discharge my pistol at the sky,
  For by this bullet Arden might not die.

Here enters GREENE.

Greene. What, is he down? is he dispatched? 550
Shakebag. Ay, in health towards Feversham, to shame us all.
Greene. The devil he is! why, sirs, how escaped he?
Shakebag. When we were ready to shoot,
  Comes my Lord Cheiny to prevent his death.
Greene. The Lord of Heaven hath preserved him.
Will. Preserved a fig! The Lord Cheiny hath preserved him,
  And bids him to a feast to his house at Shorlow.
  But by the way once more I'll meet with him,
  And, if all the Cheinies in the world say no,
  I'll have a bullet in his breast to-morrow. 560
  Therefore come, Greene, and let us to Feversham.
Greene. Ay, and excuse ourselves to Mistress Arden:
  O, how she'll chafe when she hears of this!
Shakebag. Why, I'll warrant you she'll think we dare not do it.
Will. Why, then let us go, and tell her all the matter,
  And plat the news to cut him off to-morrow. [*Exeunt.*

ACT IV

SCENE I.—ARDEN'S *House at Feversham*.

Here enters ARDEN *and his wife,* FRANKLIN, *and* MICHAEL.

Arden. See how the hours, the gardant of heaven's gate,
  Have by their toil removed the darksome clouds,
  That Sol may well discern the trampled path
  Wherein he wont to guide his golden car;
  The season fits; come, Franklin, let's away.
Alice. I thought you did pretend some special hunt,
  That made you thus cut short the time of rest.
Arden. It was no chase that made me rise so early,
  But, as I told thee yesternight, to go
  To the Isle of Sheppy, there to dine with my Lord Cheiny;
  For so his honour late commanded me.   11
Alice. Ay, such kind husbands seldom want excuses;
  Home is a wild cat to a wandering wit.
  The time hath been,—would God it were not past,—
  That honour's title nor a lord's command
  Could once have drawn you from these arms of mine.
  But my deserts or your desires decay,
  Or both; yet if true love may seem desert,
  I merit still to have thy company,
Franklin. Why, I pray you, sir, let her go along with us;   20
  I am sure his honour will welcome her
  And us the more for bringing her along.
Arden. Content; sirrah, saddle your mistress' nag.
Alice. No, begged favour merits little thanks;
  If I should go, our house would run away,
  Or else be stolen; therefore I'll stay behind.
Arden. Nay, see how mistaking you are! I pray thee, go.
Alice. No, no, not now.
Arden. Then let me leave thee satisfied in this,
  That time nor place nor persons alter me,   30
  But that I hold thee dearer than my life.
Alice. That will be seen by your quick return.

Arden. And that shall be ere night, and if I live.
  Farewell, sweet Alice, we mind to sup with thee.
                                                    [*Exit Alice.*
Franklin. Come, Michael, are our horses ready?
Michael. Ay, your horse are ready, but I am not ready, for I
  have lost my purse, with six and thirty shillings in it, with
  taking up of my master's nag.
Franklin. Why, I pray you, let us go before,
  Whilst he stays behind to seek his purse.   40
Arden. Go to, sirrah, see you follow us to the Isle of Sheppy
  To my Lord Cheiny's, where we mean to dine.
            [*Exeunt Arden and Franklin. Manet Michael.*
Michael. So, fair weather after you, for before you lies Black
  Will and Shakebag in the broom close, too close for you:
  they'll be your ferrymen to long home.

Here enters the Painter.

But who is this? the painter, my corrival, that would
  needs win Mistress Susan.
Clarke. How now, Michael? how doth my mistress and all at
  home?
Michael. Who? Susan Mosbie? she is your mistress, too?
Clarke. Ay, how doth she and all the rest?   50
Michael. All's well but Susan; she is sick.
Clarke. Sick? Of what disease?
Michael. Of a great fever.
Clarke. A fear of what?
Michael. A great fever.
Clarke. A fever? God forbid!
Michael. Yes, faith, and of a lordaine, too, as big as yourself.
Clarke. O, Michael, the spleen prickles you. Go to, you carry
  an eye over Mistress Susan.
Michael. I' faith, to keep her from the painter.   60
Clarke. Why more from a painter than from a serving creature
  like yourself?
Michael. Because you painters make but a painting table of a
  pretty wench, and spoil her beauty with blotting.
Clarke. What mean you by that?
Michael. Why, that you painters paint lambs in the lining of
  wenches' petticoats, and we serving-men put horns to them
  to make them become sheep.

Clarke. Such another word will cost you a cuff or a knock.
Michael. What, with a dagger made of a pencil? Faith, 'tis
    too weak, and therefore thou too weak to win Susan. 71
Clarke. Would Susan's love lay upon this stroke.
              [*Then he breaks Michael's head.*

      Here enters MOSBIE, GREENE, *and* ALICE.

Alice. I'll lay my life, this is for Susan's love.
    Stayed you behind your master to this end?
    Have you no other time to brable in
    But now when serious matters are in hand?—
    Say, Clarke, hast thou done the thing thou promised?
Clarke. Ay, here it is; the very touch is death.
Alice. Then this, I hope, if all the rest do fail,
    Will catch Master Arden, 80
    And make him wise in death that lived a fool.
    Why should he thrust his sickle in our corn,
    Or what hath he to do with thee, my love,
    Or govern me that am to rule myself?
    Forsooth, for credit sake, I must leave thee!
    Nay, he must leave to live that we may love,
    May live, may love; for what is life but love?
    And love shall last as long as life remains,
    And life shall end before my love depart.
Mosbie. Why, what is love without true constancy? 90
    Like to a pillar built of many stones,
    Yet neither with good mortar well compact
    Nor with cement to fasten it in the joints,
    But that it shakes with every blast of wind,
    And, being touched, straight falls unto the earth,
    And buries all his haughty pride in dust.
    No, let our love be rocks of adamant,
    Which time nor place nor tempest can asunder.
Greene. Mosbie, leave protestations now,
    And let us bethink us what we have to do. 100
    Black Will and Shakebag I have placed i' the broom,
    Close watching Arden's coming; let's to them
    And see what they have done.   [*Exeunt.*

SCENE II.—*The Kentish Coast opposite the Isle of Sheppy.*

Here enters ARDEN *and* FRANKLIN.

Arden. Oh, ferryman, where art thou?

Here enters the Ferryman.

Ferryman. Here, here, go before to the boat, and I will follow you.
Arden. We have great haste; I pray thee, come away.
Ferryman. Fie, what a mist is here!
Arden. This mist, my friend, is mystical,
 Like to a good companion's smoky brain,
 That was half drowned with new ale overnight. 110
Ferryman. 'Twere pity but his skull were opened to make more chimney room.
Franklin. Friend, what's thy opinion of this mist?
Ferryman. I think 'tis like to a curst wife in a little house, that never leaves her husband till she have driven him out at doors with a wet pair of eyes; then looks he as if his house were a-fire, or some of his friends dead.
Arden. Speaks thou this of thine own experience?
Ferryman. Perhaps, ay; perhaps, no: For my wife is as other women are, that is to say, governed by the moon. 120
Franklin. By the moon? how, I pray thee?
Ferryman. Nay, thereby lies a bargain, and you shall not have it fresh and fasting.
Arden. Yes, I pray thee, good ferryman.
Ferryman. Then for this once; let it be midsummer moon, but yet my wife has another moon.
Franklin. Another moon?
Ferryman. Ay, and it hath influences and eclipses.
Arden. Why, then, by this reckoning you sometimes play the man in the moon? 130
Ferryman. Ay, but you had not best to meddle with that moon, lest I scratch you by the face with my bramble-bush.
Arden. I am almost stifled with this fog; come, let's away.
Franklin. And, sirrah, as we go, let us have some more of your bold yeomanry.
Ferryman. Nay, by my troth, sir, but flat knavery. [*Exeunt.*

SCENE III.—*Another place on the coast.*

Here enters WILL *at one door, and* SHAKEBAG *at another.*

Shakebag. Oh, Will, where art thou?
Will. Here, Shakebag, almost in hell's mouth, where I cannot see my way for smoke.
Shakebag. I pray thee speak still that we may meet by the sound, for I shall fall into some ditch or other, unless my feet see better than my eyes. 142
Will. Didst thou ever see better weather to run away with another man's wife, or play with a wench at pot finger?
Shakebag. No; this were a fine world for chandlers, if this weather would last; for then a man should never dine nor sup without candle-light. But, sirrah Will, what horses are those that passed?
Will. Why, didst thou hear any?
Shakebag. Ay, that I did. 150
Will. My life for thine, 'twas Arden, and his companion, and then all our labour's lost.
Shakebag. Nay, say not so, for if it be they, they may haply lose their way as we have done, and then we may chance meet with them.
Will. Come, let us go on like a couple of blind pilgrims.
[*Then Shakebag falls into a ditch.*
Shakebag. Help, Will, help, I am almost drowned.

Here enters the Ferryman.

Ferryman. Who's that that calls for help?
Will. 'Twas none here, 'twas thou thyself.
Ferryman. I came to help him that called for help. 160
Why, how now? who is this that's in the ditch?
You are well enough served to go without a guide such weather as this.
Will. Sirrah, what companies hath passed your ferry this morning?
Ferryman. None but a couple of gentlemen, that went to dine at my Lord Cheiny's.
Will. Shakebag, did not I tell thee as much?
Ferryman. Why, sir, will you have any letters carried to them?

Will. No, sir; get you gone.

Ferryman. Did you ever see such a mist as this?

Will. No, nor such a fool as will rather be hought than get his way.

Ferryman. Why, sir, this is no Hough-Monday; you are deceived.
—What's his name, I pray you, sir?

Shakebag. His name is Black Will.

Ferryman. I hope to see him one day hanged upon a hill.

[*Exit Ferryman.*

Shakebag. See how the sun hath cleared the foggy mist,
Now we have missed the mark of our intent.

Here enters GREENE, MOSBIE, *and* ALICE.

Mosbie. Black Will and Shakebag, what make you here?
What, is the deed done? is Arden dead?

Will. What could a blinded man perform in arms?
Saw you not how till now the sky was dark,
That neither horse nor man could be discerned?
Yet did we hear their horses as they passed.

Greene. Have they escaped you, then, and passed the ferry?

Shakebag. Ay, for a while; but here we two will stay,
And at their coming back meet with them once more.
Zounds, I was ne'er so toiled in all my life
In following so slight a task as this.

Mosbie. How cam'st thou so beryed?

Will. With making false footing in the dark;
He needs would follow them without a guide.

Alice. Here's to pay for a fire and good cheer:
Get you to Feversham to the Flower-de-luce,
And rest yourselves until some other time.

Greene. Let me alone; it most concerns my state.

Will. Ay, Mistress Arden, this will serve the turn,
In case we fall into a second fog.

[*Exeunt Greene, Will, and Shakebag.*

Mosbie. These knaves will never do it, let us give it over.

Alice. First tell me how you like my new device:
Soon, when my husband is returning back,
You and I both marching arm in arm,
Like loving friends, we'll meet him on the way,
And boldly beard and brave him to his teeth.
When words grow hot and blows begin to rise,

SCENE IV.   Arden of Feversham   105

    I'll call those cutters forth your tenement,
    Who, in a manner to take up the fray,
    Shall wound my husband Hornsby to the death.
Mosbie. A fine device! why, this deserves a kiss.   [*Exeunt.*

SCENE IV.—*The open country.*

Here enters DICK REEDE *and a* Sailor.

Sailor. Faith, Dick Reede, it is to little end: 211
    His conscience is too liberal, and he too niggardly
    To part from any thing may do thee good.
Reede. He is coming from Shorlow as I understand;
    Here I'll intercept him, for at his house
    He never will vouchsafe to speak with me.
    If prayers and fair entreaties will not serve,
    Or make no battery in his flinty breast,

Here enters FRANKLIN, ARDEN, *and* MICHAEL.

    I'll curse the carle, and see what that will do.
    See where he comes to further my intent!—   220
    Master Arden, I am now bound to the sea;
    My coming to you was about the plat
    Of ground which wrongfully you detain from me.
    Although the rent of it be very small,
    Yet it will help my wife and children,
    Which here I leave in Feversham, God knows,
    Needy and bare: for Christ's sake, let them have it!
Arden. Franklin, hearest thou this fellow speak?
    That which he craves I dearly bought of him,
    Although the rent of it was ever mine.—   230
    Sirrah, you that ask these questions,
    If with thy clamorous impeaching tongue
    Thou rail on me, as I have heard thou dost,
    I'll lay thee up so close a twelve-month's day,
    As thou shalt neither see the sun nor moon.
    Look to it, for, as surely as I live,
    I'll banish pity if thou use me thus.
Reede. What, wilt thou do me wrong and threat me too,
    Nay, then, I'll tempt thee, Arden, do thy worst.

  God, I beseech thee, show some miracle 240
  On thee or thine, in plaguing thee for this.
  That plot of ground which thou detains from me,
  I speak it in an agony of spirit,
  Be ruinous and fatal unto thee!
  Either there be butchered by thy dearest friends,
  Or else be brought for men to wonder at,
  Or thou or thine miscarry in that place,
  Or there run mad and end thy cursèd days!
Franklin. Fie, bitter knave, bridle thine envious tongue;
  For curses are like arrows shot upright, 250
  Which falling down light on the shooter's head.
Reede. Light where they will! Were I upon the sea,
  As oft I have in many a bitter storm,
  And saw a dreadful southern flaw at hand,
  The pilot quaking at the doubtful storm,
  And all the sailors praying on their knees,
  Even in that fearful time would I fall down,
  And ask of God, whate'er betide of me,
  Vengeance on Arden or some misevent
  To show the world what wrong the carle hath done. 260
  This charge I'll leave with my distressful wife,
  My children shall be taught such prayers as these;
  And thus I go, but leave my curse with thee.
         [*Exeunt Reede and Sailor.*
Arden. It is the railingest knave in Christendom,
  And oftentimes the villain will be mad;
  It greatly matters not what he says,
  But I assure you I ne'er did him wrong.
Franklin. I think so, Master Arden.
Arden. Now that our horses are gone home before,
  My wife may haply meet me on the way. 270
  For God knows she is grown passing kind of late,
  And greatly changed from
  The old humour of her wonted frowardness,
  And seeks by fair means to redeem old faults.
Franklin. Happy the change that alters for the best!
  But see in any case you make no speech
  Of the cheer we had at my Lord Cheiny's,
  Although most bounteous and liberal,
  For that will make her think herself more wronged,
  In that we did not carry her along; 280

For sure she grieved that she was left behind.
Arden. Come, Franklin, let us strain to mend our pace,
And take her unawares playing the cook;

Here enters ALICE *and* MOSBIE.

For I believe she'll strive to mend our cheer.
Franklin. Why, there's no better creatures in the world,
Than women are when they are in good humours.
Arden. Who is that? Mosbie? what, so familiar?
Injurious strumpet, and thou ribald knave,
Untwine those arms.
Alice. Ay, with a sugared kiss let them untwine. 290
Arden. Ah, Mosbie! perjured beast! bear this and all!
Mosbie. And yet no horned beast; the horns are thine.
Franklin. O monstrous! Nay, then it is time to draw.
Alice. Help, help! they murder my husband.

Here enters WILL *and* SHAKEBAG.

Shakebag. Zounds, who injures Master Mosbie? Help, Will!
I am hurt.
Mosbie. I may thank you, Mistress Arden, for this wound.
 [*Exeunt Mosbie, Will, and Shakebag.*
Alice. Ah, Arden, what folly blinded thee?
Ah, jealous harebrained man, what hast thou done!
When we, to welcome thee with intended sport,
Came lovingly to meet thee on thy way, 300
Thou drew'st thy sword, enraged with jealousy,
And hurt thy friend whose thoughts were free from harm:
All for a worthless kiss and joining arms,
Both done but merrily to try thy patience.
And me unhappy that devised the jest,
Which, though begun in sport, yet ends in blood!
Franklin. Marry, God defend me from such a jest!
Alice. Could'st thou not see us friendly smile on thee,
When we joined arms, and when I kissed his cheek?
Hast thou not lately found me over-kind? 310
Did'st thou not hear me cry "they murder thee"?
Called I not help to set my husband free?
No, ears and all were witched; ah me accursed
To link in liking with a frantic man!

    Henceforth I'll be thy slave, no more thy wife,
    For with that name I never shall content thee.
    If I be merry, thou straightways thinks me light;
    If sad, thou sayest the sullens trouble me;
    If well attired, thou thinks I will be gadding;
    If homely, I seem sluttish in thine eye: 320
    Thus am I still, and shall be while I die.
    Poor wench abused by thy misgovernment!
Arden. But is it for truth that neither thou nor he
    Intendedst malice in your misdemeanour?
Alice. The heavens can witness of our harmless thoughts.
Arden. Then pardon me, sweet Alice, and forgive this fault!
    Forget but this and never see the like.
    Impose me penance, and I will perform it,
    For in thy discontent I find a death,—
    A death tormenting more than death itself.   330
Alice. Nay, had'st thou loved me as thou dost pretend,
    Thou wouldst have marked the speeches of thy friend,
    Who going wounded from the place, he said
    His skin was pierced only through my device;
    And if sad sorrow taint thee for this fault,
    Thou would'st have followed him, and seen him dressed,
    And cried him mercy whom thou hast misdone:
    Ne'er shall my heart be eased till this be done.
Arden. Content thee, sweet Alice, thou shalt have thy will,
    Whate'er it be. For that I injured thee,   340
    And wronged my friend, shame scourgeth my offence;
    Come thou thyself, and go along with me,
    And be a mediator 'twixt us two.
Franklin. Why, Master Arden! know you what you do?
    Will you follow him that hath dishonoured you?
Alice. Why, canst thou prove I have been disloyal?
Franklin. Why, Mosbie taunted your husband with the horn.
Alice. Ay, after he had reviled him
    By the injurious name of perjured beast:
    He knew no wrong could spite a jealous man   350
    More than the hateful naming of the horn.
Franklin. Suppose 'tis true; yet is it dangerous
    To follow him whom he hath lately hurt.
Alice. A fault confessed is more than half amends;
    But men of such ill spirit as yourself
    Work crosses and debates 'twixt man and wife.

Arden. I pray thee, gentle Franklin, hold thy peace:
　　I know my wife counsels me for the best.
　　I'll seek out Mosbie where his wound is dressed,
　　And salve this hapless quarrel if I may. 360
　　　　　　　　　　[*Exeunt Arden and Alice.*
Franklin. He whom the devil drives must go perforce.
　　Poor gentleman, how soon he is bewitched!
　　And yet, because his wife is the instrument,
　　His friends must not be lavish in their speech.
　　　　　　　　　　　　　　　[*Exit Franklin.*

ACT V

SCENE I.—*A Street in Feversham.*

Here enters WILL, SHAKEBAG, *and* GREENE.

Will. Sirrah Greene, when was I so long in killing a man?
Greene. I think we shall never do it; let us give it over.
Shakebag. Nay, Zounds! we'll kill him, though we be hanged at his door for our labour.
Will. Thou knowest, Greene, that I have lived in London this twelve years, where I have made some go upon wooden legs for taking the wall on me; divers with silver noses for saying "There goes Black Will!" I have cracked as many blades as thou hast nuts.
Greene. O monstrous lie! 10
Will. Faith, in a manner I have. The bawdy-houses have paid me tribute; there durst not a whore set up, unless she have agreed with me first for opening her shop-windows. For a cross word of a tapster I have pierced one barrel after another with my dagger, and held him by the ears till all his beer hath run out. In Thames Street a brewer's cart was like to have run over me: I made no more ado, but went to the clerk and cut all the notches of his tallies and beat them about his head. I and my company have taken the constable from his watch, and carried him about the fields on a coltstaff. I have broken a sergeant's head with his own mace, and bailed whom I list with my sword and buckler. All the tenpenny-alehouses-men would stand every morning with a quart-pot in their hand, saying, "Will it please your worship drink?" He that had not done so, had been sure to have had his sign pulled down and his lattice borne away the next night. To conclude, what have I not done? yet cannot do this; doubtless, he is preserved by miracle.

Here enters ALICE *and* MICHAEL.

Greene. Hence, Will! here comes Mistress Arden. 30
Alice. Ah, gentle Michael, art thou sure they're friends?

Michael. Why, I saw them when they both shook hands.
  When Mosbie bled, he even wept for sorrow,
  And railed on Franklin that was cause of all.
  No sooner came the surgeon in at doors,
  But my master took to his purse and gave him money,
  And, to conclude, sent me to bring you word
  That Mosbie, Franklin, Bradshaw, Adam Fowle,
  With divers of his neighbours and his friends,
  Will come and sup with you at our house this night.   40
Alice. Ah, gentle Michael, run thou back again,
  And, when my husband walks into the fair,
  Bid Mosbie steal from him and come to me;
  And this night shall thou and Susan be made sure.
Michael. I'll go tell him.
Alice. And as thou goest, tell John cook of our guests,
  And bid him lay it on, spare for no cost.   [*Exit Michael.*
Will. Nay, and there be such cheer, we will bid ourselves.—
  Mistress Arden, Dick Greene and I do mean to sup with you.
Alice. And welcome shall you be. Ah, gentlemen,   50
  How missed you of your purpose yesternight?
Greene. 'Twas 'long of Shakebag, that unlucky villain.
Shakebag. Thou dost me wrong; I did as much as any.
Will. Nay then, Mistress Arden, I'll tell you how it was:
  When he should have locked with both his hilts,
  He in a bravery flourished o'er his head;
  With that comes Franklin at him lustily,
  And hurts the slave; with that he slinks away.
 Now his way had been to have come hand and feet, one
  and two round, at his costard; he like a fool bears his
  sword-point half a yard out of danger. I lie here for my
  life; if the devil come, and he have no more strength than I
  have fence, he shall never beat me from this ward, I'll stand
  to it; a buckler in a skilful hand is as good as a castle; nay,
  'tis better than a sconce, for I have tried it.   65
  Mosbie, perceiving this, began to faint:
  With that comes Arden with his arming sword,
  And thrust him through the shoulder in a trice.
Alice. Ay, but I wonder why you both stood still.
Will. Faith, I was so amazed, I could not strike.   70
Alice. Ah, sirs, had he yesternight been slain,
  For every drop of his detested blood
  I would have crammed in angels in thy fist,

            And kissed thee, too, and hugged thee in my arms.
Will. Patient yourself, we cannot help it now.
       Greene and we two will dog him through the fair,
       And stab him in the crowd, and steal away.

                    Here enters MOSBIE.

Alice. It is unpossible; but here comes he
       That will, I hope, invent some surer means.
       Sweet Mosbie, hide thy arm, it kills my heart.   80
Mosbie. Ay, Mistress Arden, this is your favour.
Alice. Ah, say not so; for when I saw thee hurt,
       I could have took the weapon thou let'st fall,
       And run at Arden; for I have sworn
       That these mine eyes, offended with his sight,
       Shall never close till Arden's be shut up.
       This night I rose and walked about the chamber,
       And twice or thrice I thought to have murdered him.
Mosbie. What, in the night? then had we been undone.
Alice. Why, how long shall he live?   90
Mosbie. Faith, Alice, no longer than this night.—
       Black Will and Shakebag, will you two perform
       The complot that I have laid?
Will. Ay, or else think me a villain.
Greene. And rather than you shall want, I'll help myself.
Mosbie. You, Master Greene, shall single Franklin forth,
       And hold him with a long tale of strange news,
       That he may not come home till supper-time.
       I'll fetch Master Arden home, and we like friends
       Will play a game or two at tables here.   100
Alice. But what of all this? how shall he be slain?
Mosbie. Why, Black Will and Shakebag locked within the counting-house
       Shall at a certain watchword given rush forth.
Will. What shall the watchword be?
Mosbie. "Now I take you"; that shall be the word:
       But come not forth before in any case.
Will. I warrant you. But who shall lock me in?
Alice. That will I do; thou'st keep the key thyself.
Mosbie. Come, Master Greene, go you along with me.
       See all things ready, Alice, against we come.   110
Alice. Take no care for that; send you him home.
                           [*Exeunt Mosbie and Greene.*

And if he e'er go forth again, blame me.
   Come, Black Will, that in mine eyes art fair;
   Next unto Mosbie do I honour thee;
   Instead of fair words and large promises
   My hands shall play you golden harmony:
   How like you this? say, will you do it, sirs?
Will. Ay, and that bravely, too. Mark my device:
   Place Mosbie, being a stranger, in a chair,
   And let your husband sit upon a stool,   120
   That I may come behind him cunningly,
   And with a towel pull him to the ground,
   Then stab him till his flesh be as a sieve;
   That done, bear him behind the Abbey,
   That those that find him murdered may suppose
   Some slave or other killed him for his gold.
Alice. A fine device! you shall have twenty pound,
   And, when he is dead, you shall have forty more,
   And, lest you might be suspected staying here,
   Michael shall saddle you two lusty geldings;   130
   Ride whither you will, to Scotland, or to Wales,
   I'll see you shall not lack, where'er you be.
Will. Such words would make one kill a thousand men!
   Give me the key: which is the counting-house?
Alice. Here would I stay and still encourage you;
   But that I know how resolute you are.
Shakebag. Tush, you are too faint-hearted; we must do it.
Alice. But Mosbie will be there, whose very looks
   Will add unwonted courage to my thought,
   And make me the first that shall adventure on him.   140
Will. Tush, get you gone; 'tis we must do the deed.
   When this door opens next, look for his death.
                    [*Exeunt Will and Shakebag.*
Alice. Ah, would he now were here that it might open!
   I shall no more be closed in Arden's arms,
   That like the snakes of black Tisiphone
   Sting me with their embracings! Mosbie's arms
   Shall compass me, and, were I made a star,
   I would have none other spheres but those.
   There is no nectar but in Mosbie's lips!
   Had chaste Diana kissed him, she like me   150
   Would grow love-sick, and from her watery bower
   Fling down Endymion and snatch him up:

Then blame not me that slay a silly man
Not half so lovely as Endymion.

Here enters MICHAEL.

Michael. Mistress, my master is coming hard by.
Alice. Who comes with him?
Michael. Nobody but Mosbie.
Alice. That's well, Michael. Fetch in the tables, and when thou hast done, stand before the counting-house door.
Michael. Why so? 160
Alice. Black Will is locked within to do the deed.
Michael. What? shall he die to-night?
Alice. Ay, Michael.
Michael. But shall not Susan know it?
Alice. Yes, for she'll be as secret as ourselves.
Michael. That's brave. I'll go fetch the tables.
Alice. But, Michael, hark to me a word or two:
When my husband is come in, lock the street-door;
He shall be murdered, or the guests come in.
[*Exit Michael.*

Here enters ARDEN *and* MOSBIE.

Husband, what mean you to bring Mosbie home? 170
Although I wished you to be reconciled,
'Twas more for fear of you than love of him.
Black Will and Greene are his companions,
And they are cutters, and may cut you short:
Therefore I thought it good to make you friends.
But wherefore do you bring him hither now?
You have given me my supper with his sight.
Mosbie. Master Arden, methinks your wife would have me gone.
Arden. No, good master Mosbie; women will be prating.
Alice, bid him welcome; he and I are friends. 180
Alice. You may enforce me to it, if you will;
But I had rather die than bid him welcome.
His company hath purchased me ill friends,
And therefore will I ne'er frequent it more.
Mosbie. —Oh, how cunningly she can dissemble!
Arden. Now he is here, you will not serve me so.
Alice. I pray you be not angry or displeased;
I'll bid him welcome, seeing you'll have it so.
You are welcome, Master Mosbie; will you sit down?

Mosbie. I know I am welcome to your loving husband; 190
  But for yourself, you speak not from your heart.
Alice. And if I do not, sir, think I have cause.
Mosbie. Pardon me, Master Arden; I'll away.
Arden. No, good Master Mosbie.
Alice. We shall have guests enough, though you go hence.
Mosbie. I pray you, Master Arden, let me go.
Arden. I pray thee, Mosbie, let her prate her fill.
Alice. The doors are open, sir, you may be gone.
Michael. —Nay, that's a lie, for I have locked the doors.
Arden. Sirrah, fetch me a cup of wine, I'll make them friends.
  And, gentle Mistress Alice, seeing you are so stout, 201
  You shall begin! frown not, I'll have it so.
Alice. I pray you meddle with that you have to do.
Arden. Why, Alice! how can I do too much for him
  Whose life I have endangered without cause?
Alice. 'Tis true; and, seeing 'twas partly through my means,
  I am content to drink to him for this once.
  Here, Master Mosbie! and I pray you, henceforth
  Be you as strange to me as I to you.
  Your company hath purchased me ill friends, 210
  And I for you, God knows, have undeserved
  Been ill spoken of in every place;
  Therefore henceforth frequent my house no more.
Mosbie. I'll see your husband in despite of you.
  Yet, Arden, I protest to thee by heaven,
  Thou ne'er shalt see me more after this night,
  I'll go to Rome rather than be forsworn.
Arden. Tush, I'll have no such vows made in my house.
Alice. Yes, I pray you, husband, let him swear;
  And, on that condition, Mosbie, pledge me here. 220
Mosbie. Ay, as willingly as I mean to live.
Arden. Come, Alice, is our supper ready yet?
Alice. It will by then you have played a game at tables.
Arden. Come, Master Mosbie, what shall we play for?
Mosbie. Three games for a French crown, sir, and please you.
Arden. Content.
  [*Then they play at the tables. Enter Will and Shakebag.*
Will. —Can he not take him yet? what a spite is that?
Alice. —Not yet, Will; take heed he see thee not.
Will. —I fear he will spy me as I am coming.
Michael. —To prevent that, creep betwixt my legs. 230

Mosbie. One ace, or else I lose the game.
Arden. Marry, sir, there's two for failing.
Mosbie. Ah, Master Arden, "now I can take you."
[*Then Will pulls him down with a towel.*
Arden. Mosbie! Michael! Alice! what will you do?
Will. Nothing but take you up, sir, nothing else.
Mosbie. There's for the pressing iron you told me of.
[*Stabs him.*
Shakebag. And there's for the ten pound in my sleeve.
[*Stabs him.*
Alice. What! groans thou? nay, then give me the weapon!
Take this for hindering Mosbie's love and mine.
[*She stabs him.*
Michael. O, mistress! 240
Will. Ah, that villain will betray us all.
Mosbie. Tush, fear him not; he will be secret.
Michael. Why, dost thou think I will betray myself?
Shakebag. In Southwark dwells a bonny northern lass,
The widow Chambly; I'll to her house now,
And if she will not give me harborough,
I'll make booty of the quean even to her smock.
Will. Shift for yourselves; we two will leave you now.
Alice. First lay the body in the counting-house.
[*Then they lay the body in the Counting-house.*
Will. We have our gold; Mistress Alice, adieu; 250
Mosbie, farewell, and Michael, farewell too. [*Exeunt.*

Enter SUSAN.

Susan. Mistress, the guests are at the doors.
Hearken, they knock: what, shall I let them in?
Alice. Mosbie, go thou and bear them company. [*Exit Mosbie.*
And, Susan, fetch water and wash away this blood.
Susan. The blood cleaveth to the ground and will not out.
Alice. But with my nails I'll scrape away the blood;—
The more I strive, the more the blood appears!
Susan. What's the reason, Mistress, can you tell?
Alice. Because I blush not at my husband's death. 260

Here enters MOSBIE.

Mosbie. How now? what's the matter? is all well?
Alice. Ay, well, if Arden were alive again.
In vain we strive, for here his blood remains.

Mosbie. Why, strew rushes on it, can you not?
  This wench doth nothing: fall unto the work.
Alice. 'Twas thou that made me murder him.
Mosbie. What of that?
Alice. Nay, nothing, Mosbie, so it be not known.
Mosbie. Keep thou it close, and 'tis unpossible.
Alice. Ah, but I cannot! was he not slain by me?   270
  My husband's death torments me at the heart.
Mosbie. It shall not long torment thee, gentle Alice;
  I am thy husband, think no more of him.

Here enters ADAM FOWLE *and* BRADSHAW.

Bradshaw. How now, Mistress Arden? what ail you weep?
Mosbie. Because her husband is abroad so late.
  A couple of ruffians threatened him yesternight,
  And she, poor soul, is afraid he should be hurt.
Adam. Is't nothing else? tush, he'll be here anon.

Here enters GREENE.

Greene. Now, Mistress Arden, lack you any guests?
Alice. Ah, Master Greene, did you see my husband lately?   280
Greene. I saw him walking behind the Abbey even now.

Here enters FRANKLIN.

Alice. I do not like this being out so late.—
  Master Franklin, where did you leave my busband?
Franklin. Believe me I saw him not since morning.
  Fear you not, he'll come anon; meantime
  You may do well to bid his guests sit down.
Alice. Ay, so they shall; Master Bradshaw, sit you there;
  I pray you, be content, I'll have my will.
  Master Mosbie, sit you in my husband's seat.
Michael. —Susan, shall thou and I wait on them?   290
  Or, an thou sayest the word, let us sit down too.
Susan. —Peace, we have other matters now in hand.
  I fear me, Michael, all will be bewrayed.
Michael. —Tush, so it be known that I shall marry thee in the
  morning, I care not though I be hanged ere night. But to
  prevent the worst, I'll buy some ratsbane.
Susan. —Why, Michael, wilt thou poison thyself?

Michael. —No, but my mistress, for I fear she'll tell.
Susan. —Tush, Michael; fear not her, she's wise enough.
Mosbie. Sirrah Michael, give's a cup of beer.— 300
 Mistress Arden, here's to your husband.
Alice. My husband!
Franklin. What ails you, woman, to cry so suddenly?
Alice. Ah, neighbours, a sudden qualm came o'er my heart;
 My husband being forth torments my mind.
 I know something's amiss, he is not well;
 Or else I should have heard of him ere now.
Mosbie. —She will undo us through her foolishness.
Greene. Fear not, Mistress Arden, he's well enough.
Alice. Tell not me; I know he is not well: 310
 He was not wont for to stay thus late.
 Good Master Franklin, go and seek him forth,
 And if you find him, send him home to me,
 And tell him what a fear he hath put me in.
Franklin. —I like not this; I pray God all be well.
 I'll seek him out, and find him if I can.
       [*Exeunt Franklin, Mosbie, and Greene.*
Alice. —Michael, how shall I do to rid the rest away?
Michael. —Leave that to my charge, let me alone.
 'Tis very late, Master Bradshaw,
 And there are many false knaves abroad, 320
 And you have many narrow lanes to pass.
Bradshaw. Faith, friend Michael, and thou sayest true.
 Therefore I pray thee light's forth and lend's a link.
       [*Exeunt Bradshaw, Adam, and Michael.*
Alice. Michael, bring them to the doors, but do not stay;
 You know I do not love to be alone.
 —Go, Susan, and bid thy brother come:
 But wherefore should he come? Here is nought but fear;
 Stay, Susan, stay, and help to counsel me.
Susan. Alas, I counsel! fear frights away my wits.
      [*Then they open the counting-house door,
       and look upon Arden.*
Alice. See, Susan, where thy quondam master lies, 330
 Sweet Arden, smeared in blood and filthy gore.
Susan. My brother, you, and I shall rue this deed.
Alice. Come, Susan, help to lift his body forth,
 And let our salt tears be his obsequies.

Here enters Mosbie *and* Greene.

Mosbie. Now now, Alice, whither will you bear him?
Alice. Sweet Mosbie, art thou come? Then weep that will:
    I have my wish in that I joy thy sight.
Greene. Well, it behoves us to be circumspect.
Mosbie. Ay, for Franklin thinks that we have murdered him.
Alice. Ay, but he cannot prove it for his life. 340
    We'll spend this night in dalliance and in sport.

Here enters Michael.

Michael. O mistress, the Mayor and all the watch
    Are coming towards our house with glaives and bills.
Alice. Make the door fast; let them not come in.
Mosbie. Tell me, sweet Alice, how shall I escape?
Alice. Out at the back-door, over the pile of wood,
    And for one night lie at the Flower-de-luce.
Mosbie. That is the next way to betray myself.
Greene. Alas, Mistress Arden, the watch will take me here,
    And cause suspicion, where else would be none. 350
Alice. Why, take that way that Master Mosbie doth;
    But first convey the body to the fields.
        [*Then they bear the body into the fields.*
Mosbie. Until to-morrow, sweet Alice, now farewell:
    And see you confess nothing in any case.
Greene. Be resolute, Mistress Alice, betray us not,
    But cleave to us as we will stick to you.
        [*Exeunt* Mosbie *and* Greene.
Alice. Now, let the judge and juries do their worst:
    My house is clear, and now I fear them not.
Susan. As we went, it snowed all the way,
    Which makes me fear our footsteps will be spied. 360
Alice. Peace, fool, the snow will cover them again.
Susan. But it had done before we came back again.
Alice. Hark, hark, they knock! go, Michael, let them in.

Here enters the Mayor *and the* Watch.

    How now, Master Mayor, have you brought my husband home?
Mayor. I saw him come into your house an hour ago.

Alice. You are deceived; it was a Londoner.
Mayor. Mistress Arden, know you not one that is called Black
    Will?
Alice. I know none such: what mean these questions?
Mayor. I have the Council's warrant to apprehend him.
Alice. —I am glad it is no worse. 370
    Why, Master Mayor, think you I harbour any such?
Mayor. We are informed that here he is;
    And therefore pardon us, for we must search.
Alice. Ay, search, and spare you not, through every room:
    Were my husband at home, you would not offer this.

Here enters FRANKLIN.

    Master Franklin, what mean you come so sad?
Franklin. Arden, thy husband and my friend, is slain.
Alice. Ah, by whom? Master Franklin, can you tell?
Franklin. I know not; but behind the Abbey
    There he lies murdered in most piteous case. 380
Mayor. But, Master Franklin, are you sure 'tis he?
Franklin. I am too sure; would God I were deceived.
Alice. Find out the murderers, let them be known.
Franklin. Ay, so they shall: come you along with us.
Alice. Wherefore?
Franklin. Know you this hand-towel and this knife?
Susan. —Ah, Michael, through this thy negligence
    Thou hast betrayed and undone us all.
Michael. —I was so afraid I knew not what I did:
    I thought I had thrown them both into the well. 390
Alice. It is the pig's blood we had to supper.
    But wherefore stay you? find out the murderers.
Mayor. I fear me you'll prove one of them yourself.
Alice. I one of them? what mean such questions?
Franklin. I fear me he was murdered in this house
    And carried to the fields; for from that place
    Backwards and forwards may you see
    The print of many feet within the snow.
    And look about this chamber where we are,
    And you shall find part of his guiltless blood; 400
    For in his slipshoe did I find some rushes,
    Which argueth he was murdered in this room.
Mayor. Look in the place where he was wont to sit.

See, see! his blood! it is too manifest.
Alice. It is a cup of wine that Michael shed.
Michael. Ay, truly.
Franklin. It is his blood, which, strumpet, thou hast shed.
   But if I live, thou and thy 'complices
   Which have conspired and wrought his death shall rue it.
Alice. Ah, Master Franklin, God and heaven can tell   410
   I loved him more than all the world beside.
   But bring me to him, let me see his body.
Franklin. Bring that villain and Mosbie's sister too;
   And one of you go to the Flower-de-luce,
   And seek for Mosbie, and apprehend him too.   [*Exeunt.*

SCENE II.—*An obscure street in London.*

Here enters SHAKEBAG *solus.*

Shakebag. The widow Chambly in her husband's days I kept;
   And now he's dead, she is grown so stout
   She will not know her old companions.
   I came thither, thinking to have had harbour
   As I was wont,   420
   And she was ready to thrust me out at doors;
   But whether she would or no, I got me up,
   And as she followed me, I spurned her down the stairs,
   And broke her neck, and cut her tapster's throat,
   And now I am going to fling them in the Thames.
   I have the gold; what care I though it be known!
   I'll cross the water and take sanctuary.   [*Exit.*

SCENE III.—*Arden's house at Feversham.*

Here enters the MAYOR, MOSBIE, ALICE, FRANKLIN, MICHAEL, *and* SUSAN.

Mayor. See, Mistress Arden, where your husband lies;
   Confess this foul fault and be penitent.
Alice. Arden, sweet husband, what shall I say?   430
   The more I sound his name, the more he bleeds;
   This blood condemns me, and in gushing forth
   Speaks as it falls, and asks me why I did it.
   Forgive me, Arden: I repent me now,

And, would my death save thine, thou should'st not die.
Rise up, sweet Arden, and enjoy thy love,
And frown not on me when we meet in heaven:
In heaven I'll love thee, though on earth I did not.
Mayor. Say, Mosbie, what made thee murder him?
Franklin. Study not for an answer; look not down· 440
His purse and girdle found at thy bed's head
Witness sufficiently thou didst the deed;
It bootless is to swear thou didst it not.
Mosbie. I hired Black Will and Shakebag, ruffians both,
And they and I have done this murderous deed.
But wherefore stay we? Come and bear me hence.
Franklin. Those ruffians shall not escape; I will up to London,
And get the Council's warrant to apprehend them.
[*Exeunt.*

SCENE IV.—*The Kentish Coast.*

Here enters WILL.

Will. Shakebag, I hear, hath taken sanctuary,
But I am so pursued with hues and cries 450
For petty robberies that I have done,
That I can come unto no sanctuary.
Therefore must I in some oyster-boat
At last be fain to go on board some hoy,
And so to Flushing. There is no staying here.
At Sittingburgh the watch was like to take me,
And had not I with my buckler covered my head,
And run full blank at all adventures,
I am sure I had ne'er gone further than that place;
For the constable had twenty warrants to apprehend me,
Besides that, I robbed him and his man once at Gadshill.
Farewell, England; I'll go to Flushing now. 462
[*Exit Will.*

SCENE V.—*Justice-room at Feversham.*

Here enters the MAYOR, MOSBIE, ALICE, MICHAEL, SUSAN, *and*
BRADSHAW.

Mayor. Come, make haste, and bring away the prisoners.
Bradshaw. Mistress Arden, you are now going to God,
And I am by the law condemned to die

About a letter I brought from Master Greene.
I pray you, Mistress Arden, speak the truth:
Was I ever privy to your intent or no.
Alice. What should I say? You brought me such a letter,
But I dare swear thou knewest not the contents. 470
Leave now to trouble me with worldly things,
And let me meditate upon my saviour Christ,
Whose blood must save me for the blood I shed.
Mosbie. How long shall I live in this hell of grief?
Convey me from the presence of that strumpet.
Alice. Ah, but for thee I had never been a strumpet.
What cannot oaths and protestations do,
When men have opportunity to woo?
I was too young to sound thy villainies,
But now I find it and repent too late. 480
Susan. Ah, gentle brother, wherefore should I die?
I knew not of it till the deed was done.
Mosbie. For thee I mourn more than for myself;
But let it suffice, I cannot save thee now.
Michael. And if your brother and my mistress
Had not promised me you in marriage,
I had ne'er given consent to this foul deed.
Mayor. Leave to accuse each other now,
And listen to the sentence I shall give.
Bear Mosbie and his sister to London straight, 490
Where they in Smithfield must be executed;
Bear Mistress Arden unto Canterbury,
Where her sentence is she must be burnt;
Michael and Bradshaw in Feversham must suffer death.
Alice. Let my death make amends for all my sins.
Mosbie. Fie upon women! this shall be my song;
But bear me hence, for I have lived too long.
Susan. Seeing no hope on earth, in heaven is my hope.
Michael. Faith, I care not, seeing I die with Susan.
Bradshaw. My blood be on his head that gave the sentence. 500
Mayor. To speedy execution with them all! [*Exeunt.*

SCENE VI.

Here enters FRANKLIN.

Franklin. Thus have you seen the truth of Arden's death.
As for the ruffians, Shakebag and Black Will,

The one took sanctuary, and, being sent for out,
Was murdered in Southwark as he passed
To Greenwich, where the Lord Protector lay.
Black Will was burned in Flushing on a stage;
Greene was hanged at Osbridge in Kent;
The painter fled and how he died we know not.
But this above the rest is to be noted: 510
Arden lay murdered in that plot of ground
Which he by force and violence held from Reede;
And in the grass his body's print was seen
Two years and more after the deed was done.
Gentlemen, we hope you'll pardon this naked tragedy,
Wherein no filèd points are foisted in
To make it gracious to the ear or eye;
For simple truth is gracious enough,
And needs no other points of glosing stuff. [*Exit.*

DAVID AND BETHSABE

The love of King David and Fair Bethsabe. With the Tragedie of Absalon. As it hath ben diuers times plaied on the stage. Written by George Peele. London, Printed by Adam Islip. 1599. 4to.

This play was reprinted by Hawkins in the second volume of *The Origin of the English Drama*, 1773; and, excepting one or two errors of the press, the text was, on the whole, accurately given. Octavius Gilchrist (*Letter to Gifford on Ford's Works*, p. 11), talks rather too contemptuously of Hawkins.

DAVID AND BETHSABE

DRAMATIS PERSONÆ

DAVID.
AMNON, *son of David by Ahinoam.*
CHILEAB, *son of David by Abigail.*
ABSALON, *son of David by Maacah.*
ADONIA, *son of David by Haggith.*
SALOMON, *son of David by Bethsabe.*
JOAB, *captain of the host to David,* } *nephews of David and sons of his sister Zeruiah.*
ABISAI,
AMASA, *nephew of David and son of his sister Abigail; captain of the host to Absalon.*
JONADAB, *nephew of David and son of his brother Shimeah; friend to Amnon.*
URIAS, *husband of Bethsabe, and a warrior in David's army.*
NATHAN, *a prophet.*
SADOC, *high-priest.*[1]
AHIMAAS, *his son.*

ABIATHAR, *a priest.*
JONATHAN, *his son.*
ACHITOPHEL, *chief counsellor to Absalon.*
CUSAY.
ITHAY.
SEMEI.
JETHRAY.
HANON, *King of Ammon.*
MACHAAS, *King of Gath.*
Messenger, Soldiers, Shepherds, and Attendants.

THAMAR, *daughter of David by Maacah.*
BETHSABE, *wife of Urias.*
Woman of Thecoa.
Concubines to *David.*
Maid to *Bethsabe.*

Chorus.

THE LOVE OF DAVID AND FAIR BETHSABE, WITH THE TRAGEDY OF ABSALON.

PROLOGUS

Of Israel's sweetest singer now I sing,
His holy style and happy victories;
Whose Muse was dipt in that inspiring dew
Arch-angels stillèd from the breath of Jove,[2]
Decking her temples with the glorious flowers
Heavens rain'd on tops of Sion and Mount Sinai.

---

[1] So he is described in the play, p. 157—
    " *Sadoc, high-priest*, preserver of the ark," etc.
The 4to gives no list of *Dram. Pers.*
[2] Equivalent to—Jehovah. See note on Marlowe's *Works*, p. 80, ed. Dyce, 1858, and note on Shakespeare's *Works*, vol. iv. p. 203, ed. Dyce.

Upon the bosom of his ivory lute
The cherubins and angels laid their breasts;
And, when his consecrated fingers struck
The golden wires of his ravishing harp,   10
He gave alarum to the host of heaven,
That, wing'd with lightning, brake the clouds, and cast
Their crystal armour at his conquering feet.
Of this sweet poet, Jove's musician,
And of his beauteous son, I prease [1] to sing.
Then help, divine Adonai, to conduct
Upon the wings of my well-temper'd verse
The hearers' minds above the towers of heaven,
And guide them so in this thrice-haughty flight,
Their mounting feathers scorch not with the fire   20
That none can temper but thy holy hand:
To thee for succour flies my feeble Muse,
And at thy feet her iron pen doth use.

The Prologue-speaker, *before going out, draws a curtain and discovers* BETHSABE, *with her* Maid, *bathing over a spring : she sings, and* DAVID *sits above viewing her.*

THE SONG.

Hot sun, cool fire, temper'd with sweet air,
Black shade, fair nurse, shadow my white hair:
Shine, sun; burn, fire; breathe, air, and ease me;
Black shade, fair nurse, shroud me, and please me:
Shadow, my sweet nurse, keep me from burning,
Make not my glad cause cause of [my] mourning.
    Let not my beauty's fire   30
    Inflame unstaid desire,
    Nor pierce any bright eye
    That wandereth lightly.

Beth. Come, gentle Zephyr, trick'd with those perfumes
That erst in Eden sweeten'd Adam's love,
And stroke my bosom with thy [2] silken fan:
This shade, sun-proof, is yet no proof for thee;
Thy body, smoother than this waveless spring,
And purer than the substance of the same,

---

[1] *i.e.*, press.   [2] The 4to " the."

> Can creep through that his lances cannot pierce: 40
> Thou, and thy sister, soft and sacred Air,
> Goddess of life, and governess of health,
> Keep every fountain fresh and arbour sweet;
> No brazen gate her passage can repulse,
> Nor bushy [1] thicket bar thy subtle breath:
> Then deck thee with thy loose delightsome robes,
> And on thy wings bring delicate perfumes,
> To play the wanton [2] with us through the leaves.
>
> *Dav.* What tunes, what words, what looks, what wonders pierce
> My soul, incensèd with a sudden fire? 50
> What tree, what shade, what spring, what paradise,
> Enjoys the beauty of so fair a dame?
> Fair Eva, plac'd in perfect happiness,
> Lending her praise-notes to the liberal heavens,
> Struck with the accents of arch-angels' tunes,
> Wrought not more pleasure to her husband's thoughts
> Than this fair woman's words and notes to mine.
> May that sweet plain that bears her pleasant weight
> Be still enamell'd with discolour'd [3] flowers;
> That precious fount bear sand of purest gold; 60
> And, for the pebble, let the silver streams
> That pierce earth's bowels to maintain the source,
> Play upon rubies, sapphires, chrysolites;
> The brims let be embrac'd with golden curls
> Of moss that sleeps with sound the waters make
> For joy to feed the fount with their recourse;
> Let all the grass that beautifies her bower
> Bear manna every morn instead of dew,
> Or let the dew be sweeter far than that
> That hangs, like chains of pearl, on Hermon hill, 70
> Or balm which trickled from old Aaron's beard.—
> Cusay, come up, and serve thy lord the king.

Enter CUSAY *above.*

Cu. What service doth my lord the king command?
Dav. See, Cusay, see the flower of Israel,
> The fairest daughter that obeys the king
> In all the land the Lord subdu'd to me;

---

[1] The 4to "bushly."—Qy. "busky "=bosky?
[2] The 4to "wantons." [3] *i.e.,* variously coloured.

          Fairer than Isaac's lover at the well,
          Brighter than inside-bark of new-hewn cedar,
          Sweeter than flames of fine-perfumèd[1] myrrh,
          And comelier than the silver clouds that dance   80
          On Zephyr's[2] wings before the King of Heaven
Cu. Is it not Bethsabe the Hethite's wife,
          Urias, now at Rabbah[3] siege with Joab?
Dav. Go know, and bring her quickly to the king;
          Tell her, her graces have found grace with him.
Cu. I will, my lord.   [*Exit.*
Dav. Bright Bethsabe shall wash, in David's bower,
          In water mix'd with purest almond-flower,
          And bathe her beauty in the milk of kids:
          Bright Bethsabe gives earth to my desires;[4]   90
          Verdure to earth; and to that verdure flowers;
          To flowers sweet odours; and to odours wings
          That carry pleasures to the hearts of kings.

          Enter CUSAY, *below, to* BETHSABE, *she starting as something affright.*

Cu. Fair Bethsabe, the King of Israel
          From forth his princely tower hath seen thee bathe;
          And thy sweet graces have found grace with him:
          Come, then, and kneel unto him where he stands;
          The king is gracious, and hath liberal hands.
Beth. Ah, what is Bethsabe to please the king?
          Or what is David, that he should desire,   100
          For fickle beauty's sake, his servant's wife?
Cu. David, thou know'st, fair dame, is wise and just,
          Elected to the heart of Israel's God;
          Then do not thou expostulate with him
          For any action that contents his soul.
Beth. My lord the king, elect to God's own heart,

---

[1] *England's Parnassus*, 1600 (where this passage is given, p. 397, under the head "*Descriptions of Beauty and Personage*"), "fire-*perfumed.*"
[2] *England's Parnassus*, "Zephyrus'."
[3] In the earlier part of our play the 4to spells the name of this city "Rabath."
[4] Here "*earth*" (in spite of the repetitions, "*earth, earth*"; "*verdure, verdure*"; "*flowers, flowers*"; "*odours, odours*") seems unintelligible; but assuredly the right reading is not "birth"—as Mr. Collier boldly asserts that it is, *Hist. of the Engl. Stage*, p. 34, note, *Shakespeare*, vol. i. ed. 1858.

Should not his gracious jealousy incense
Whose thoughts are chaste: I hate incontinence.
Cu. Woman, thou wrong'st the king, and doubt'st his honour,
 Whose truth maintains the crown of Israel, 110
 Making him stay that bade me bring thee straight.
Beth. The king's poor handmaid will obey my lord.
Cu. Then come, and do thy duty to his grace;
 And do what seemeth favour in his sight.
    [*Exit, below, with* BETHSABE.
Dav. Now comes my lover tripping like the roe,
 And brings my longings tangled in her hair.
 To joy[1] her love I'll build a kingly bower,
 Seated in hearing of a hundred streams,
 That, for their homage to her sovereign joys,[2]
 Shall, as the serpents fold into their nests 120
 In oblique turnings, wind their[3] nimble waves
 About the circles of her curious walks;
 And with their murmur summon easeful sleep
 To lay his golden sceptre on her brows.—
 Open the doors, and entertain my love;
 Open, I say, and, as you open, sing,
 Welcome, fair Bethsabe, King David's darling.

Enter, above, CUSAY, *with* BETHSABE.

Welcome, fair Bethsabe, King David's darling.
Thy bones' fair covering, erst discover'd fair,
And all mine eyes[4] with all thy beauties pierc'd: 130
As heaven's bright eye burns most when most he climbs
The crookèd zodiac with his fiery sphere,
And shineth furthest from this earthly globe;
So, since thy beauty scorch'd my conquer'd soul,
I call'd thee nearer for my nearer cure.
Beth. Too near, my lord, was your unarmèd heart
 When furthest off my hapless beauty pierc'd;
 And would this dreary day had turn'd to night,
 Or that some pitchy cloud had cloak'd the sun,

---

[1] *i.e.*, enjoy.
[2] Is not this an error originating in the word "*joy*" a little above?
The sense seems to require "charms."
[3] Walker's correction, *Crit. Exam. of the text of Shakespeare*, etc., vol. ii.
p. 231.—The 4to "the."
[4] To connect this with what precedes, a friend would read "Have *all
mine eyes*," etc.: but the probability is, that a line has dropt out.

        Before their lights had caus'd my lord to see   140
        His name disparag'd and my chastity!
Dav. My love, if want of love have left thy soul
    A sharper sense of honour than thy king,
    (For love leads princes sometimes from their seats,)
    As erst my heart was hurt, displeasing thee,
    So come and taste thy ease with easing me.
Beth. One medicine cannot heal our different harms;
    But rather make both rankle at the bone:
    Then let the king be cunning in his cure,
    Lest flattering both, both perish in his hand.   150
Dav. Leave it to me, my dearest Bethsabe,
    Whose skill is conversant in deeper cures.—
    And, Cusay, haste thou to my servant Joab,
    Commanding him to send Urias home
    With all the speed can possibly be us'd.
Cu. Cusay will fly about the king's desire.   *[Exeunt.*

Enter JOAB, ABISAI, URIAS, *and others, with drum and ensign.*

Joab. Courage, ye mighty men of Israel,
    And charge your fatal instruments of war
    Upon the bosoms of proud Ammon's sons,
    That have disguis'd your king's ambassadors,   160
    Cut half their beards and half their garments off,
    In spite of Israel and his daughters' sons!
    Ye fight the holy battles of Jehovah,
    King David's God, and ours, and Jacob's God,
    That guides your weapons to their conquering strokes,
    Orders your footsteps, and directs your thoughts
    To stratagems that harbour victory:
    He casts his sacred eyesight from on high,
    And sees your foes run seeking for their deaths,
    Laughing their labours and their hopes to scorn;   170
    While 'twixt your bodies and their blunted swords
    He puts on armour of his honour's proof,
    And makes their weapons wound the senseless winds.
Abis. Before this city Rabbah we will lie,
    And shoot forth shafts as thick and dangerous
    As was the hail that Meses mix'd with fire,
    And threw with fury round about the fields,
    Devouring Pharaoh's friends and Egypt's fruits.

David and Bethsabe

Ur. First, mighty captains, Joab and Abisai,
    Let us assault, and scale this kingly tower,   180
    Where all their conduits and their fountains are;
    Then we may easily take the city too.
Joab. Well hath Urias counsell'd our attempts;
    And as he spake us, so assault the tower:
    Let Hanon now, the king of Ammon's sons,[1]
    Repulse our conquering passage if he dare.

Enter HANON, MACHAAS, *and others, upon the walls.*

Ha. What would the shepherd's-dogs of Israel
    Snatch from the mighty issue of King Ammon,
    The valiant Ammonites and haughty Syrians?
    'Tis not your late successive victories   190
    Can make us yield, or quail our courages;
    But if ye dare assay to scale this tower,
    Our angry swords shall smite ye to the ground,
    And venge our losses on your hateful lives.
Joab. Hanon, thy father Nahas gave relief
    To holy David in his hapless exile,
    Livèd his fixèd date, and died in peace:
    But thou, instead of reaping his reward,
    Hast trod it under foot, and scorn'd our king;
    Therefore thy days shall end with violence,   200
    And to our swords thy vital blood shall cleave.
Mach. Hence, thou that bear'st poor Israel's shepherd's-hook,
    The proud lieutenant of that base-born king,
    And keep within the compass of his fold;
    For, if ye seek to feed on Ammon's fruits,
    And stray into the Syrians' fruitful meads,
    The mastives of our land shall worry[2] ye,
    And pull the weesels[3] from your greedy throats.
Abis. Who can endure these pagans' blasphemies?
Ur. My soul repines at this disparagement.   210
Joab. Assault, ye valiant men of David's host,
    And beat these railing dastards from their doors.

---

[1] The 4to "sonne."—Compare the third line of Joab's first speech in this scene, and more particularly, line 431, page 140.
[2] The 4to "werry."
[3] *i.e.*, weasands. (This word is spelt by some of our old writers "*wesils*.")

Assault, and they win the tower; and then JOAB *speaks above.*

> Thus have we won the tower, which we will keep,
> Maugre the sons of Ammon and of Syria.

Enter CUSAY *below.*

Cu. Where is Lord Joab, leader of the host?
Joab. Here is Lord Joab, leader of the host.
    Cusay, come up, for we have won the hold.
Cu. In happy hour,[1] then, is Cusay come.

CUSAY *goes up.*

Joab. What news, then, brings Lord Cusay from the king?
Cu. His majesty commands thee out of hand   220
    To send him home Urias from the wars,
    For matter of some service he should do.
Ur. 'Tis for no choler hath surpris'd the king,
    I hope, Lord Cusay, 'gainst his servant's truth?
Cu. No; rather to prefer Urias' truth.
Joab. Here, take him with thee, then, and go in peace;
    And tell my lord the king that I have fought
    Against the city Rabbah with success,
    And scalèd where the royal palace is,
    The conduit-heads and all their sweetest springs: 230
    Then let him come in person to these walls,
    With all the soldiers he can bring besides,
    And take the city as his own exploit,
    Lest I surprise it, and the people give
    The glory of the conquest to my name.
Cu. We will, Lord Joab; and great Israel's God
    Bless in thy hands the battles of our king!
Joab. Farewell, Urias; haste away the king.
Ur. As sure as Joab breathes a victor here,
    Urias will haste him and his own return.   240
                                  [*Exeunt Cusay and Urias.*
Abis. Let us descend, and ope the palace' gate,
    Taking our soldiers in to keep the hold.
Joab. Let us, Abisai:—and, ye sons of Judah,
    Be valiant, and maintain your victory.   [*Exeunt.*

[1] A dissyllable here (and so spelt in the 4to—" hower ").

Enter AMNON,[1] JONADAB, JETHRAY, *and* AMNON's Page.

Jonad. What means my lord, the king's belovèd son,
　That wears upon his right triumphant arm
　The power of Israel for a royal favour,
　That holds upon the tables of his hands
　Banquets of honour and all thought's content,
　To suffer pale and grisly abstinence
　To sit and feed upon his fainting cheeks,
　And suck away the blood that cheers his looks?
Am. Ah, Jonadab, it is my sister's looks,
　On whose sweet beauty I bestow my blood,
　That make me look so amorously lean;
　Her beauty having seiz'd upon my heart,
　So merely[2] consecrate to her content,
　Sets now such guard about his vital blood,
　And views the passage with such piercing eyes,
　That none can scape to cheer my pining cheeks,
　But all is thought too little for her love.
Jonad. Then from her heart thy looks shall be reliev'd,
　And thou shalt joy[3] her as thy soul desires.
Am. How can it be, my sweet friend Jonadab,
　Since Thamar is a virgin and my sister?
Jonad. Thus it shall be: lie down upon thy bed,
　Feigning thee fever-sick and ill-at-ease;
　And when the king shall come to visit thee,
　Desire thy sister Thamar may be sent
　To dress some dainties for thy malady:
　Then when thou hast her solely with thyself,
　Enforce some favour to thy manly love.
　See where she comes: entreat her in with thee.

Enter THAMAR.

Tha. What aileth Amnon, with such sickly looks
　To daunt the favour[4] of his lovely face?
Am. Sweet Thamar, sick, and wish some wholesome cates
　Dress'd with the cunning of thy dainty hands.

---

[1] The 4to throughout "Ammon."
[2] *i.e.*, wholly, absolutely.—The 4to "merrily."
[3] *i.e.*, enjoy.
[4] *ie.*, beauty.

Tha. That hath the king commanded at my hands:
   Then come and rest thee, while I make thee ready
   Some dainties easeful to thy crazèd soul.   280
Am. I go, sweet sister, easèd with thy sight.
         [*Exeunt Thamar, Amnon, Jethray, and Page.*
Jonad. Why should a prince, whose power may command,
   Obey the rebel passions of his love,
   When they contend but 'gainst his conscience,
   And may be govern'd or suppress'd by will?
   Now, Amnon, loose those loving knots of blood,
   That suck'd the courage from thy kingly heart,
   And give it passage to thy wither'd cheeks.
   Now, Thamar, ripen'd are the holy fruits
   That grew on plants of thy virginity;   290
   And rotten is thy name in Israel:
   Poor Thamar, little did thy lovely hands
   Foretell an action of such violence
   As to contend with Amnon's lusty arms
   Sinew'd with vigour of his kindless [1] love:
   Fair Thamar, now dishonour hunts thy foot,
   And follows thee through every covert shade,
   Discovering thy shame and nakedness,
   Even from the valleys of Jehosaphat
   Up to the lofty mounts of Lebanon;   300
   Where cedars, stirr'd with anger of the winds,
   Sounding in storms the tale of thy disgrace,
   Tremble with fury, and with murmur shake
   Earth with their feet and with their heads the heavens,
   Beating the clouds into their swiftest rack,[2]
   To bear this wonder round about the world.   [*Exit.*

Re-enter AMNON *thrusting out* THAMAR, *and* JETHRAY.

Am. Hence from my bed, whose sight offends my soul
   As doth the parbreak [3] of disgorgèd bears!
Tha. Unkind, unprincely, and unmanly Amnon,
   To force, and then refuse [4] thy sister's love,   310
   Adding unto the fright of thy offence

---

[1] *i.e.*, unnatural.

[2] *i.e.*, moving masses of vapour. "The winds in the upper region which move the clouds above (which we call the *rack*)," etc.—Bacon's *Sylva Sylvarum, or A Naturall Historie*, § 115, p. 32, ed. 1658.

[3] *i.e.*, vomit.   [4] *i.e.*, reject.

David and Bethsabe

    The baneful torment of my publish'd shame!
    O, do not this dishonour to thy love,
    Nor clog thy soul with such increasing sin!
    This second evil far exceeds the first.
Am. Jethray, come thrust this woman from my sight,
    And bolt the door upon her if she strive.   [*Exit.*
Jeth. Go, madam, go; away; you must be gone;
    My lord hath done with you: I pray, depart.
                         [*Shuts her out.—Exit.*
Tha. Whither, alas, ah, whither shall I fly,   320
    With folded arms and all-amazèd soul?
    Cast as was Eva from that glorious soil,
    (Where all delights sat bating, wing'd with thoughts,
    Ready to nestle in her naked breasts,)
    To bare and barren vales with floods made waste,
    To desert woods, and hills with lightning scorch'd,
    With death, with shame, with hell, with horror sit;[1]
    There will I wander from my father's face;
    There Absalon, my brother Absalon,
    Sweet Absalon shall hear his sister mourn;   330
    There will I lure[2] with my windy sighs
    Night-ravens and owls to rend my bloody side,
    Which with a rusty weapon I will wound,
    And make them passage to my panting heart.
    Why talk'st thou, wretch, and leav'st the deed undone?
    Rend hair and garments, as thy heart is rent
    With inward fury of a thousand griefs,
    And scatter them by these unhallow'd doors,
    To figure Amnon's resting cruelty,
    And tragic spoil of Thamar's chastity.   340

Enter ABSALON.

Abs. What causeth Thamar to exclaim so much?
Tha. The cause that Thamar shameth to disclose.
Abs. Say; I thy brother will revenge that cause.
Tha. Amnon, our father's son, hath forcèd me,
    And thrusts me from him as the scorn of Israel.
Abs. Hath Amnon forcèd thee? by David's hand,
    And by the covenant God hath made with him,

---

[1] An error, I believe: but qy. as to the right reading?
[2] Lure is here a dissyllable. The 4to " liue."

                Amnon shall bear his violence to hell;
                Traitor to heaven, traitor to David's throne,
                Traitor to Absalon and Israel.   350
                This fact hath Jacob's ruler seen from heaven,
                And through a cloud of smoke and tower of fire,
                As he rides vaunting him upon the greens,
                Shall tear his chariot-wheels with violent winds,
                And throw his body in the bloody sea;
                At him the thunder shall discharge his bolt;
                And his fair spouse, with bright and fiery wings,[1]
                Sit ever burning on his hateful bones:
                Myself, as swift as thunder or his spouse,
                Will hunt occasion with a secret hate,   360
                To work false Amnon an ungracious end.—
                Go in, my sister; rest thee in my house;
                And God in time shall take this shame from thee.
Tha. Nor God nor time will do that good for me.   [*Exit.*

Enter DAVID *with his train.*

Dav. My Absalon, what mak'st thou here alone,
    And bear'st such discontentment in thy brows?
Abs. Great cause hath Absalon to be displeas'd,
    And in his heart to shroud the wounds of wrath.
Dav. 'Gainst whom should Absalon be thus displeas'd?
Abs. 'Gainst wicked Amnon, thy ungracious son,   370
    My brother and fair Thamar's by the king,
    My step-brother by mother and by kind:[2]
    He hath dishonour'd David's holiness,
    And fix'd a blot of lightness on his throne,
    Forcing my sister Thamar when he feign'd
    A sickness, sprung from root of heinous lust.
Dav. Hath Amnon brought this evil on my house,
    And suffer'd sin to smite his father's bones?
    Smite, David, deadlier than the voice of heaven,
    And let hate's fire be kindled in thy heart: 380
    Frame in the arches of thy angry brows,
    Making thy forehead, like a comet, shine,
    To force false Amnon tremble at thy looks.

---

[1] Hawkins (Preface to *The Origin of the English Drama*, vol. i. p. 11) thinks this "a metaphor worthy of Æschylus."
[2] *i.e.*, nature.

David and Bethsabe

Sin, with his sevenfold crown and purple robe,
Begins his triumphs in my guilty throne;
There sits he watching with his hundred eyes
Our idle minutes and our wanton thoughts;
And with his baits, made of our frail desires,
Gives us the hook that hales our souls to hell:
But with the spirit of my kingdom's God   390
I'll thrust the flattering tyran [1] from his throne,
And scourge his bondslaves from my hallow'd court
With rods of iron and thorns of sharpen'd steel.
Then, Absalon, revenge not thou this sin;
Leave it to me, and I will chasten him.
Abs. I am content: then grant, my lord the king,
Himself with all his other lords would come
Up to my sheep-feast on the plain of Hazor.
Dav. Nay, my fair son, myself with all my lords
Will bring thee too much charge; yet some shall go.   400
Abs. But let my lord the king himself take pains;
The time of year is pleasant for your grace,
And gladsome summer in her shady robes,
Crownèd with roses and with painted [2] flowers,
With all her nymphs, shall entertain my lord,
That, from the thicket of my verdant groves,
Will sprinkle honey-dews about his breast,
And cast sweet balm upon his kingly head:
Then grant thy servant's boon, and go, my lord.
Dav. Let it content my sweet son Absalon,   410
That I may stay, and take my other lords.
Abs. But shall thy best-belovèd Amnon go?
Dav. What needeth it, that Amnon go with thee?
Abs. Yet do thy son and servant so much grace.
Dav. Amnon shall go, aud all my other lords,
Because I will give grace to Absalon.

Enter CUSAY *and* URIAS, *with others.*

Cu. Pleaseth my lord the king, his servant Joab
Hath sent Urias from the Syrian wars.
Dav. Welcome, Urias, from the Syrian wars,
Welcome to David as his dearest lord.   420

---
[1] Tyran, for *tyrant*, is a form frequently used by our old poets.
[2] The 4to " planted."

Ur. Thanks be to Israel's God and David's grace,
    Urias finds such greeting with the king.
Dav. No other greeting shall Urias find
    As long as David sways th' elected seat
    And consecrated throne of Israel.
    Tell me, Urias, of my servant Joab;
    Fights he with truth the battles of our God,
    And for the honour of the Lord's anointed?
Ur. Thy servant Joab fights the chosen wars
    With truth, with honour, and with high success,   430
    And, 'gainst the wicked king of Ammon's sons,
    Hath, by the finger of our sovereign's God,
    Besieg'd the city Rabbah, and achiev'd
    The court of waters, where the conduits run,
    And all the Ammonites' delightsome springs:
    Therefore he wisheth David's mightiness
    Should number out the host of Israel,
    And come in person to the city Rabbah,
    That so her conquest may be made the king's,
    And Joab fight as his inferior.   440
Dav. This hath not God and Joab's prowess done
    Without Urias' valour,[1] I am sure,
    Who, since his true conversion from a Hethite
    To an adopted son of Israel,
    Hath fought like one whose arms were lift by heaven,
    And whose bright sword was edg'd with Israel's wrath.
    Go, therefore, home, Urias, take thy rest;
    Visit thy wife and household with the joys
    A victor and a favourite of the king's
    Should exercise with honour after arms.   450
Ur. Thy servant's bones are yet not half so craz'd,
    Nor constitute on such a sickly mould,
    That for so little service he should faint,
    And seek, as cowards, refuge of his home:
    Nor are his thoughts so sensually stirr'd,
    To stay the arms with which the Lord would smite
    And fill their circle with his conquer'd foes,
    For wanton bosom of a flattering wife.
Dav. Urias hath a beauteous sober wife,
    Yet young, and fram'd of tempting flesh and blood;   460
    Then, when the king hath summon'd thee from arms,

---

[1] The 4to "valours."

David and Bethsabe

<blockquote>

If thou unkindly shouldst refrain her bed,
Sin might be laid upon Urias' soul,
If Bethsabe by frailty hurt her fame:
Then go, Urias, solace in her love;
Whom God hath knit to thee, tremble to loose.

Ur. The king is much too tender of my ease:
The ark and Israel and Judah dwell
In palaces and rich pavilions;
But Joab and his brother in the fields,   470
Suffering the wrath of winter and the sun:
And shall Urias (of more shame than they)
Banquet, and loiter in the work of heaven?
As sure [1] as thy soul doth live, my lord,
Mine ears shall never lean to such delight,
When holy labour calls me forth to fight.

Dav. Then be it with Urias' manly heart
As best his fame may shine in Israel.

Ur. Thus shall Urias' heart be best content,
Till thou dismiss me back to Joab's bands: 480
This ground before the king my master's doors
Shall be my couch, and this unwearied arm
The proper pillow of a soldier's head;   [*Lies down.*
For never will I lodge within my house,
Till Joab triumph in my secret vows.

Dav. Then fetch some flagons of our purest wine,
That we may welcome home our hardy friend
With full carouses to his fortunes past
And to the honours of his future arms;
Then will I send him back to Rabbah siege,   490
And follow with the strength of Israel.

Enter one with flagons of wine.

Arise, Urias; come and pledge the king.

Ur. If David think me worthy such a grace,
I will be bold and pledge my lord the king.   [*Rises.*

Dav. Absalon and Cusay both shall drink
To good Urias and his happiness.

Abs. We will, my lord, to please Urias' soul.

Dav. I will begin, Urias, to thyself,
And all the treasure of the Ammonites,
</blockquote>

[1] A dissyllable here.

Which here I promise to impart to thee, 500
And bind that promise with a full carouse. [*Drinks.*

Ur. What seemeth pleasant in my sovereign's eyes,
That shall Urias do till he be dead.
Dav. Fill him the cup. [*Urias drinks.*]—Follow, ye lords that love
Your sovereign's health, and do as he hath done.
Abs. Ill may he thrive, or live in Israel,
That loves not David, or denies his charge.—
Urias, here is to Abisai's health,
Lord Joab's brother and thy loving friend. [*Drinks.*
Ur. I pledge Lord Absalon and Abisai's health. 510
[*Drinks.*

Cu. Here now, Urias, to the health of Joab,
And to the pleasant journey we shall have
When we return to mighty Rabbah siege. [*Drinks.*
Ur. Cusay, I pledge thee all with all my heart.—
Give me some drink, ye servants of the king;
Give me my drink. [*Drinks.*
Dav. Well done, my good Urias! drink thy fill,
That in thy fulness David may rejoice.
Ur. I will, my lord.
Abs. Now, Lord Urias, one carouse to me. 520
Ur. No, sir, I'll drink to the king;
Your father is a better man than you.
Dav. Do so, Urias; I will pledge thee straight.
Ur. I will indeed, my lord and sovereign;
I'll[1] once in my days be so bold.
Dav. Fill him his glass.
Ur. Fill me my glass.[2]
Dav. Quickly, I say.
Ur. Quickly, I say.—Here, my lord, by your favour now I drink to you. [*Drinks.*
Dav. I pledge thee, good Urias, presently. [*Drinks.*
Abs. Here, then, Urias, once again for me, 532
And to the health of David's children. [*Drinks.*
Ur. David's children!
Abs. Ay, David's children: wilt thou pledge me, man?

---

[1] The 4to "I."
[2] Here the 4to has a stage direction "*He giues him the glasse,*" which means, I suppose, that Urias gives the glass to the person who pours out the wine, to be filled.

David and Bethsabe

Ur. Pledge me, man!
Abs. Pledge me, I say, or else thou lov'st us not.
Ur. What, do you talk? do you talk? I'll no more; I'll lie down here.
Dav. Rather, Urias, go thou home and sleep. 540
Ur. O, ho, sir! would you make me break my sentence? [*Lies down.*] Home, sir! no, indeed, sir: I'll sleep upon mine arm, like a soldier; sleep like a man as long as I live in Israel.
Dav. [*aside.*] If naught will serve to save his wife's renown,
    I'll send him with a letter unto Joab
    To put him in the forefront of the wars,
    That so my purposes may take effect.—
    Help him in, sirs.   [*Exeunt David and Absalon.*
Cu. Come, rise, Urias; get thee in and sleep. 550
Ur. I will not go home, sir; that's flat.
Cu. Then come and rest thee upon David's bed.
Ur. On, afore, my lords, on, afore.   [*Exeunt.*

Enter CHORUS.

Chorus. O proud revolt of a presumptuous man,
    Laying his bridle in the neck of sin,
    Ready to bear him past his grave to hell!
    Like as the fatal raven,[1] that in his voice
    Carries the dreadful summons of our deaths,
    Flies by the fair Arabian spiceries,
    Her pleasant gardens and delightsome parks,[2] 560

---

[1] Imitated from Du Bartas:
    " Ainsi que les corbeaux d'vne penne venteuse
    Passans les bois pleurans de l'Arabie heureuse,
    Mesprisent les iardins et parcs delicieux,
    Qui de fleurs esmaillez vont parfumant les cieux,
    Et s'arrestent, gloutons, sur la salle carcasse
    D'vn criminel rompu n'aguere à coups de masse," etc.
    L'Arche,—Premiere Partie au Second Jour de la Seconde Semaine, p. 270, ed. 1632, 12°.

(In Chapman and Shirley's *Chabot, Admiral of France,* act iv. sc. 1, we find—

    " like crows and carrion birds,
    They fly o'er flowery meads, clear springs, fair gardens,
    And stoop at carcasses "—

which I formerly supposed (see my note on Shirley's *Works,* vi. 132) to have been borrowed from the passage of our text, as I was not then acquainted with the lines of Du Bartas just cited.)

[2] *England's Parnassus,* 1600 (where several lines of his Chorus are given, p. 195, under the head " *Man* "), has " delightfull parts."

Seeming to curse them with his hoarse exclaims,
And yet doth stoop with hungry violence
Upon a piece of hateful carrion;
So wretched man, displeas'd with those delights
Would yield a quickening savour to his soul,
Pursues with eager and unstanchèd thirst
The greedy longings of his loathsome flesh.
If holy David so shook hands with sin,
What shall our baser spirits glory in?
This kingly [1] giving lust her rein 570
Pursues the sequel with a greater ill.
Urias in the forefront of the wars
Is murder'd by the hateful heathens' sword,
And David joys his too dear Bethsabe.
Suppose this past, and that the child is born,
Whose death the prophet solemnly doth mourn. [*Exit.*

Enter BETHSABE *with her* Maid.[2]

Beth. Mourn, Bethsabe, bewail thy foolishness,
   Thy sin, thy shame, the sorrow of thy soul:
   Sin, shame, and sorrow swarm about thy soul;
   And, in the gates and entrance of my heart, 580
   Sadness, with wreathèd arms, hangs her complaint.
   No comfort from the ten-string'd instrument,
   The tinkling [3] cymbal, or the ivory lute;
   Nor doth the sound of David's kingly harp
   Make glad the broken heart of Bethsabe:
   Jerusalem is fill'd with thy complaint,
   And in the streets of Sion sits thy grief.
   The babe is sick, sick to the death, I fear,
   The fruit that sprung from thee to David's house;
   Nor may the pot of honey and of oil 590
   Glad David or his handmaid's countenance.
   Urias—wo is me to think hereon!
   For who is it among the sons of men
   That saith not to my soul, "The king hath sinn'd;
   David hath done amiss, and Bethsabe
   Laid snares of death unto Urias' life"?

---

[1] A mutilated line. (In my former eds. I queried if "*kingly*" should be "*king by.*")
[2] Here the 4to "handmaid;" but see *ante*, p. 128.
[3] The 4to "twinckling."

David and Bethsabe

    My sweet Urias, fall'n into the pit
Art thou, and gone even to the gates of hell
For Bethsabe, that wouldst not shroud her shame.
O, what is it to serve the lust of kings!   600
How lion-like th[e]y rage when we resist!
But, Bethsabe, in humbleness attend
The grace that God will to his handmaid send.   [*Exeunt.*

Enter DAVID *in his gown, walking sadly;* Servants *attending.*

Dav. [*aside.*] The babe is sick, and sad is David's heart,
    To see the guiltless bear the guilty's pain.
    David, hang up thy harp; hang down thy head;
    And dash thy ivory lute against the stones.
    The dew, that on the hill of Hermon falls,
    Rains not on Sion's tops and lofty towers;
    The plains of Gath and Askaron rejoice,[1]   610
    And David's thoughts are spent in pensiveness:
    The babe is sick, sweet babe, that Bethsabe
    With woman's pain brought forth to Israel.

Enter NATHAN.

    But what saith Nathan to his lord the king?
Na. Thus Nathan saith unto his lord the king.
    There were two men both dwellers in one town:
    The one was mighty, and exceeding rich
    In oxen, sheep, and cattle of the field;
    The other poor, having nor ox, nor calf,
    Nor other cattle, save one little lamb   620
    Which he had bought and nourish'd by the hand;
    And it grew up, and fed with him and his,
    And eat and drank as he and his were wont,
    And in his bosom slept, and was to him [2]
    As was his daughter or his dearest child.
    There came a stranger to this wealthy man;
    And he refus'd and spar'd to take his own,
    Or of his store to dress or make him meat,
    But took the poor man's sheep, partly, poor man's store.[3]
    And dress'd it for this stranger in his house.   630
    What, tell me, shall be done to him for this?

---

[1] This and the next line are transposed in the 4to.
[2] The 4to "liue."   [3] Some deep corruption here.

Dav. Now, as the Lord doth live, this wicked man
　　Is judg'd and shall become the child of death;
　　Fourfold to the poor man shall he restore,
　　That without mercy took his lamb away.
Na. Thou art the man; and thou hast judg'd thyself.
　　David, thus saith the Lord thy God by me:
　　I thee anointed king in Israel,
　　And sav'd thee from the tyranny of Saul;
　　Thy master's house I gave thee to possess;　　　　　640
　　His wives into thy bosom did I give,
　　And Judah and Jerusalem withal;
　　And might, thou know'st, if this had been too small,
　　Have given thee more:
　　Wherefore, then, hast thou gone so far astray,
　　And hast done evil, and sinnèd in my sight?
　　Urias thou hast killèd with the sword;
　　Yea, with the sword of the uncircumcis'd
　　Thou hast him slain: wherefore, from this day forth,
　　The sword shall never go from thee and thine;　　650
　　For thou hast ta'en this Hethite's wife to thee:
　　Wherefore, behold, I will, saith Jacob's God,
　　In thine own house stir evil up to thee;
　　Yea, I before thy face will take thy wives,
　　And give them to thy neighbour to possess:
　　This shall be done to David in the day,
　　That Israel openly may see thy shame,
Dav. Nathan, I have against the Lord, I have
　　Sinnèd; O, sinnèd grievously! and, lo,
　　From heaven's throne doth David throw himself,　　660
　　And groan and grovel to the gates of hell! [*Falls down.*
Na. [*raising him.*] David, stand up: thus saith the Lord by me:
　　David the king shall live, for he hath seen
　　The true repentant sorrow of thy heart;
　　But, for thou hast in this misdeed of thine
　　Stirr'd up the enemies of Israel
　　To triumph, and blaspheme the God of Hosts,
　　And say, he set a wicked man to reign
　　Over his lovèd people and his tribes,—
　　The child shall surely die, that erst was born,　　670
　　His mother's sin, his kingly father's scorn.[1]　　[*Exit.*

---

[1] *i.e.*, " disgrace, reproach." Walker's *Crit. Exam. of the text of Shakespeare*, etc., vol. ii. p. 81.

David and Bethsabe

Dav. How just is Jacob's God in all his works!
    But must it die that David loveth so?
    O, that the Mighty One of Israel
    Nill [1] change his doom, and says the babe must die!
    Mourn, Israel, and weep in Sion-gates;
    Wither, ye cedar-trees of Lebanon;
    Ye sprouting almonds, with your flowering tops,
    Droop, drown, and drench in Hebron's fearful streams:
    The babe must die that was to David born,   680
    His mother's sin, his kingly father's scorn.   [*Sits sadly.*

Enter CUSAY.

First Serv. What tidings bringeth Cusay to the king?
Cu. To thee, the servant of King David's court,
    This bringeth Cusay, as the prophet spake;
    The Lord hath surely stricken to the death
    The child new-born by that Urias' wife,
    That by the sons of Ammon erst was slain.
First Serv. Cusay, be still; the king is vexèd sore:
    How shall he speed that brings this tidings first,
    When, while the child was yet alive, we spake,   690
    And David's heart would not be comforted?
Dav. Yea, David's heart will not be comforted!
    What murmur ye, the servants of the king?
    What tidings telleth Cusay to the king?
    Say, Cusay, lives the child, or is he dead?
Cu. The child is dead, that of Urias' wife
    David begat.
Dav. Urias' wife, saist thou?
    The child is dead, then ceaseth David's shame:
    Fetch me to eat, and give me wine to drink;   700
    Water to wash, and oil to clear my looks;
    Bring down your shalms, your cymbals, and your pipes;
    Let David's harp and lute, his hand and voice,
    Give laud to him that loveth Israel,
    And sing his praise that shendeth [2] David's fame,

---

[1] *i.e.*, will not.

[2] "In the following passage," says Nares in his *Glossary*, "it [*shend*] seems to mean to protect, which must be considered as an error, being contrary to all analogy—
    'This I must succour, this I must defend,
      And from the wild boare's rooting ever *shend*.'
                  Brown, *Brit. Past.* part ii. p. 144."
In the passage just cited "*shend*" is certainly equivalent to "defend," as in our text "*shendeth*" is equivalent to "defendeth."

That put away his sin from out his sight,
And sent his shame into the streets of Gath.
Bring ye to me the mother of the babe,
That I may wipe the tears from off her face,
And give her comfort with this hand of mine, 710
And deck fair Bethsabe with ornaments,
That she may bear to me another son,
That may be lovèd of the Lord of Hosts;
For where he is, of force must David go,
But never may he come where David is.

They bring in water, wine, and oil. Music and a banquet; and enter BETHSABE.

Fair Bethsabe, sit thou, and sigh no more:—
And sing and play, you servants of the king:
Now sleepeth David's sorrow with the dead,
And Bethsabe liveth to Israel.

They use all solemnities together and sing, etc.

Now arms and warlike engines for assault 720
Prepare at once, ye men of Israel,
Ye men of Judah and Jerusalem,
That Rabbah may be taken by the king,
Lest it be callèd after Joab's name,
Nor David's glory shine in Sion streets.
To Rabbah marcheth David with his men,
To chàstise Ammon and the wicked ones. [*Exeunt.*

Enter ABSALON *with several others.*

Abs. Set up your mules, and give them well to eat,
And let us meet our brothers at the feast.
Accursèd is the master of this feast, 730
Dishonour of the house of Israel,
His sister's slander, and his mother's shame:
Shame be his share that could such ill contrive,
To ravish Thamar, and, without a pause,
To drive her shamefully from out his house:
But may his wickedness find just reward!
Therefore doth Absalon conspire with you,
That Amnon die what time he sits to eat;

For in the holy temple have I sworn
Wreak of his villany in Thamar's rape.   740
And here he comes: bespeak him gently, all,
Whose death is deeply gravèd in my heart.

Enter AMNON, ADONIA, *and* JONADAB.

Am. Our shearers are not far from hence, I wot;
  And Amnon to you all his brethren
  Giveth such welcome as our fathers erst
  Were wont in Judah and Jerusalem;—
  But, specially, Lord Absalon, to thee,
  The honour of thy house and progeny:
  Sir down and dine with me, King David's son,
  Thou fair young man, whose hairs shine in mine eye   750
  Like golden wires of David's ivory lute.
Abs. Amnon, where be thy shearers and thy men,
  That we may pour-in plenty of thy wines,[1]
  And eat thy goats'-milk, and rejoice with thee?
Am. Here cometh Amnon's shearers and his men:—
  Absalon, sit and [2] rejoice with me.

Enter a company of Shepherds, *who dance and sing.*

  Drink, Absalon, in praise of Israel;
  Welcome to Amnon's fields from David's court.
Abs. [*stabbing Amnon.*] Die with thy draught; perish, and die accurs'd;
  Dishonour to the honour of us all;   760
  Die for the villany to Thamar done,
  Unworthy thou to be King David's son! [*Exit with others.*
Jonad. O, what hath Absalon for Thamar done,
  Murder'd his brother, great King David's son!
Ad. Run, Jonadab, away, and make it known,
  What cruelty this Absalon hath shown.
  Amnon, thy brother Adonia shall
  Bury thy body 'mong the dead men's bones;
  And we will make complaint to Israel
  Of Amnon's death and pride of Absalon.   770
  [*Exeunt.*

---

[1] The 4to "vines."   [2] Qy. "*sit* down *and*," etc.?

Enter DAVID, JOAB, ABISAI, CUSAY, *and others, with drum and ensign against* RABBAH.

Dav. This is the town of the uncircumcis'd,
　The city of the kingdom, this is it,
　Rabbah, where wicked Hanon sitteth king.
　Despoil this king, this Hanon of his crown;
　Unpeople Rabbah and the streets thereof;
　For in their blood, and slaughter of the slain,
　Lieth the honour of King David's line.
　Joab, Abisai, and the rest of you,
　Fight ye this day for great Jerusalem.

Enter HANON *and others on the walls.*

Joab. And see where Hanon shows him on the walls;　　780
　Why, then, do we forbear to give assault,
　That Israel may, as it is promisèd,
　Subdue the daughters of the Gentiles' tribes?
　All this must be perform'd by David's hand.
Dav. Hark to me, Hanon, and remember well:
　As sure as He doth live that kept my host,
　What time our young men, by the pool of Gibeon,
　Went forth against the strength of Isboseth,
　And twelve to twelve did with their weapons play;
　So sure[1] art thou and thy men of war　　790
　To feel the sword of Israel this day,
　Because thou hast defièd Jacob's God,
　And suffer'd Rabbah with the Philistine
　To rail upon the tribe of Benjamin.
Ha. Hark, man: as sure as Saul thy master fell,
　And gor'd his sides upon the mountain-tops,
　And Jonathan, Abinadab, and Melchisua,
　Water'd the dales and deeps of Askaron
　With bloody streams, that from Gilboa ran
　In channels through the wilderness of Ziph,　　800
　What time the sword of the uncircumcis'd
　Was drunken with the blood of Israel;
　So sure shall David perish with his men
　Under the walls of Rabbah, Hanon's town.

[1] **A** dissyllable here.

Joab. Hanon, the God of Israel hath said,
   David the king shall wear that crown of thine
   That weighs a talent of the finest gold,
   And triumph in the spoil of Hanon's town,
   When Israel shall hale thy people hence,
   And turn them to the tile-kiln, man and child,   810
   And put them under harrows made of iron,
   And hew their bones with axes, and their limbs
   With iron swords divide and tear in twain.
   Hanon, this shall be done to thee and thine,
   Because thou hast defièd Israel.—
   To arms, to arms, that Rabbah feel revenge,
   And Hanon's town become King David's spoil!

Alarum, excursions, assault; exeunt. Then the trumpets sound, and re-enter DAVID *with* HANON'S *crown,* JOAB, *etc.*

Dav. Now clattering arms and wrathful storms of war
   Have thunder'd over Rabbah's razèd towers;
   The wreakful ire of great Jehovah's arm,   820
   That for his people made the gates to rend,
   And cloth'd the cherubins in fiery coats
   To fight against the wicked Hanon's town.
   Pay thanks, ye men of Judah, to the King,
   The God of Sion and Jerusalem,
   That hath exalted Israel to this,
   And crownèd David with this diadem.
Joab. Beauteous and bright is he among the tribes;
   As when the sun,[1] attir'd in glistering robe,
   Comes dancing from his oriental gate,   830
   And bridegroom-like hurls through the gloomy air
   His radiant beams, such doth King David show,
   Crown'd with the honour of his enemies' town,
   Shining in riches like the firmament,
   The starry vault that overhangs the earth:

---

[1] Hawkins, who (Preface to *The Origin of the English Drama,* vol. i. p. 11) justly praises this simile, had forgotten the following lines of Spenser:

> "At last, the golden orientall gate
> Of greatest heaven gan to open fayre;
> And Phœbus, fresh as brydegrome to his mate,
> Came dauncing forth, shaking his deawie hayre;
> And hurld his glistring beames through gloomy ayre."
>   *The Faerie Queene,* B. 1. c. 5, st. 2.

So looketh David King of Israel.
Abis. Joab, why doth not David mount his throne
Whom heaven hath beautified with Hanon's crown?
Sound trumpets, shalms, and instruments of praise,
To Jacob's God for David's victory. 840
[*Trumpets, etc.*

Enter JONADAB.

Jonad. Why doth the King of Israel rejoice?
Why sitteth David crown'd with Rabbah's rule?
Behold, there hath great heaviness befall'n
In Amnon's fields by Absalon's misdeed;
And Amnon's shearers and their feast of mirth
Absalon hath o'erturnèd with his sword;
Nor liveth any of King David's sons
To bring this bitter tidings to the king.
Dav. Ay me, how soon are David's triumphs dash'd,
How suddenly declineth David's pride! 850
As doth the daylight settle in the west,
So dim is David's glory and his gite.[1]
Die, David; for to thee is left no seed
That may revive thy name in Israel.
Jonad. In Israel is left of David's seed.
Comfort your lord, you servants of the king.—
Behold, thy sons return in mourning weeds,
And only Amnon Absalon hath slain.

Enter ADONIA *with other* Sons *of* DAVID.

Dav. Welcome, my sons; dearer to me you are
Than is this golden crown or Hanon's spoil. 860
O, tell me, then, tell me, my sons, I say,
How cometh it to pass that Absalon
Hath slain his brother Amnon with the sword?
Ad. Thy sons, O king, went up to Amnon's fields,
To feast with him and eat his bread and oil;
And Absalon upon his mule doth come,
And to his men he saith, "When Amnon's heart
Is merry and secure, then strike him dead,

---

[1] Gite in the present passage, as well as in the following line of our author's *Tale of Troy*, seems to mean—splendour, brightness:

"Done is thy pride, dim is thy glorious *gite*."

David and Bethsabe

 Because he forcèd Thamar shamefully,
 And hated her, and threw her forth his doors."   870
 And this did he; and they with him conspire,
 And kill thy son in wreak of Thamar's wrong.
Dav. How long shall Judah and Jerusalem
 Complain, and water Sion with their tears!
 How long shall Israel lament in vain,
 And not a man among the mighty ones
 Will hear the sorrows of King David's heart!
 Amnon, thy life was pleasing to thy lord,
 As to mine ears the music of my lute,
 Or songs that David tuneth to his harp;   880
 And Absalon hath ta'en from me away
 The gladness of my sad distressèd soul.
     [*Exeunt Joab and some others.*[1]

Enter Woman of Thecoa.[2]

Wo. of T. [*kneeling.*] God save King David, King of Israel,
 And bless the gates of Sion for his sake!
Dav. Woman, why mournest thou? rise from the earth;
 Tell me what sorrow hath befall'n thy soul.
Wo. of T. [*rising.*] Thy servant's soul, O king, is troubled sore,
 And grievous is the anguish of her heart;
 And from Thecoa doth thy handmaid come.
Dav. Tell me, and say, thou woman of Thecoa,   890
 What aileth thee or what is come to pass.
Wo. of T. Thy servant is a widow in Thecoa.
 Two sons thy handmaid had; and they, my lord,
 Fought in the field, where no man went betwixt,
 And so the one did smite and slay the other.
 And, lo, behold, the kindred doth arise,
 And cry on him[3] that smote his brother,
 That he therefóre may be the child of death;
 " For we will follow and destroy the heir."
 So will they quench that sparkle that is left,   900
 And leave nor name nor issue on the earth

---

[1] The 4to has " *Exeunt* omnes. *Manet David.*" But see David's last speech on page 155, line 957.
[2] The 4to " *widdow of Thecoa* ": but she is only *a pretended widow*.
[3] Some slight omission here. The words of Scripture are: " And they said, Deliver him that smote his brother, that we may kill him for the life of his brother whom he slew; and we will destroy the heir also," etc. —*Sec. Samuel*, xiv. 7.

        To me or to thy handmaid's husband dead.
Dav. Woman, return; go home unto thy house:
    I will take order that thy son be safe.
    If any man say otherwise than well,
    Bring him to me, and I shall chástise him;
    For, as the Lord doth live, shall not a hair
    Shed from thy son or fall upon the earth.
    Woman, to God alone belongs revenge:
    Shall, then, the kindred slay him for his sin?   910
Wo. of T. Well hath King David to his handmaid spoke:
    But wherefore, then, hast thou determinèd
    So hard a part against the righteous tribes,
    To follow and pursue the banishèd,
    Whenas [1] to God alone belongs revenge?
    Assuredly thou saist against thyself:
    Therefore call home again the banishèd;
    Call home the banishèd, that he may live,
    And raise to thee some fruit in Israel.
Dav. Thou woman of Thecoa, answer me,   920
    Answer me one thing I shall ask of thee:
    Is not the hand of Joab in this work?
    Tell me, is not his finger in this fact?
Wo. of T. It is, my lord; his hand is in this work:
    Assure thee, Joab, captain of thy host,
    Hath put these words into thy handmaid's mouth;
    And thou art as an angel from on high,
    To understand the meaning of my heart:
    Lo, where he cometh to his lord the king.

Re-enter JOAB.

Dav. Say, Joab, didst thou send this woman in   930
    To put this parable for Absalon?
Joab. Joab, my lord, did bid this woman speak,
    And she hath said; and thou hast understood.
Dav. I have, and am content to do the thing.
    Go fetch my son, that he may live with me.
Joab. [*kneeling.*] Now God be blessèd for King David's life!
    Thy servant Joab hath found grace with thee,
    In that thou sparest Absalon thy child.   [*Rises.*
    A beautiful and fair young man is he,

[1] *i.e.,* When.

David and Bethsabe

> In all his body is no blemish seen; 940
> His hair is like the wire of David's harp,
> That twines about his bright and ivory neck;
> In Israel is not such a goodly man;
> And here I bring him to entreat for grace.

Joab brings in Absalon.

Dav. Hast thou [1] slain in the fields of Hazor——
> Ah, Absalon, my son! ah, my son, Absalon!
> But wherefore do I vex thy spirit so?
> Live, and return from Gesur to thy house;
> Return from Gesur to Jerusalem:
> What boots it to be bitter to thy soul? 950
> Amnon is dead, and Absalon survives.

Abs. Father, I have offended Israel,
> I have offended David and his house;
> For Thamar's wrong hath Absalon misdone:
> But David's heart is free from sharp revenge,
> And Joab hath got grace for Absalon.

Dav. Depart with me, you men of Israel,
> You that have follow'd Rabbah with the sword,
> And ransack Ammon's richest treasuries.—
> Live, Absalon, my son, live once in peace: 960
> Peace [be] with thee, and with Jerusalem!
> *[Exeunt all except Absalon.*

Abs. David is gone, and Absalon remains,
> Flowering in pleasant spring-time of his youth:
> Why liveth Absalon and is not honour'd
> Of tribes and elders and the mightiest ones,
> That round about his temples he may wear
> Garlands and wreaths set on with reverence;
> That every one that hath a cause to plead
> Might come to Absalon and call for right?
> Then in the gates of Sion would I sit, 970
> And publish laws in great Jerusalem;
> And not a man should live in all the land
> But Absalon would do him reason's due:
> Therefore I shall address me, as I may,
> To love the men and tribes of Israel.   *[Exit.*

---

[1] Qy. "*Hast thou slain* Amnon *in the fields of Hazor?*" for I cannot think that this line of nine syllables is to be defended on the supposition that David here avoids mentioning the name of his murdered son.

Enter DAVID, ITHAY, SADOC, AHIMAAS, JONATHAN, *and others;*
  DAVID *barefoot, with some loose covering over his head; and
  all mourning.*

Dav. Proud lust, the bloodiest traitor to our souls,
  Whose greedy throat nor earth, air, sea, or heaven,
  Can glut or satisfy with any store,
  Thou art the cause these torments suck my blood,
  Piercing with venom of thy poison'd eyes   980
  The strength and marrow of my tainted bones.
  To punish Pharaoh and his cursèd host,
  The waters shrunk [1] at great Adonai's voice,
  And sandy bottom of the sea appear'd,
  Offering his service at his servant's feet;
  And, to inflict a plague on David's sin,
  He makes his bowels traitors to his breast,
  Winding about his heart with mortal gripes.
  Ah, Absalon, the wrath of heaven inflames
  Thy scorchèd bosom with ambitious heat,   990
  And Satan sets thee on a lofty [2] tower,
  Showing thy thoughts the pride of Israel,
  Of choice to cast thee on her ruthless stones!—
  Weep with me, then, ye sons of Israel;
  Lie down with David, and with David mourn
  Before the Holy One that sees our hearts;
        [*Lies down, and all the rest after him.*
  Season this heavy soil with showers of tears,
  And fill the face of every flower with dew;
  Weep, Israel, for David's soul dissolves,
  Lading the fountains of his drownèd eyes,   1000
  And pours her substance on the senseless earth.

Sa. Weep, Israel; O, weep for David's soul,
  Strewing the ground with hair and garments torn,
  For tragic witness of your hearty woes!

Ahi. O, would our eyes were conduits to our hearts,
  And that our hearts were seas of liquid blood,
  To pour in streams upon this holy mount,
  For witness we would die for David's woes!

Jonath. Then should this Mount of Olives seem a plain
  Drown'd with a sea, that with our sighs should roar, 1010

---

[1] The 4to "shrinke."   [2] The 4to "lustie."

> And, in the murmur of his mounting waves,
> Report our bleeding sorrows to the heavens,
> For witness we would die for David's woes.
Ith. Earth cannot weep enough for David's woes:
> Then weep, you heavens, and, all you clouds, dissolve,
> That piteous stars may see our miseries,
> And drop their golden tears upon the ground,
> For witness how they weep for David's woes.
Sa. Now let my sovereign raise his prostrate bones,
> And mourn not as a faithless man would do;   1020
> But be assur'd that Jacob's righteous God,
> That promis'd never to forsake your throne,
> Will still be just and pure [1] in his vows.
Dav. Sadoc, high-priest, preserver of the ark,
> Whose sacred virtue keeps the chosen crown,
> I know my God is spotless in his vows,
> And that these hairs shall greet my grave in peace:
> But that my son should wrong his tender'd soul,
> And fight against his father's happiness,
> Turns all my hopes into despair of him,   1030
> And that despair feeds all my veins with grief.
Ith. Think of it, David, as a fatal plague
> Which grief preserveth, but preventeth not;
> And turn thy drooping eyes upon the troops
> That, of affection to thy worthiness,
> Do swarm about the person of the king:
> Cherish their valours and their zealous loves
> With pleasant looks and sweet encouragements.
Dav. Methinks the voice of Ithay fills mine ears.
Ith. Let not the voice of Ithay loathe thine ears,   1040
> Whose heart would balm thy bosom with his tears.
Dav. But wherefore go'st thou to the wars with us?
> Thou art a stranger here in Israel,
> And son to Achis, mighty King of Gath;
> Therefore return, and with thy father stay:
> Thou cam'st but yesterday; and should I now
> Let thee partake these troubles here with us?
> Keep both thyself and all thy soldiers safe:
> Let me abide the hazards of these arms,
> And God requite the friendship thou hast show'd.   1050
Ith. As sure as Israel's God gives David life,

---

[1] A dissyllable here.

What place or peril shall contain the king,
The same will Ithay share in life and death.
Dav. Then, gentle Ithay, be thou still with us,
A joy to David, and a grace to Israel.—
Go, Sadoc, now, and bear the ark of God
Into the great Jerusalem again:
If I find favour in his gracious eyes,
Then will he lay his hand upon my heart
Yet once again before I visit death; 1060
Giving it strength, and virtue to mine eyes,
To taste the comforts and behold the form
Of his fair ark and holy tabernacle:
But, if he say, " My wonted love is worn,
And I have no delight in David now,"
Here lie I armèd with an humble heart
T' embrace the pains that anger shall impose,
And kiss the sword my lord shall kill me with.
Then, Sadoc, take Ahimaas thy son,
With Jonathan son to Abiathar; 1070
And in these fields will I repose myself,
Till they return from you some certain news.
Sa. Thy servants will with joy obey the king,
And hope to cheer his heart with happy news.
                    [*Exeunt Sadoc, Ahimaas, and Jonathan.*
Ith. Now that it be no grief unto the king,
Let me for good inform his majesty,
That, with unkind and graceless Absalon,
Achitophel your ancient counsellor
Directs the state of this rebellion.
Dav. Then doth it aim with danger at my crown.— 1080
O thou, that hold'st his raging bloody bound
Within the circle of the silver moon,
That girds earth's centre with his watery scarf,
Limit the counsel of Achitophel,
No bounds extending to my soul's distress,
But turn his wisdom into foolishness!

Enter CUSAY *with his coat turned and head covered.*

Cu. Happiness and honour to my lord the king!
Dav. What happiness or honour may betide
His state that toils in my extremities?

David and Bethsabe

Cu. O, let my gracious sovereign cease these griefs, 1090
    Unless he wish his servant Cusay's death,
    Whose life depends upon my lord's relief!
    Then let my presence with my sighs perfume
    The pleasant closet of my sovereign's soul.
Dav. No, Cusay, no; thy presence unto me
    Will be a burden, since I tender thee,
    And cannot brook [1] thy sighs for David's sake:
    But if thou turn to fair Jerusalem,
    And say to Absalon, as thou hast been
    A trusty friend unto his father's seat, 1100
    So thou wilt be to him, and call him king,
    Achitophel's counsel may be brought to naught.
    Then having Sadoc and Abiathar,
    All three may learn the secrets of my son,
    Sending the message by Ahimaas,
    And friendly Jonathan, who both are there.
Cu. Then rise, referring the success to heaven.[2]
Dav. Cusay, I rise; though with unwieldy bones
    I carry arms against my Absalon.   [*Exeunt.*

ABSALON, AMASA, ACHITOPHEL, *with the* Concubines *of* DAVID, *and others, are discovered in great state ;* ABSALON *crowned.*

Abs. Now you that were my father's concubines, 1110
    Liquor to his inchaste and lustful fire,
    Have seen his honour shaken in his house,
    Which I possess in sight of all the world;
    I bring ye forth for foils to my renown,
    And to eclipse the glory of your king,
    Whose life is with his honour fast enclos'd
    Within the entrails of a jetty cloud,
    Whose dissolution shall pour down in showers
    The substance of his life and swelling pride:
    Then shall the stars light earth with rich aspécts, 1120
    And heaven shall burn in love with Absalon,
    Whose beauty will suffice to chase [3] all mists,
    And clothe the sun's sphere with a triple fire,
    Sooner than his clear eyes should suffer stain,
    Or be offended with a lowering day.

---

[1] The 4to " breake."   [2] This line is given in the 4to to David.
[3] The 4to " chast."

First Conc. Thy father's honour, graceless Absalon,
　　And ours thus beaten with thy violent arms,
　　Will cry for vengeance to the host of heaven,
　　Whose power is ever arm'd against the proud,
　　And will dart plagues at thy aspiring head　　　　1130
　　For doing this disgrace to David's throne.
Second Conc. To David's throne, to David's holy throne,
　　Whose sceptre angels guard with swords of fire,
　　And sit as eagles on his conquering fist,
　　Ready to prey upon his enemies:
　　Then think not thou, the captain of his foes,
　　Wert thou much swifter than Azahell [1] was,
　　That could outpace the nimble-footed roe,
　　To scape the fury of their thumping beaks
　　Or dreadful scope of their commanding wings.　　1140
Ach. Let not my lord the King of Israel
　　Be angry with a silly woman's threats;
　　But, with the pleasure he hath erst enjoy'd,
　　Turn them into their cabinets again,
　　Till David's conquest be their overthrow.
Abs. Into your bowers, ye daughters of disdain,
　　Gotten by fury of unbridled lust,
　　And wash your couches with your mourning tears,
　　For grief that David's kingdom is decay'd.
First Conc. No, Absalon, his kingdom is enchain'd　　1150
　　Fast to the finger of great Jacob's God,
　　Which will not loose it for a rebel's love.

　　　　　　　　　　　　　　　　[*Exeunt Concubines.*

Ama. If I might give advice unto the king,
　　These concubines should buy their taunts with blood.
Abs. Amasa, no; but let thy martial sword
　　Empty the veins [2] of David's armèd men,
　　And let these foolish women scape our hands
　　To recompense the shame they have sustain'd.
　　First, Absalon was by the trumpet's sound
　　Proclaim'd through Hebron King of Israel;　　　　1160
　　And now is set in fair Jerusalem
　　With cómplete state and glory of a crown:
　　Fifty fair footmen by my chariot run,

---

[1] "And there were three sons of Zeruiah there, Joab, and Abishai, and Asahel: and Asahel was as light of foot as a wild roe."—*Sec. Samuel*, ii. 18.
[2] The 4to "paines."

And to the air whose rupture rings my fame,
Where'er I ride, they offer reverence.
Why should not Absalon, that in his face
Carries the final purpose of his God,
That is, to work him grace in Israel,
Endeavour to achieve with all his strength
The state that most may satisfy his joy,   1170
Keeping his statutes and his covenants pure?
His thunder is entangled in my hair,
And with my beauty is his lightning quench'd:
I am the man he made to glory in,
When by the errors of my father's sin
He lost the path that led into the land
Wherewith our chosen ancestors were bless'd.

Enter CUSAY.

Cu. Long may the beauteous King of Israel live,
 To whom the people do by thousands swarm!
Abs. What meaneth Cusay so to greet his foe?   1180
 Is this the love thou show'st [1] to David's soul,
 To whose assistance thou hast vow'd thy life?
 Why leav'st thou him in this extremity?
Cu. Because the Lord and Israel chooseth thee;
 And as before I serv'd thy father's turn
 With counsel acceptable in his sight,
 So likewise will I now obey his son.
Abs. Then welcome, Cusay, to King Absalon.—
 And now, my lords and loving counsellors,
 I think it time to exercise our arms   1190
 Against forsaken David and his host.
 Give counsel first, my good Achitophel,
 What times and orders we may best observe
 For prosperous manage of these high exploits.
Ach. Let me choose out twelve thousand valiant men:
 And, while the night hides with her sable mists
 The close endeavours cunning soldiers use,
 I will assault thy discontented sire;
 And, while with weakness of their weary arms,
 Surcharg'd with toil, to shun thy sudden power, 1200
 The people fly in huge disorder'd troops

[1] The 4to " shewdst."

> To save their lives, and leave the king alone,
> Then will I smite him with his latest wound,
> And bring the people to thy feet in peace.
>
> *Abs.* Well hath Achitophel given his advice.
> Yet let us hear what Cusay counsels us,
> Whose great experience is well worth the ear.
>
> *Cu.* Though wise Achitophel be much more meet
> To purchase hearing with my lord the king,
> For all his former counsels, than myself,   1210
> Yet, not offending Absalon or him,
> This time it is not good nor worth pursuit;
> For, well thou know'st, thy father's men are strong,
> Chafing as she-bears robbèd of their whelps:
> Besides, the king himself a valiant man,
> Train'd up in feats and stratagems of war;
> And will not, for prevention of the worst,
> Lodge with the common soldiers in the field;
> But now, I know, his wonted policies
> Have taught him lurk within some secret cave,   1220
> Guarded with all his stoutest soldiers;
> Which, if the forefront of his battle faint,
> Will yet give out that Absalon doth fly,
> And so thy soldiers be discouragèd:
> David himself withal, whose angry heart
> Is as a lion's letted of his walk,
> Will fight himself, and all his men to one,
> Before a few shall vanquish him by fear.
> My counsel therefore is, with trumpet's sound
> To gather men from Dan to Bersabe,   1230
> That they may march in number like sea-sands,
> That nestle close in [one] another's neck:
> So shall we come upon him in our strength,
> Like to the dew that falls in showers from heaven,
> And leave him not a man to march withal.
> Besides, if any city succour him,
> The numbers of our men shall fetch us ropes,
> And we will pull it down the river's stream,
> That not a stone be left to keep us out.
>
> *Abs.* What says my lord to Cusay's counsel now?   1240
>
> *Ama.* I fancy Cusay's counsel better far
> Than that is given us from Achitophel;
> And so, I think, doth every soldier here.

All. Cusay's counsel is better than Achitophel's.
Abs. Then march we after Cusay's counsel all:
 Sound trumpets through the bounds of Israel,
 And muster all the men will serve the king,
 That Absalon may glut his longing soul
 With sole fruition of his father's crown.
Ach. [*aside.*] Ill shall they fare that follow thy attempts, 1250
 That scorns the counsel of Achitophel.
   [*Exeunt all except Cusay.*
Cu. Thus hath the power of Jacob's jealous God
 Fulfill'd his servant David's drifts by me,
 And brought Achitophel's advice to scorn.

Enter SADOC, ABIATHAR, AHIMAAS, *and* JONATHAN.

Sa. God save Lord Cusay, and direct his zeal
 To purchase David's conquest 'gainst his son!
Abi. What secrets hast thou glean'd from Absalon?
Cu. These, sacred priests that bear the ark of God:—
 Achitophel advis'd him in the night
 To let him choose twelve thousand fighting men, 1260
 And he would come on David at unwares,
 While he was weary with his violent toil:
 But I advis'd to get a greater host,
 And gather men from Dan to Bersabe,
 To come upon him strongly in the fields.
 Then send Ahimaas and Jonathan
 To signify these secrets to the king,
 And will [1] him not to stay this night abroad;
 But get him over Jordan presently,
 Lest he and all his people kiss the sword. 1270
Sa. Then go, Ahimaas and Jonathan,
 And straight convey this message to the king.
Ahi. Father, we will, if Absalon's chief spies
 Prevent not this device, and stay us here.   [*Exeunt.*

Enter Semei.

Sem. The man of Israel that hath rul'd as king,
 Or rather as the tyrant of the land,
 Bolstering his hateful head upon the throne

[1] *i.e.,* desire.

That God unworthily hath bless'd him with,
Shall now, I hope, lay it as low as hell,
And be depos'd from his detested chair. 1280
O, that my bosom could by nature bear
A sea of poison, to be pour'd upon
His cursèd head that sacred balm hath grac'd
And consecrated King of Israel!
Or would my breath were made the smoke of hell,
Infected with the sighs of damnèd souls,
Or with the reeking of that serpent's gorge
That feeds on adders, toads, and venomous roots,
That, as I open'd my revenging lips
To curse the shepherd for his tyranny, 1290
My words might cast rank poison to his pores,
And make his swoln and rankling sinews crack,
Like to the combat-blows that break the clouds
When Jove's [1] stout champions fight with fire.
See where he cometh that my soul abhors!
I have prepar'd my pocket full of stones
To cast at him, mingled with earth and dust,
Which, bursting with disdain, I greet him with.

Enter DAVID, JOAB, ABISAI, ITHAY, *and others.*

Come forth, thou murderer and wicked man:
The lord hath brought upon thy cursèd head 1300
The guiltless blood of Saul and all his sons,
Whose royal throne thy baseness hath usurp'd;
And, to revenge it deeply on thy soul,
The Lord hath given the kingdom to thy son,
And he shall wreak the traitorous wrongs of Saul:
Even as thy sin hath still importun'd heaven,
So shall thy murders and adultery
Be punish'd in the sight of Israel,
As thou deserv'st, with blood, with death, and hell.
Hence, murderer, hence! 1310
  [*Throws* [2] *stones and earth at David.*
Abis. Why doth [t]his dead dog curse my lord the king?
Let me alone to take away his head.

[1] A mutilated line.
[2] In the 4to this stage direction and the end of the speech are confounded thus:
  "*Hence murtherer, hence, he threw at him.*"

Dav. Why meddleth thus the son of Zeruia
    To interrupt the action of our God?
    Semei useth me with this reproach
    Because the Lord hath sent him to reprove
    The sins of David, printed in his brows
    With blood, that blusheth for his conscience' guilt;
    Who dares, then, ask him why he curseth me?
Sem. If, then, thy conscience tell thee thou hast sinn'd,   1320
    And that thy life is odious to the world,
    Command thy followers to shun thy face;
    And by thyself here make away thy soul,
    That I may stand and glory in thy shame.
Dav. I am not desperate, Semei, like thyself,
    But trust unto the covenant of my God,
    Founded on mercy, with repentance built,
    And finish'd with the glory of my soul.
Sem. A murderer, and hope for mercy in thy end!
    Hate and destruction sit upon thy brows   1330
    To watch the issue of thy damnèd ghost,
    Which with thy latest gasp they'll take and tear,
    Hurling in every pain of hell a piece.
    Hence, murderer, thou shame to Israel,
    Foul lecher, drunkard, plague to heaven and earth!
        [*Throws again at David.*
Joab. What, is it piety in David's thoughts,
    So to abhor from laws of policy
    In this extremity of his distress,
    To give his subjects cause of carelessness?
    Send hence the dog with sorrow to his grave.   1340
Dav. Why should the sons of Zeruia seek to check [1]
    His spirit, which the Lord hath thus inspir'd?
    Behold, my son which issu'd from my flesh,
    With equal fury seeks to take my life:
    How much more then the son of Jemini,
    Chiefly since he doth naught but God's command?
    It may be, he will look on me this day
    With gracious eyes, and for his cursing bless
    The heart of David in his bitterness.
Sem. What, dost thou fret my soul with sufferance?   1350

---

[1] "The sons of Zeruia," be it remembered, are Abisai (who a little before has said "Let me alone to take away his [Semei's] head") and Joab.—In this line "*seek to*" would seem to be an interpolation.

O, that the souls of Isboseth and Abner,
Which thou sent'st swimming to their graves in blood,
With wounds fresh bleeding, gasping for revenge,
Were here to execute my burning hate!
But I will hunt thy foot with curses still:
Hence, monster, murderer, mirror of contempt!
              [*Throws again at David.*

Enter AHIMAAS *and* JONATHAN.

Ahi. Long life to David, to his enemies death!
Dav. Welcome, Ahimaas and Jonathan:
  What news sends Cusay to thy lord the king?
Ahi. Cusay would wish [1] my lord the king   1360
  To pass the river Jordan presently,
  Lest he and all his people perish here;
  For wise Achitophel hath counsell'd Absalon
  To take advantage of your weary arms,
  And come this night upon you in the fields.
  But yet the Lord hath made his counsel scorn,
  And Cusay's policy with praise preferr'd;
  Which was to number every Israelite,
  And so assault you in their pride of strength.
Jonath. Abiathar besides entreats the king   1370
  To send his men of war against his son,
  And hazard not his person in the field.
Dav. Thanks to Abiathar, and to you both,
  And to my Cusay, whom the Lord requite;
  But ten times treble thanks to his soft hand
  Whose pleasant touch hath made my heart to dance,
  And play him praises in my zealous breast,
  That turn'd the counsel of Achitophel
  After the prayers of his servant's lips.
  Now will we pass the river all this night,   1380
  And in the morning sound the voice of war,
  The voice of bloody and unkindly war.
Joab. Then tell us how thou wilt divide thy men,
  And who shall have the special charge herein.
Dav. Joab, thyself shall for thy charge conduct
  The first third part of all my valiant men;
  The second shall Abisai's valour lead;

---

[1] Another mutilated line.

The third fair Ithay, which I most should grace
For comfort he hath done to David's woes;
And I myself will follow in the midst.   1390
Ith. That let not David; for, though we should fly,
Ten thousand of us were not half so much
Esteem'd with David's enemies as himself:
Thy people, loving thee, deny thee this.
Dav. What seems them best, then, that will David do.
But now, my lords and captains, hear his voice
That never yet pierc'd piteous heaven in vain;
Then let it not slip lightly through your ears;—
For my sake spare the young man Absalon.
Joab, thyself didst once use friendly words   1400
To reconcile my heart incens'd to him;
If, then, thy love be to thy kinsman sound,
And thou wilt prove a perfect Israelite,
Friend him with deeds, and touch no hair of him,—
Not that fair hair with which the wanton winds
Delight to play, and love to make it curl,
Wherein the nightingales would build their nests,
And make sweet bowers in every golden tress
To sing their lover every night asleep:
O, spoil not, Joab, Jove's fair ornaments,   1410
Which he hath sent to solace David's soul!
The best, ye see, my lords, are swift to sin;
To sin our feet are wash'd with milk of roes,[1]
And dried again with coals of lightning.[2]
O Lord, thou see'st the proudest sin's poor slave,
And with his bridle[3] pull'st him to the grave!
For my sake, then, spare lovely Absalon.
Ith. We will, my lord, for thy sake favour him.   [*Exeunt.*

---

[1] Walker, who (*Shakespeare's Versification*, etc., p. 18) quotes this as if the reading of the old copy was "*milk of* roses," justly calls it "a strange passage."

[2] Lightning is here a trisyllable. (Indeed, the 4to has "lightening.")

[3] Mr. Collier, quoting the present passage in his *Hist. of Eng. Dram. Poetry*, iii. 204, gives,

"*And with his bridle* pulls *him to the grave;*"

remarking (*ibid*): "This line, as printed by the Rev. Mr. Dyce, exhibits almost the solitary verbal blemish of his edition: it there stands,

'And with his bridle pull'st him to the grave:'

as if David, addressing the Lord, said, 'Thou pull'st man to the grave with the bridle of sin;' whereas the meaning is, that 'sin with his bridle pulls man to the grave.' The passage would read better, could we alter *and* in the last line to 'who.'"

Enter ACHITOPHEL *with a halter.*

Ach. Now hath Achitophel order'd his house,
    And taken leave of every pleasure there: 1420
    Hereon depend Achitophel's delights,
    And in this circle must his life be clos'd.
    The wise Achitophel, whose counsel prov'd
    Ever as sound for fortunate success
    As if men ask'd the oracle of God,
    Is now us'd like the fool of Israel:
    Then set thy angry soul upon her wings,
    And let her fly into the shade of death;
    And for my death let heaven for ever weep,
    Making huge floods upon the land I leave, 1430
    To ravish them and all their fairest fruits.
    Let all the sighs I breath'd for this disgrace,
    Hang on my hedges like eternal mists,
    As mourning garments for their master's death.
    Ope, earth, and take thy miserable son
    Into the bowels of thy cursèd womb:
    Once in a surfeit thou didst spew him forth;
    Now for fell hunger suck him in again,
    And be his body poison to thy veins.
    And now, thou hellish instrument of heaven, 1440
    Once execute th' arrest of Jove's just doom,
    And stop his breath [1] that curseth Israel. [*Exit.*

Enter ABSALON, *with* AMASA *and the rest of his train.*

Abs. Now for the crown and throne of Israel,
    To be confirm'd with virtue of my sword,
    And writ with David's blood upon the blade.
    Now, Jove, let forth the golden firmament,
    And look on him, with all thy fiery eyes,
    Which thou hast made to give their glories light:
    To show thou lov'st the virtue of thy hand,
    Let fall a wreath of stars upon my head, 1450
    Whose influence may govern Israel
    With state exceeding all her other kings.
    Fight, lords and captains, that your sovereign's face

---

[1] The 4to " breast."

David and Bethsabe

May shine in honour brighter than the sun;
And with the virtue of my beauteous rays
Make this fair land as fruitful as the fields
That with sweet milk and honey overflow'd.
God, in the whizzing of a pleasant wind,
Shall march upon the tops of mulberry-trees,[1]
To cool all breasts that burn with any griefs,　　　　　1460
As whilom he was good to Moses' men.
By day the Lord shall sit within a cloud,
To guide your footsteps to the fields of joy;
And in the night a pillar, bright as fire,
Shall go before you, like a second sun,
Wherein the essence of his godhead is;
That day and night you may be brought to peace,
And never swerve from that delightsome path
That leads your souls to perfect happiness.
This shall he do for joy when I am king.　　　　　　1470
Then fight, brave captains, that these joys may fly
Into your bosoms with sweet victory.　　　　　[*Exeunt.*

The battle; and then ABSALON *hangs by the hair.*[2]

Abs. What angry angel, sitting in these shades,
Hath laid his cruel hands upon my hair,
And holds my body thus 'twixt heaven and earth?
Hath Absalon no soldier near his hand
That may untwine me this unpleasant curl,
Or wound this tree that ravisheth his lord?
O God, behold the glory of thy hand,
And choicest fruit of nature's workmanship,　　　　　1480
Hang, like a rotten branch, upon this tree,
Fit for the axe and ready for the fire!
Since thou withhold'st all ordinary help
To loose my body from this bond of death,
O, let my beauty fill these senseless plants
With sense and power to loose me from this plague,

---

[1] " And it shall be, when thou shalt hear a sound of going in the tops of the mulberry-trees, that then thou shalt go out to battle: for God is gone first before thee," etc.—*First Chron.* xiv. 15.

[2] The following entry occurs in Henslowe's *Diary*, under Octr. 1602:
" Pd for poleyes and workmanshipp for to hange Absalome . xiiijd." p. 241, ed. Shake. Soc. Does Henslowe allude to the present play, or to some other drama in which Absalon was " hung "?

And work some wonder to prevent his death
Whose life thou mad'st a special miracle!

Enter JOAB *with a* Soldier.

Sold. My lord, I saw the young Prince Absalon
    Hang by the hair upon a shady oak,   1490
    And could by no means get himself unloos'd.
Joab. Why slew'st thou not the wicked Absalon,
    That rebel to his father and to heaven,
    That so I might have given thee for thy pains
    Ten silver shekels [1] and a golden waist? [2]
Sold. Not for a thousand shekels would I slay
    The son of David, whom his father charg'd
    Nor thou, Abisai, nor the son of Gath,[3]
    Should touch with stroke of deadly violence.
    The charge was given in hearing of us all;   1500
    And, had I done it, then, I know, thyself,
    Before thou wouldst abide the king's rebuke,
    Wouldst have accus'd me as a man of death.
Joab. I must not now stand trifling here with thee.
Abs. Help, Joab, help, O, help thy Absalon!
    Let not thy angry thoughts be laid in blood,
    In blood of him that sometimes nourish'd thee,
    And soften'd thy sweet heart with friendly love:
    O, give me once again my father's sight,
    My dearest father and my princely sovereign!   1510
    That, shedding tears of blood before his face,
    The ground may witness, and the heavens record,
    My last submission sound and full of ruth.
Joab. Rebel to nature, hate to heaven and earth!
    Shall I give help to him that thirsts the soul
    Of his dear father and my sovereign lord?
    Now see, the Lord hath tangled in a tree
    The health and glory of thy stubborn heart,
    And made thy pride curb'd with a senseless plant:
    Now, Absalon, how doth the Lord regard   1520
    The beauty whereupon thy hope was built,
    And which thou thought'st his grace did glory in?
    Find'st thou not now, with fear of instant death,

---

[1] The 4to "sickles."   [2] *i.e.*, girdle.—The 4to "wast."
[3] *i.e.*, the native of Gath, viz. Ithay (Ittai).

>   That God affects not any painted shape
>   Or goodly personage, when the virtuous soul
>   Is stuff'd with naught but pride and stubbornness?
>   But, preach I to thee, while I should revenge
>   Thy cursèd sin that staineth Israel,
>   And makes her fields blush with her children's blood?
>   Take that as part of thy deservèd plague,   1530
>   Which worthily no torment can inflict.   [*Stabs him*
> *Abs.* O Joab, Joab, cruel, ruthless Joab!
>   Herewith thou wound'st thy kingly sovereign's heart,
>   Whose heavenly temper hates his children's blood,
>   And will be sick, I know, for Absalon.
>   O, my dear father, that thy melting eyes
>   Might pierce this thicket to behold thy son,
>   Thy dearest son, gor'd with a mortal dart!
>   Yet, Joab, pity me: pity my father, Joab;
>   Pity his soul's distress that mourns my life,   1540
>   And will be dead, I know, to hear my death.
> *Joab.* If he were so remorseful [1] of thy state,
>   Why sent he me against thee with the sword?
>   All Joab means to pleasure thee withal
>   Is, to despatch thee quickly of thy pain:
>   Hold, Absalon, Joab's pity is in this;
>   In this, proud Absalon, is Joab's love.
>   [*Stabs him again; and then exit with Soldier.*
> *Abs.* Such love, such pity Israel's God send thee,
>   And for his love to David pity me!
>   Ah, my dear father, see thy bowels bleed;   1550
>   See death assault thy dearest Absalon;
>   See, pity, pardon, pray for Absalon!

Enter five or six Soldiers.

> *First Sold.* See where the rebel in his glory hangs.—
>   Where is the virtue of thy beauty, Absalon?
>   Will any of us here now fear thy looks,
>   Or be in love with that thy golden hair
>   Wherein was wrapt rebellion 'gainst thy sire,
>   And cords prepar'd to stop thy father's breath?
>   Our captain Joab hath begun to us;
>   And here's an end to thee and all thy sins.   1560
>   [*They stab Absalon; who dies.*

[1] *i.e.*, compassionate.

> Come, let us take the beauteous rebel down,
> And in some ditch, amids this darksome wood,
> Bury his bulk [1] beneath a heap of stones,
> Whose stony heart did hunt his father's death.

Re-enter, in triumph with drum and ensign, JOAB; ABISAI *and* Soldiers.

Joab. Well done, tall [2] soldiers! take the traitor down,
  And in this miry ditch inter his bones,
  Covering his hateful breast with heaps of stones.
  This shady thicket of dark Ephraim
  Shall ever lower on his cursèd grave;
  Night-ravens and owls shall ring his fatal knell,   1570
  And sit exclaiming on his damnèd soul;
  There shall they heap their preys of carrion,
  Till all his grave be clad with stinking bones,
  That it may loathe the sense of every man:
  So shall his end breed horror to his name,
  And to his traitorous fact eternal shame.   [*Exeunt.*

Enter Chorus.

Chorus. O dreadful precedent of his just doom,
  Whose holy heart is never touch'd with ruth
  Of fickle beauty or of glorious shape,[3]
  But with the virtue of an upright soul,   1580
  Humble and zealous in his inward thoughts,
  Though in his person loathsome and deform'd!
  Now, since this story lends us other store,
  To make a third discourse of David's life,
  Adding thereto his most renownèd death,
  And all their deaths that at his death he judg'd,
  Here end we this, and what here wants to please,
  We will supply with treble willingness.[4]   [*Exit.*

---

[1] *i.e.*, body.   [2] *i.e.*, brave.   [3] The 4to "shapes."
[4] In the 4to, after this speech of the Chorus, the page ends with the following fragment, which belongs to some earlier scene of the play that has been lost:

> "*Absalon with three or foure of his seruants or gentlemen.*
>
>   *Abs.* What boots it Absalon, vnhappie Absalon,
>   Sighing I say what boots it Absalon,
>   To haue disclos'd a farre more worthy wombe
>
>   Then "

Trumpets sound. Enter JOAB, AHIMAAS, CUSAY; AMASA, *with
    all the other followers of* ABSALON.

Joab. Soldiers of Israel, and ye sons of Judah,
    That have contended in these irksome broils,   1590
    And ript old Israel's bowels with your swords;
    The godless general of your stubborn arms
    Is brought by Israel's helper to the grave,
    A grave of shame, and scorn of all the tribes:
    Now, then, to save your honours from the dust,
    And keep your bloods in temper by your bones,
    Let Joab's ensign shroud your manly heads,
    Direct your eyes, your weapons, and your hearts,
    To guard the life of David from his foes.
    Error hath mask'd your much-too-forward minds,   1600
    And you have sinn'd against the chosen state,
    Against his life, for whom your lives are bless'd,
    And follow'd an usurper to the field;
    In whose just death your deaths are threatenèd;
    But Joab pities your disorder'd souls,
    And therefore offers pardon, peace, and love,
    To all that will be friendly reconcil'd
    To Israel's weal, to David, and to heaven.
    Amasa, thou art leader of the host
    That under Absalon have rais'd their arms;   1610
    Then be a captain wise and politic,
    Careful and loving for thy soldiers' lives,
    And lead them to this honourable league.
Ama. I will;[1] at least, I'll do my best:
    And for the gracious offer thou hast made
    I give thee thanks, as much as for my head.—
    Then, you deceiv'd poor souls of Israel,
    Since now ye see the errors you incurr'd,
    With thanks and due submission be appeas'd;
    And as ye see your captain's precedent,   1620
    Here cast we, then, our swords at Joab's feet,
    Submitting with all zeal and reverence
    Our goods and bodies to his gracious hands.
                                                   [*Kneels with others.*
Joab. Stand up, and take ye all your swords again:
                                                           [*All stand up.*

---

[1] Qy. " Joab, *I will,*" etc.? or " *I will,* my lord," etc.

  David and Joab shall be bless'd herein.
Ahi. Now let me go inform my lord the king
  How God hath freed him from his enemies.
Joab. Another time, Ahimaas, not now.—
  But, Cusay, go thyself, and tell the king
  The happy message of our good success.   1630
Cu. I will, my lord, and thank thee for thy grace.   [*Exit.*
Ahi. What if thy servant should go too, my lord?
Joab. What news hast thou to bring since he is gone?
Ahi. Yet do Ahimaas so much content,
  That he may run about so sweet a charge.
Joab. Run, if thou wilt; and peace be with thy steps.
           [*Exit Ahimaas.*
  Now follow, that you may salute the king
  With humble hearts and reconcilèd souls.
Ama. We follow, Joab, to our gracious king;
  And him our swords shall honour to our deaths.   1640
           [*Exeunt.*

Enter DAVID, BETHSABE, SALOMON, NATHAN, ADONIA, CHILEAB,
     with their train.

Beth. What means my lord, the lamp of Israel,
  From whose bright eyes all eyes receive their light,
  To dim the glory of his sweet aspéct,[1]
  And paint his countenance with his heart's distress?
  Why should his thoughts retain a sad conceit,
  When every pleasure kneels before his throne,
  And sues for sweet acceptance with his grace?
  Take but your lute, and make the mountains dance,
  Retrieve the sun's sphere, and restrain the clouds,
  Give ears to trees, make savage lions tame,   1650
  Impose still silence to the loudest winds,
  And fill the fairest day with foulest storms:
  Then why should passions of much meaner power
  Bear head against the heart of Israel?
Dav. Fair Bethsabe, thou mightst increase the strength
  Of these thy arguments, drawn from my skill,
  By urging thy sweet sight to my conceits,
  Whose virtue ever serv'd for sacred balm
  To cheer my pinings past all earthly joys:
  But, Bethsabe, the daughter of the Highest,   1660

     [1] The 4to " aspects."

> Whose beauty builds the towers of Israel,
> She that in chains of pearl and unicorn
> Leads at her train the ancient golden world,
> The world that Adam held in paradise,
> Whose breath refineth all infectious airs,
> And makes the meadows smile at her repair,—
> She, she, my dearest [1] Bethsabe,
> Fair Peace, the goddess of our graces here,
> Is fled the streets of fair Jerusalem,
> The fields of Israel, and the heart of David, 1670
> Leading my comforts in her golden chains,
> Link'd to the life and soul of Absalon.
>
> *Beth.* Then is the pleasure of my sovereign's heart
> So wrapt within the bosom of that son,
> That Salomon, whom Israel's God affects,
> And gave the name unto him for his love,
> Should be no salve to comfort David's soul?
>
> *Dav.* Salomon, my love, is David's lord; [2]
> Our God hath nam'd him lord of Israel:
> In him (for that, and since he is thy son,) 1680
> Must David needs be pleasèd at the heart;
> And he shall surely sit upon my throne.
> But Absalon, the beauty of my bones,
> Fair Absalon, the counterfeit [3] of love,
> Sweet Absalon, the image of content,
> Must claim a portion in his father's care,
> And be in life and death King David's son.
>
> *Nath.* Yet, as my lord hath said, let Salomon reign,
> Whom God in naming hath anointed king.
> Now is he apt to learn th' eternal laws, 1690
> Whose knowledge being rooted in his youth
> Will beautify his age with glorious fruits;
> While Absalon, incens'd with graceless pride,
> Usurps and stains the kingdom with his sin:
> Let Salomon be made thy staff of age,
> Fair Israel's rest, and honour of thy race.
>
> *Dav.* Tell me, my Salomon, wilt thou embrace
> Thy father's precepts gravèd in thy heart,
> And satisfy my zeal to thy renown
> With practice of such sacred principles 1700

---

[1] Qy. "*She, she,* alas, *my dearest*," etc.?
[2] Corrupted.
[3] *i.e.*, portrait.

        As shall concern the state of Israel?
Sal. My royal father, if the heavenly zeal,
    Which for my welfare feeds upon your soul,
    Were not sustain'd with virtue of mine own;
    If the sweet accents of your cheerful voice
    Should not each hour [1] beat upon mine ears
    As sweetly as the breath of heaven to him
    That gaspeth scorchèd with the summer's sun;
    I should be guilty of unpardon'd sin,
    Fearing the plague of heaven and shame of earth: 1710
    But since I vow myself to learn the skill
    And holy secrets of his mighty hand
    Whose cunning tunes the music of my soul,
    It would content me, father, first to learn
    How the Eternal fram'd the firmament;
    Which bodies lend [2] their influence by fire,
    And which are fill'd with hoary winter's ice;
    What sign is rainy, and what star is fair;
    Why by the rules of true proportion
    The year is still divided into months,   1720
    The months to days, the days to certain hours;
    What fruitful race shall fill the future world;
    Or for what time shall this round building stand;
    What magistrates, what kings shall keep in awe
    Men's minds with bridles of th' eternal law.
Dav. Wade not too far, my boy, in waves so [3] deep:
    The feeble eyes of our aspiring thoughts
    Behold things present, and record things past;
    But things to come exceed our human reach,
    And are not painted yet in angels' eyes: 1730
    For those, submit thy sense, and say—" Thou power,
    That now art framing of the future world,
    Know'st all to come, not by the course of heaven,
    By frail conjectures of inferior signs,
    By monstrous floods, by flights and flocks of birds,
    By bowels of a sacrificèd beast,
    Or by the figures of some hidden art;
    But by a true and natural presage,
    Laying the ground and perfect architect [4]

---

[1] A dissyllable here. (The 4to " hower.")
[2] The 4to " lead."   [3] The 4to " too."
[4] Qy. " archetype "? unless Peele uses the former word in the sense of the latter.

>   Of all our actions now before thine eyes, 1740
>   From Adam to the end of Adam's seed:
>   O heaven, protect my weakness with thy strength!
>   So look on me that I may view thy face,
>   And see these secrets written in thy brows.
>   O sun, come dart thy rays upon my moon!
>   That now mine eyes, eclipsèd to the earth,
>   May brightly be refin'd and shine to heaven;
>   Transform me from this flesh, that I may live,
>   Before my death, regenerate with thee.
>   O thou great God, ravish my earthly sprite! 1750
>   That for the time a more than human skill
>   May feed the organons of all my sense;
>   That, when I think, thy thoughts may be my guide,
>   And, when I speak, I may be made by choice
>   The perfect echo of thy heavenly voice."
>   Thus say, my son, and thou shalt learn them all.
> *Sal.* A secret fury ravisheth my soul,
>   Lifting my mind above her human bounds;
>   And, as the eagle, rousèd from her stand
>   With violent hunger, towering in the air, 1760
>   Seizeth her feather'd prey, and thinks to feed,
>   But seeing then a cloud beneath her feet,
>   Lets fall the fowl, and is emboldenèd
>   With eyes intentive to bedare [1] the sun,
>   And styeth [2] close unto his stately sphere;
>   So Salomon, mounted on the burning wings
>   Of zeal divine, lets fall his mortal food,
>   And cheers his senses with celestial air,
>   Treads in the golden starry labyrinth,
>   And holds his eyes fix'd on Jehovah's brows. 1770
>   Good father, teach me further what to do.
> *Nath.* See, David, how his haughty spirit mounts,
>   Even now of height to wield a diadem:
>   Then make him promise that he may succeed,
>   And rest old Israel's bones from broils of war.
> *Dav.* Nathan, thou prophet, sprung from Jesse's root,
>   I promise thee and lovely Bethsabe,
>   My Salomon shall govern after me.
> *Beth.* He that hath touch'd thee with this righteous thought
>   Preserve the harbour of thy thoughts in peace! 1780

[1] *i.e.*, defy.   [2] *i.e.*, soareth, ascendeth.

Enter Messenger.

Mess. My lord, thy servants of the watch have seen
    One running hitherward from forth the wars.
Dav. If he be come alone, he bringeth news.
Mess. Another hath thy servant seen, my lord,
    Whose running much resembles Sadoc's son.
Dav. He is a good man, and good tidings brings.

Enter AHIMAAS.

Ahi. Peace and content be with my lord the king,
    Whom Israel's God hath bless'd with victory.
Dav. Tell me, Ahimaas, lives my Absalon?
Ahi. I saw a troop of soldiers gatherèd,   1790
    But know not what the tumult might import.
Dav. Stand by, until some other may inform
    The heart of David with a happy truth.

Enter CUSAY.

Cu. Happiness and honour live with David's soul,
    Whom God hath bless'd with conquest of his foes.
Dav. But, Cusay, lives the young man Absalon?
Cu. The stubborn enemies to David's peace,
    And all that cast their darts against his crown,
    Fare ever like the young man Absalon!
    For as he rid the woods of Ephraim,   1800
    Which fought for thee as much as all thy men,
    His hair was tangled in a shady oak;
    And hanging there, by Joab and his men
    Sustain'd the stroke of well deservèd death.
Dav. Hath Absalon sustain'd the stroke of death?
    Die, David, for the death of Absalon,
    And make these cursèd news the bloody darts
    That through his bowels rip thy wretched breast.
    Hence, David, walk the solitary woods,
    And in some cedar's shade the thunder slew,   1810
    And fire from heaven hath made his branches black,
    Sit mourning the decease of Absalon:
    Against the body of that blasted plant
    In thousand shivers break thy ivory lute,

Hanging thy stringless harp upon his boughs;
And through the hollow sapless sounding trunk
Bellow the torments that perplex thy soul.
There let the winds sit sighing till they burst;
Let tempest, muffled with a cloud of pitch,
Threaten the forests with her hellish face, 1820
And, mounted fiercely on her iron wings,
Rend up the wretched engine by the roots
That held my dearest Absalon to death.
Then let them toss my broken lute to heaven,
Even to his hands that beats me with the strings,
To show how sadly his poor shepherd sings.
            [*Goes to his pavilion and sits close a while.*
Beth. Die, Bethsabe, to see thy David mourn,
  To hear his tunes of anguish and of hell.
  O, help, my David, help thy Bethsabe,
  Whose heart is piercèd with thy breathy swords,[1] 1830
  And bursts with burden of ten thousand griefs!
                                        [*Lies down.*
  Now sit thy sorrows sucking of my blood:
  O, that it might be poison to their powers,
  And that their lips might draw my bosom dry,
  So David's love might ease him, though she die!
Nath. These violent passions come not from above;
  David and Bethsabe offend the Highest,
  To mourn in this immeasurable sort.
Dav. [*looking forth.*] O Absalon, Absalon! O my son, my son!
  Would God that I had died for Absalon! 1840
  But he is dead; ah, dead! Absalon is dead:
  And David lives to die for Absalon. [*Sits close again.*

Enter JOAB, ABISAI, ITHAY, *and their train.*

Joab. Why lies the queen so prostrate on the ground?
  Why is this company so tragic-hu'd?
  Why is the king now absent from his men,

---

[1] " We suggest whether it should not be ' breathed words;' but if the text is suffered to remain, we can only say, that ' thy breathy swords,' for ' the swords of thy breath,' is more barbaric than anything which we have met with in Peele." *Rev. J. Mitford—Gent. Mag.* for Feb., 1833, p. 103. " Barbaric " as the expression may be, I nevertheless believe that it is the genuine reading.

And marcheth not in triumph through the gates?
[*Unfolds the pavilion.*
David, awake; if sleep have shut thine eyes,
Sleep of affection, that thou canst not see
The honour offer'd to the victor's head:
Joab brings conquest piercèd on his spear, 1850
And joy from all the tribes of Israel.
Dav. Thou man of blood, thou sepulchre of death,
Whose marble breast intombs [1] my bowels quick,
Did I not charge thee, nay, entreat thy hand,
Even for my sake, to spare my Absalon?
And hast thou now, in spite of David's health,
And scorn to do my heart some happiness,
Given him the sword and spilt his purple soul?
Joab. What, irks it David, that he victor breathes,
That Juda and the fields of Israel 1860
Should cleanse their faces from their children's blood?
What, art thou weary of thy royal rule?
Is Israel's throne a serpent in thine eyes,
And he that set thee there so far from thanks,
That thou must curse his servant for his sake?
Hast thou not said that, as the morning light,
The cloudless morning, so should be thine house,
And not as flowers by the brightest rain
Which grow up quickly and as quickly fade?
Hast thou not said, the wicked are as thorns, 1870
That cannot be preservèd [2] with the hand,
And that the man shall touch them must be arm'd
With coats of iron and garments made of steel,
Or with the shaft of a defencèd spear?

---

[1] The 4to "intombe."

[2] *Qy.* "repressèd"?—The passage of Scripture to which our author here alludes is as follows:

"And he shall be as the light of the morning, when the sun riseth, even a morning without clouds; as the tender grass springing out of the earth by clear shining after rain.

"Although my house be not so with God; yet he hath made with me an everlasting covenant, ordered in all things and sure: for this is all my salvation, and all my desire, although he make it not to grow.

"But the sons of Belial shall be all of them as thorns thrust away, because they cannot be taken with hands [The Vulgate "*quæ non tolluntur manibus*"]:

"But the man that shall touch them must be fenced with iron and the staff of a spear," etc.—*Sec. Samuel,* xxiii. 4, sqq.

David and Bethsabe

And art thou angry he is now cut off
That led the guiltless swarming to their deaths,
And was more wicked than an host of men?
Advance thee from thy melancholy den,
And deck thy body with thy blissful robes,
Or, by the Lord that sways the heaven I swear, 1880
I'll lead thine armies to another king
Shall cheer them for their princely chivalry,
And not sit daunted, frowning in the dark,
When his fair looks, with oil and wine refresh'd,
Should dart into their bosoms gladsome beams,
And fill their stomachs with triumphant feasts;
That when elsewhere stern war shall sound his trump,
And call another battle to the field,
Fame still may bring thy valiant soldiers home,
And for their service happily confess 1890
She wanted worthy trumps to sound their prowess:
Take thou this course and live; refuse and die.
Abis. Come, brother, let him sit there till he sink;
Some other shall advance the name of Joab.
    [*Offers to go out with Joab.*
Beth. [*rising.*] O, stay, my lords, stay! David mourns no more,
But riseth to give honour to your acts.
Dav. [*rising, and coming from his pavilion.*] Then happy art thou,
    David's fairest son,
That, freèd from the yoke of earthly toils,
And séquester'd from sense of human sins,
Thy soul shall joy[1] the sacred cabinet 1900
Of those divine ideas that present
Thy changèd spirit with a heaven of bliss.
Then thou art gone; ah, thou art gone, my son!
To heaven, I hope, my Absalon is gone:
Thy soul there plac'd in honour of the saints,
Or angels clad with immortality,
Shall reap a sevenfold grace for all thy griefs;
Thy eyes, now no more eyes but shining stars,
Shall deck the flaming heavens with novel lamps;
There shalt thou taste the drink of seraphins, 1910
And cheer thy feelings with archangels' food;
Thy day of rest, thy holy sabbath-day,
Shall be eternal; and, the curtain drawn,

[1] *i.e.*, enjoy.

  Thou shalt behold thy sovereign face to face,
  With wonder, knit in triple unity,
  Unity infinite and innumerable.——
  Courage, brave captains! Joab's tale hath stirr'd,
  And made the suit of Israel preferr'd.
Joab. Bravely resolv'd, and spoken like a king:
  Now may old Israel and his daughters sing.   1920
           [*Exeunt omnes.*

THE SPANISH TRAGEDY

DRAMATIS PERSONÆ

Ghost of Andrea, a Spanish nobleman, } *Chorus.*
Revenge.

KING OF SPAIN.
CYPRIAN DUKE OF CASTILE, *his brother.*
LORENZO, *the Duke's son.*
BELLIMPERIA, *Lorenzo's sister.*

VICEROY OF PORTUGAL.
BALTHAZAR, *his son.*
DON PEDRO, *the Viceroy's brother.*

HIERONIMO, *Marshal of Spain.*
ISABELLA, *his wife.*
HORATIO, *their son.*

Spanish General.
Deputy.
DON BAZULTO, *an old man.*
Three Citizens.

Portuguese Ambassador.

ALEXANDRO, } *Portuguese Noblemen.*
VILLUPPO,
Two Portuguese.

PEDRINGANO, *Bellimperia's servant.*
CHRISTOPHIL, *Bellimperia's custodian.*
Lorenzo's Page.
SERBERINE, *Balthazar's servant.*
Isabella's Maid.
Messenger.
Hangman.
Three Kings and three Knights in the first Dumb-show.
Hymen and two torch-bearers in the second.

BAZARDO, *a Painter.*
PEDRO and JAQUES, *Hieronimo's servants.*

Army. Banquet. Royal suites. Noblemen. Halberdiers. Officers. Three Watchmen. Trumpets. Servants, etc.

THE SPANISH TRAGEDY

ACT I

SCENE I.—*Induction.*

Enter the Ghost of Andrea, *and with him* Revenge.

Ghost. When this eternal substance of my soul
    Did live imprison'd in my wanton flesh,
    Each in their function serving other's need,
    I was a courtier in the Spanish court:
    My name was Don Andrea; my descent,
    Though not ignoble, yet inferior far
    To gracious fortunes of my tender youth.
    For there in prime and pride of all my years,
    By duteous service and deserving love,
    In secret I possess'd a worthy dame,   10
    Which hight sweet Bellimperia by name.
    But, in the harvest of my summer joys,
    Death's winter nipp'd the blossoms of my bliss,
    Forcing divorce betwixt my love and me.
    For in the late conflict with Portingal
    My valour drew me into danger's mouth,
    Till life to death made passage through my wounds.
    When I was slain, my soul descended straight
    To pass the flowing stream of Acheron;
    But churlish Charon, only boatman there,   20
    Said that, my rites of burial not perform'd,
    I might not sit amongst his passengers.
    Ere Sol had slept three nights in Thetis' lap,
    And slak'd his smoking chariot in her flood,
    By Don Horatio, our knight marshal's son,
    My funerals and obsequies were done.
    Then was the ferryman of hell content
    To pass me over to the slimy strand,
    That leads to fell Avernus' ugly waves.

There, pleasing Cerberus with honey'd speech,   30
I pass'd the perils of the foremost porch.
Not far from hence, amidst ten thousand souls,
Sat Minos, Aeacus, and Rhadamanth;
To whom no sooner 'gan I make approach,
To crave a passport for my wand'ring ghost,
But Minos, in graven leaves of lottery,
Drew forth the manner of my life and death.
" This knight," quoth he, " both liv'd and died in love;
And for his love tried fortune of the wars;
And by war's fortune lost both love and life."   40
" Why then," said Aeacus, " convey him hence,
To walk with lovers in our fields of love,
And spend the course of everlasting time
Under green myrtle-trees and cypress shades."
" No, no," said Rhadamanth, " it were not well,
With loving souls to place a martialist:
He died in war, and must to martial fields,
Where wounded Hector lives in lasting pain,
And Achilles' Myrmidons do scour the plain."
Then Minos, mildest censor of the three,   50
Made this device to end the difference·
" Send him," quoth he, " to our infernal king,
To doom him as best seems his majesty."
To this effect my passport straight was drawn.
In keeping on my way to Pluto's court,
Through dreadful shades of ever-glooming night,
I saw more sights than thousand tongues can tell,
Or pens can write, or mortal hearts can think.
Three ways there were: that on the right-hand side
Was ready way unto the 'foresaid fields,   60
Where lovers live and bloody martialists;
But either sort contain'd within his bounds.
The left-hand path, declining fearfully,
Was ready downfall to the deepest hell,
Where bloody Furies shake their whips of steel,
And poor Ixion turns an endless wheel;
Where usurers are chok'd with melting gold,
And wantons are embrac'd with ugly snakes,
And murd'rers groan with never-killing wounds,
And perjur'd wights scalded in boiling lead,   70
And all foul sins with torments overwhelm'd.

       'Twixt these two ways I trod the middle path,
       Which brought me to the fair Elysian green,
       In midst whereof there stands a stately tower,
       The walls of brass, the gates of adamant:
       Here finding Pluto with his Proserpine,
       I show'd my passport, humbled on my knee;
       Whereat fair Proserpine began to smile,
       And begg'd that only she might give my doom:
       Pluto was pleas'd, and seal'd it with a kiss.   80
       Forthwith, Revenge, she rounded thee in th' ear,
       And bad thee lead me through the gates of horn,
       Where dreams have passage in the silent night.
       No sooner had she spoke, but we were here—
       I wot not how—in twinkling of an eye.
Revenge. Then know, Andrea, that thou art arriv'd
       Where thou shalt see the author of thy death,
       Don Balthazar, the prince of Portingal,
       Depriv'd of life by Bellimperia.
       Here sit we down to see the mystery,   90
       And serve for Chorus in this tragedy.

SCENE II.—*The Court of Spain.*

Enter SPANISH KING, General, CASTILE, *and* HIERONIMO.

King. Now say, lord General, how fares our camp?
Gen. All well, my sovereign liege, except some few
    That are deceas'd by fortune of the war.
King. But what portends thy cheerful countenance,
    And posting to our presence thus in haste?
    Speak, man, hath fortune given us victory?
Gen. Victory, my liege, and that with little loss.
King. Our Portingals will pay us tribute then?
Gen. Tribute and wonted homage therewithal.   100
King. Then bless'd be heaven and guider of the heavens,
    From whose fair influence such justice flows.
Cast. *O multum dilecte Deo, tibi militat aether,*
    Et conjuratae curvato poplite gentes
    Succumbunt; recti soror est victoria juris.
King. Thanks to my loving brother of Castile.
    But, General, unfold in brief discourse

Your form of battle and your war's success,
That, adding all the pleasure of thy news
Unto the height of former happiness, 110
With deeper wage and greater dignity
We may reward thy blissful chivalry.
Gen. Where Spain and Portugal do jointly knit
Their frontiers, leaning on each other's bound,
There met our armies in their proud array:
Both furnish'd well, both full of hope and fear,
Both menacing alike with daring shows,
Both vaunting sundry colours of device,
Both cheerly sounding trumpets, drums, and fifes,
Both raising dreadful clamours to the sky, 120
That valleys, hills, and rivers made rebound,
And heav'n itself was frighted with the sound.
Our battles both were pitch'd in squadron form,
Each corner strongly fenc'd with wings of shot;
But ere we join'd and came to push of pike,
I brought a squadron of our readiest shot
From out our rearward, to begin the fight:
They brought another wing t' encounter us.
Meanwhile, our ordnance play'd on either side,
And captains strove to have their valours tried. 130
Don Pedro, their chief horsemen's colonel,
Did with his cornet bravely make attempt
To break the order of our battle ranks:
But Don Rogero, worthy man of war,
March'd forth against him with our musketeers,
And stopp'd the malice of his fell approach.
While they maintain hot skirmish to and fro,
Both battles join, and fall to handy-blows,
Their violent shot resembling th' ocean's rage,
When, roaring loud, and with a swelling tide, 140
It beats upon the rampiers of huge rocks,
And gapes to swallow neighbour-bounding lands.
Now while Bellona rageth here and there,
Thick storms of bullets ran like winter's hail,
And shiver'd lances dark the troubled air,
    Pede pes et cuspide cuspis;
Arma sonant armis, vir petiturque viro.
On every side drop captains to the ground,
And soldiers, some ill-maim'd, some slain outright:

    Here falls a body sunder'd from his head, 150
    There legs and arms lie bleeding on the grass,
    Mingled with weapons and unbowell'd steeds,
    That scatt'ring overspread the purple plain.
    In all this turmoil, three long hours and more,
    The victory to neither part inclin'd;
    Till Don Andrea, with his brave lanciers,
    In their main battle made so great a breach,
    That, half dismay'd, the multitude retir'd:
    But Balthazar, the Portingals' young prince,
    Brought rescue, and encourag'd them to stay. 160
    Here-hence the fight was eagerly renew'd,
    And in that conflict was Andrea slain:
    Brave man at arms, but weak to Balthazar.
    Yet while the prince, insulting over him,
    Breath'd out proud vaunts, sounding to our reproach,
    Friendship and hardy valour, join'd in one,
    Prick'd forth Horatio, our knight marshal's son,
    To challenge forth that prince in single fight.
    Not long between these twain the fight endur'd,
    But straight the prince was beaten from his horse, 170
    And forc'd to yield him prisoner to his foe.
    When he was taken, all the rest they fled,
    And our carbines pursu'd them to the death,
    Till, Phœbus waving to the western deep,
    Our trumpeters were charg'd to sound retreat.
King. Thanks, good lord General, for these good news;
    And for some argument of more to come,
    Take this and wear it for thy sovereign's sake.
                                      [Gives him his chain.
    But tell me now, hast thou confirm'd a peace?
Gen. No peace, my liege, but peace conditional, 180
    That if with homage tribute be well paid,
    The fury of your forces will be stay'd:
    And to this peace their viceroy hath subscrib'd,
                                  [Gives the King a paper.
    And made a solemn vow that, during life,
    His tribute shall be truly paid to Spain.
King. These words, these deeds, become thy person well.
    But now, knight marshal, frolic with thy king,
    For 'tis thy son that wins this battle's prize.
Hier. Long may he live to serve my sovereign liege,

  And soon decay, unless he serve my liege.   190
King. Nor thou, nor he, shall die without reward.
           [A tucket afar off.
  What means the warning of this trumpet's sound?
Gen. This tells me that your grace's men of war,
  Such as war's fortune hath reserv'd from death,
  Come marching on towards your royal seat,
  To show themselves before your majesty:
  For so I gave in charge at my depart.
  Whereby by demonstration shall appear,
  That all, except three hundred or few more,
  Are safe return'd, and by their foes enrich'd.   200

The Army enters; BALTHAZAR, *between* LORENZO *and* HORATIO,
captive.

King. A gladsome sight! I long to see them here.
         [They enter and pass by
  Was that the warlike prince of Portingal,
  That by our nephew was in triumph led?
Gen. It was, my liege, the prince of Portingal.
King. But what was he that on the other side
  Held him by th' arm, as partner of the prize?
Hier. That was my son, my gracious sovereign;
  Of whom though from his tender infancy
  My loving thoughts did never hope but well,
  He never pleas'd his father's eyes till now,   210
  Nor fill'd my heart with over-cloying joys.
King. Go, let them march once more about these walls,
  That, staying them, we may confer and talk
  With our brave prisoner and his double guard.
  Hieronimo, it greatly pleaseth us
  That in our victory thou have a share,
  By virtue of thy worthy son's exploit.   *[Enter again.*
  Bring hither the young prince of Portingal:
  The rest march on; but, ere they be dismiss'd,
  We will bestow on every soldier   220
  Two ducats and on every leader ten,
  That they may know our largess welcomes them.
     [Exeunt all but Balthazar, Lorenzo, and Horatio
  Welcome, Don Balthazar! welcome, nephew!
  And thou, Horatio, thou art welcome too.

> Young prince, although thy father's hard misdeeds,
> In keeping back the tribute that he owes,
> Deserve but evil measure at our hands,
> Yet shalt thou know that Spain is honourable.

Bal. The trespass that my father made in peace
   Is now controll'd by fortune of the wars; 230
   And cards once dealt, it boots not ask why so.
   His men are slain, a weak'ning to his realm;
   His colours seiz'd, a blot unto his name;
   His son distress'd, a cor'sive to his heart:
   These punishments may clear his late offence.

King. Ay, Balthazar, if he observe this truce,
   Our peace will grow the stronger for these wars.
   Meanwhile live thou, though not in liberty,
   Yet free from bearing any servile yoke;
   For in our hearing thy deserts were great, 240
   And in our sight thyself art gracious.

Bal. And I shall study to deserve this grace.

King. But tell me—for their holding makes me doubt—
   To which of these twain art thou prisoner?

Lor. To me, my liege.

Hor.   To me, my sovereign.

Lor. This hand first took his courser by the reins.

Hor. But first my lance did put him from his horse.

Lor. I seiz'd his weapon, and enjoy'd it first.

Hor. But first I forc'd him lay his weapons down.

King. Let go his arm, upon our privilege. 250
   [*They let him go.*
   Say, worthy prince, to whether did'st thou yield?

Bal. To him in courtesy, to this perforce:
   He spake me fair, this other gave me strokes;
   He promis'd life, this other threaten'd death;
   He won my love, this other conquer'd me,
   And, truth to say, I yield myself to both.

Hier. But that I know your grace for just and wise,
   And might seem partial in this difference,
   Enforc'd by nature and by law of arms
   My tongue should plead for young Horatio's right: 260
   He hunted well that was a lion's death,
   Not he that in a garment wore his skin;
   So hares may pull dead lions by the beard.

King. Content thee, marshal, thou shalt have no wrong;

And, for thy sake, thy son shall want no right.
Will both abide the censure of my doom?
Lor. I crave no better than your grace awards.
Hor. Nor I, although I sit beside my right.
King. Then, by my judgment, thus your strife shall end:
    You both deserve, and both shall have reward.   270
    Nephew, thou took'st his weapon and his horse:
    His weapons and his horse are thy reward.
    Horatio, thou did'st force him first to yield:
    His ransom therefore is thy valour's fee;
    Appoint the sum, as you shall both agree.
    But, nephew, thou shalt have the prince in guard,
    For thine estate best fitteth such a guest:
    Horatio's house were small for all his train.
    Yet, in regard thy substance passeth his,
    And that just guerdon may befall desert,   280
    To him we yield the armour of the prince.
    How likes Don Balthazar of this device?
Bal. Right well, my liege, if this proviso were,
    That Don Horatio bear us company,
    Whom I admire and love for chivalry.
King. Horatio, leave him not that loves thee so.—
    Now let us hence to see our soldiers paid,
    And feast our prisoner as our friendly guest.   [*Exeunt.*

SCENE III.—*The Court of Portugal.*

Enter VICEROY, ALEXANDRO, VILLUPPO.

Vic. Is our ambassador despatch'd for Spain?
Alex. Two days, my liege, are past since his depart.   290
Vic. And tribute-payment gone along with him?
Alex. Ay, my good lord.
Vic. Then rest we here awhile in our unrest,
    And feed our sorrows with some inward sighs;
    For deepest cares break never into tears.
    But wherefore sit I in a regal throne?
    This better fits a wretch's endless moan.
                          [*Falls to the ground.*
    Yet this is higher than my fortunes reach,
    And therefore better than my state deserves.

Ay, ay, this earth, image of melancholy,
Seeks him whom fates adjudge to misery.
Here let me lie; now am I at the lowest.
    Qui jacet in terra, non habet unde cadat.
    In me consumpsit vires fortuna nocendo:
    Nil superest ut jam possit obesse magis.
Yes, Fortune may bereave me of my crown:
Here, take it now;—let Fortune do her worst,
She will not rob me of this sable weed:
O no, she envies none but pleasant things.
Such is the folly of despiteful chance!
Fortune is blind, and sees not my deserts;
So is she deaf, and hears not my laments;
And could she hear, yet is she wilful-mad,
And therefore will not pity my distress.
Suppose that she could pity me, what then?
What help can be expected at her hands
Whose foot is standing on a rolling stone,
And mind more mutable than fickle winds?
Why wail I then, where's hope of no redress?
O yes, complaining makes my grief seem less.
My late ambition hath distain'd my faith;
My breach of faith occasion'd bloody wars;
Those bloody wars have spent my treasure;
And with my treasure my people's blood;
And with their blood, my joy and best belov'd,
My best belov'd, my sweet and only son.
O, wherefore went I not to war myself?
The cause was mine; I might have died for both:
My years were mellow, his but young and green;
My death were natural, but his was forc'd.

Alex. No doubt, my liege, but still the prince survives.
Vic. Survives! ay, where?
Alex. In Spain—a prisoner by mischance of war.
Vic. Then they have slain him for his father's fault.
Alex. That were a breach to common law of arms.
Vic. They reck no laws that meditate revenge.
Alex. His ransom's worth will stay from foul revenge.
Vic. No; if he liv'd, the news would soon be here.
Alex. Nay, evil news fly faster still than good.
Vic. Tell me no more of news; for he is dead.
Vil. My sovereign, pardon the author of ill news,

  And I'll bewray the fortune of thy son.
Vic. Speak on, I'll guerdon thee, whate'er it be:
  Mine ear is ready to receive ill news;
  My heart grown hard 'gainst mischief's battery.
  Stand up, I say, and tell thy tale at large.
Vil. Then hear that truth which these mine eyes have seen:
  When both the armies were in battle join'd,
  Don Balthazar, amidst the thickest troops,
  To win renown did wondrous feats of arms: 350
  Amongst the rest I saw him, hand to hand,
  In single fight with their lord-general;
  Till Alexandro, that here counterfeits,
  Under the colour of a duteous friend
  Discharg'd his pistol at the prince's back,
  As though he would have slain their general:
  But therewithal Don Balthazar fell down;
  And when he fell, then we began to fly:
  But, had he liv'd, the day had sure been ours.
Alex. O wicked forgery! O trait'rous miscreant!   360
Vic. Hold thou thy peace! But now, Villuppo, say,
  Where then became the carcase of my son?
Vil. I saw them drag it to the Spanish tents.
Vic. Ay, ay, my nightly dreams have told me this.—
  Thou false, unkind, unthankful, trait'rous beast,
  Wherein had Balthazar offended thee
  That thou shouldst thus betray him to our foes?
  Was't Spanish gold that bleared so thine eyes
  That thou couldst see no part of our deserts?
  Perchance, because thou art Terceira's lord,   370
  Thou hadst some hope to wear this diadem,
  If first my son and then myself were slain;
  But thy ambitious thought shall break thy neck.
  Ay, this was it that made thee spill his blood:
     [*Takes the crown and puts it on again.*
  But I'll now wear it till thy blood be spilt.
Alex. Vouchsafe, dread sovereign, to hear me speak.
Vic. Away with him; his sight is second hell.
  Keep him till we determine of his death:
  If Balthazar be dead, he shall not live.
  Villuppo, follow us for thy reward.   [*Exit Viceroy.*
Vil. Thus have I with an envious, forged tale   381
  Deceiv'd the king, betray'd mine enemy,
  And hope for guerdon of my villany.   [*Exit.*

SCENE IV

Enter HORATIO *and* BELLIMPERIA.

Bel. Signior Horatio, this is the place and hour,
    Wherein I must entreat thee to relate
    The circumstance of Don Andrea's death,
    Who, living, was my garland's sweetest flower,
    And in his death hath buried my delights.
Hor. For love of him and service to yourself,
    I nill refuse this heavy doleful charge;   390
    Yet tears and sighs, I fear, will hinder me.
    When both our armies were enjoin'd in fight,
    Your worthy chevalier amidst the thickest,
    For glorious cause still aiming at the fairest,
    Was at the last by young Don Balthazar
    Encounter'd hand to hand: their fight was long,
    Their hearts were great, their clamours menacing,
    Their strength alike, their strokes both dangerous.
    But wrathful Nemesis, that wicked power,
    Envying at Andrea's praise and worth,   400
    Cut short his life, to end his praise and worth.
    She, she herself, disguis'd in armour's mask—
    As Pallas was before proud Pergamus—
    Brought in a fresh supply of halberdiers,
    Which paunch'd his horse, and ding'd him to the ground.
    Then young Don Balthazar with ruthless rage,
    Taking advantage of his foe's distress,
    Did finish what his halberdiers begun,
    And left not, till Andrea's life was done.
    Then, though too late, incens'd with just remorse,   410
    I with my band set forth against the prince,
    And brought him prisoner from his halberdiers.
Bel. Would thou hadst slain him that so slew my love!
    But then was Don Andrea's carcase lost?
Hor. No, that was it for which I chiefly strove,
    Nor stepp'd I back till I recover'd him:
    I took him up, and wound him in mine arms;
    And wielding him unto my private tent,
    There laid him down, and dew'd him with my tears,

       And sigh'd and sorrow'd as became a friend.   420
       But neither friendly sorrow, sighs, nor tears
       Could win pale Death from his usurpèd right.
       Yet this I did, and less I could not do:
       I saw him honour'd with due funeral.
       This scarf I pluck'd from off his lifeless arm,
       And wear it in remembrance of my friend.
Bel. I know the scarf: would he had kept it still;
       For had he liv'd, he would have kept it still,
       And worn it for his Bellimperia's sake:
       For 'twas my favour at his last depart.   430
       But now wear thou it both for him and me;
       For after him thou hast deserv'd it best.
       But for thy kindness in his life and death,
       Be sure, while Bellimperia's life endures,
       She will be Don Horatio's thankful friend.
Hor. And, madam, Don Horatio will not slack
       Humbly to serve fair Bellimperia.
       But now, if your good liking stand thereto,
       I'll crave your pardon to go seek the prince;
       For so the duke, your father, gave me charge.   440
Bel. Ay, go, Horatio, leave me here alone;
       For solitude best fits my cheerless mood.   [*Exit Hor.*
       Yet what avails to wail Andrea's death,
       From whence Horatio proves my second love?
       Had he not lov'd Andrea as he did,
       He could not sit in Bellimperia's thoughts.
       But how can love find harbour in my breast,
       Till I revenge the death of my belov'd?
       Yes, second love shall further my revenge!
       I'll love Horatio, my Andrea's friend,   450
       The more to spite the prince that wrought his end,
       And where Don Balthazar, that slew my love,
       Himself now pleads for favour at my hands,
       He shall, in rigour of my just disdain,
       Reap long repentance for his murd'rous deed.
       For what was 't else but murd'rous cowardice,
       So many to oppress one valiant knight,
       Without respect of honour in the fight?
       And here he comes that murder'd my delight.

Enter LORENZO *and* BALTHAZAR.

Lor. Sister, what means this melancholy walk? 460
Bel. That for a while I wish no company.
Lor. But here the prince is come to visit you.
Bel. That argues that he lives in liberty.
Bal. No, madam, but in pleasing servitude.
Bel. Your prison then, belike, is your conceit.
Bal. Ay, by conceit my freedom is enthrall'd.
Bel. Then with conceit enlarge yourself again.
Bal. What, if conceit have laid my heart to gage?
Bel. Pay that you borrow'd, and recover it.
Bal. I die, if it return from whence it lies. 470
Bel. A heartless man, and live? A miracle!
Bal. Ay, lady, love can work such miracles.
Lor. Tush, tush, my lord! let go these ambages,
And in plain terms acquaint her with your love.
Bel. What boots complaint, when there's no remedy?
Bal. Yes, to your gracious self must I complain,
In whose fair answer lies my remedy;
On whose perfection all my thoughts attend;
On whose aspect mine eyes find beauty's bower;
In whose translucent breast my heart is lodg'd. 480
Bel. Alas, my lord, these are but words of course,
And but device to drive me from this place.
      [*She, in going in, lets fall her glove, which
           Horatio, coming out, takes up.*

Hor. Madam, your glove.
Bel. Thanks, good Horatio; take it for thy pains.
Bal. Signior Horatio stoop'd in happy time!
Hor. I reap'd more grace than I deserv'd or hop'd.
Lor. My lord, be not dismay'd for what is past:
You know that women oft are humorous;
These clouds will overblow with little wind:
Let me alone, I'll scatter them myself. 490
Meanwhile, let us devise to spend the time
In some delightful sports and revelling.
Hor. The king, my lords, is coming hither straight,
To feast the Portingal ambassador;
Things were in readiness before I came.
Bal. Then here it fits us to attend the king,

> To welcome hither our ambassador,
> And learn my father and my country's health.

SCENE V

Enter the Banquet, Trumpets, the KING, *and Ambassador.*

King. See, lord Ambassador, how Spain entreats
    Their prisoner Balthazar, thy viceroy's son: 500
    We pleasure more in kindness than in wars.
Amb. Sad is our king, and Portingal laments,
    Supposing that Don Balthazar is slain.
Bal. So am I!—slain by beauty's tyranny.
    You see, my lord, how Balthazar is slain:
    I frolic with the Duke of Castile's son,
    Wrapp'd every hour in pleasures of the court,
    And grac'd with favours of his majesty.
King. Put off your greetings, till our feast be done;
    Now come and sit with us, and taste our cheer.   510
                                    [*Sit to the banquet.*
    Sit down, young prince, you are our second guest;
    Brother, sit down; and, nephew, take your place.
    Signior Horatio, wait thou upon our cup;
    For well thou hast deservèd to be honour'd.
    Now, lordings, fall to; Spain is Portugal,
    And Portugal is Spain: we both are friends;
    Tribute is paid, and we enjoy our right.
    But where is old Hieronimo, our marshal?
    He promis'd us, in honour of our guest,
    To grace our banquet with some pompous jest.   520

Enter HIERONIMO *with a drum, three knights, each his scutcheon; then he fetches three kings, they take their crowns and them captive.*

    Hieronimo, this masque contents mine eye,
    Although I sound not well the mystery.
Hier. The first arm'd knight, that hung his scutcheon up,
                        [*He takes the scutcheon and gives it to the King.*
    Was English Robert, Earl of Gloucester,
    Who, when King Stephen bore sway in Albion,

Arriv'd with five and twenty thousand men
In Portingal, and by success of war
Enforc'd the king, then but a Saracen,
To bear the yoke of the English monarchy.
King. My lord of Portingal, by this you see
That which may comfort both your king and you,
And make your late discomfort seem the less.
But say, Hieronimo, what was the next?
Hier. The second knight, that hung his scutcheon up,
[*He doth as he did before.*
Was Edmond, Earl of Kent in Albion,
When English Richard wore the diadem.
He came likewise, and razèd Lisbon walls,
And took the King of Portingal in fight;
For which and other such-like service done
He after was created Duke of York.
King. This is another special argument,
That Portingal may deign to bear our yoke,
When it by little England hath been yok'd.
But now, Hieronimo, what were the last?
Hier. The third and last, not least, in our account,
[*Doing as before.*
Was, as the rest, a valiant Englishman,
Brave John of Gaunt, the Duke of Lancaster,
As by his scutcheon plainly may appear.
He with a puissant army came to Spain,
And took our King of Castile prisoner.
Amb. This is an argument for our viceroy
That Spain may not insult for her success,
Since English warriors likewise conquer'd Spain,
And made them bow their knees to Albion.
King. Hieronimo, I drink to thee for this device,
Which hath pleas'd both the ambassador and me:
Pledge me, Hieronimo, if thou love thy king.
[*Takes the cup of Horatio.*
My lord, I fear we sit but over-long,
Unless our dainties were more delicate;
But welcome are you to the best we have.
Now let us in, that you may be despatch'd:
I think our council is already set. [*Exeunt omnes.*

SCENE VI

Ghost of Andrea, Revenge.

Andrea. Come we for this from depth of underground,
　　To see him feast that gave me my death's wound?
　　These pleasant sights are sorrow to my soul:
　　Nothing but league, and love, and banqueting?
Revenge. Be still, Andrea; ere we go from hence,
　　I'll turn their friendship into fell despite,
　　Their love to mortal hate, their day to night,
　　Their hope into despair, their peace to war,　　　　570
　　Their joys to pain, their bliss to misery.

ACT II

SCENE I

Enter LORENZO *and* BALTHAZAR.

Lor. My lord, though Bellimperia seem thus coy,
  Let reason hold you in your wonted joy:
  In time the savage bull sustains the yoke,
  In time all haggard hawks will stoop to lure,
  In time small wedges cleave the hardest oak,
  In time the flint is pierc'd with softest shower,
  And she in time will fall from her disdain,
  And rue the suff'rance of your friendly pain.
Bal. No, she is wilder, and more hard withal,
  Than beast, or bird, or tree, or stony wall. 10
  But wherefore blot I Bellimperia's name?
  It is my fault, not she, that merits blame.
  My feature is not to content her sight,
  My words are rude, and work her no delight.
  The lines I send her are but harsh and ill,
  Such as do drop from Pan and Marsyas' quill.
  My presents are not of sufficient cost,
  And being worthless, all my labour's lost.
  Yet might she love me for my valiancy:
  Ay, but that's slander'd by captivity. 20
  Yet might she love me to content her sire:
  Ay, but her reason masters his desire.
  Yet might she love me as her brother's friend:
  Ay, but her hopes aim at some other end.
  Yet might she love me to uprear her state:
  Ay, but perhaps she hopes some nobler mate.
  Yet might she love me as her beauty's thrall:
  Ay, but I fear she cannot love at all.
Lor. My lord, for my sake leave this ecstasy,
  And doubt not but we'll find some remedy. 30
  Some cause there is that lets you not be lov'd;
  First that must needs be known, and then remov'd.

      What, if my sister love some other knight?
Bal. My summer's day will turn to winter's night.
Lor. I have already found a stratagem,
      To sound the bottom of this doubtful theme.
      My lord, for once you shall be rul'd by me;
      Hinder me not, whate'er you hear or see.
      By force or fair means will I cast about
      To find the truth of all this question out.   40
      Ho, Pedringano!
Ped. Signior!
Lor. Vien qui presto.

Enter PEDRINGANO.

Ped. Hath your lordship any service to command me?
Lor. Ay, Pedringano, service of import;
      And—not to spend the time in trifling words—
      Thus stands the case: It is not long, thou know'st,
      Since I did shield thee from my father's wrath,
      For thy conveyance in Andrea's love,
      For which thou wert adjudg'd to punishment: 50
      I stood betwixt thee and thy punishment,
      And since, thou know'st how I have favour'd thee.
      Now to these favours will I add reward,
      Not with fair words, but store of golden coin,
      And lands and living join'd with dignities,
      If thou but satisfy my just demand:
      Tell truth, and have me for thy lasting friend.
Ped. Whate'er it be your lordship shall demand,
      My bounden duty bids me tell the truth,
      If case it lie in me to tell the truth.   60
Lor. Then, Pedringano, this is my demand:
      Whom loves my sister Bellimperia?
      For she reposeth all her trust in thee.
      Speak, man, and gain both friendship and reward:
      I mean, whom loves she in Andrea's place?
Ped. Alas, my lord, since Don Andrea's death
      I have no credit with her as before;
      And therefore know not, if she love or no.
Lor. Nay, if thou dally, then I am thy foe,   [*Draws his sword.*
      And fear shall force what friendship cannot win: 70
      Thy death shall bury what thy life conceals;

  Thou diest for more esteeming her than me.
Ped. O, stay, my lord.
Lor. Yet speak the truth, and I will guerdon thee,
  And shield thee from whatever can ensue,
  And will conceal whate'er proceeds from thee.
  But if thou dally once again, thou diest.
Ped. If madam Bellimperia be in love——
Lor. What, villain! ifs and ands?
Ped. O, stay, my lord, she loves Horatio.   80
          [*Balthazar starts back.*
Lor. What, Don Horatio, our knight marshal's son?
Ped. Even him, my lord.
Lor. Now say, but how know'st thou he is her love?
  And thou shalt find me kind and liberal:
  Stand up, I say, and fearless tell the truth.
Ped. She sent him letters, which myself perus'd,
  Full-fraught with lines and arguments of love,
  Preferring him before Prince Balthazar.
Lor. Swear on this cross that what thou say'st is true;
  And that thou wilt conceal what thou hast told.   90
Ped. I swear to both, by him that made us all.
Lor. In hope thine oath is true, here's thy reward:
  But if I prove thee perjur'd and unjust,
  This very sword, whereon thou took'st thine oath,
  Shall be the worker of thy tragedy.
Ped. What I have said is true, and shall—for me—
  Be still conceal'd from Bellimperia.
  Besides, your honour's liberality
  Deserves my duteous service, ev'n till death.
Lor. Let this be all that thou shalt do for me: 100
  Be watchful, when and where these lovers meet,
  And give me notice in some secret sort.
Ped. I will, my lord.
Lor. Then shalt thou find that I am liberal.
  Thou know'st that I can more advance thy state
  Than she; be therefore wise, and fail me not.
  Go and attend her, as thy custom is,
  Lest absence make her think thou dost amiss.
            [*Exit Pedringano.*
  Why so: *tam armis quam ingenio:*
  Where words prevail not, violence prevails;   110
  But gold doth more than either of them both.

How likes Prince Balthazar this stratagem?
Bal. Both well and ill; it makes me glad and sad:
Glad, that I know the hind'rer of my love;
Sad, that I fear she hates me whom I love.
Glad, that I know on whom to be reveng'd;
Sad, that she'll fly me, if I take revenge.
Yet must I take revenge, or die myself,
For love resisted grows impatient.
I think Horatio be my destin'd plague: 120
First, in his hand he brandishèd a sword,
And with that sword he fiercely wagèd war,
And in that war he gave me dang'rous wounds,
And by those wounds he forcèd me to yield,
And by my yielding I became his slave.
Now in his mouth he carries pleasing words,
Which pleasing words do harbour sweet conceits,
Which sweet conceits are lim'd with sly deceits,
Which sly deceits smooth Bellimperia's ears,
And through her ears dive down into her heart,   130
And in her heart set him, where I should stand.
Thus hath he ta'en my body by his force,
And now by sleight would captivate my soul:
But in his fall I'll tempt the destinies,
And either lose my life, or win my love.
Lor. Let's go, my lord; your staying stays revenge.
Do you but follow me, and gain your love:
Her favour must be won by his remove.   [*Exeunt.*

SCENE II

Enter HORATIO *and* BELLIMPERIA.

Hor. Now, madam, since by favour of your love
Our hidden smoke is turn'd to open flame,   140
And that with looks and words we feed our thought
(Two chief contents, where more cannot be had):
Thus, in the midst of love's fair blandishments,
Why show you sign of inward languishments?
[*Pedringano showeth all to the Prince and
Lorenzo, placing them in secret.*
Bel. My heart, sweet friend, is like a ship at sea:

She wisheth port, where, riding all at ease,
She may repair what stormy times have worn.
And leaning on the shore, may sing with joy,
That pleasure follows pain, and bliss annoy.
Possession of thy love is th' only port, 150
Wherein my heart, with fears and hopes long toss'd,
Each hour doth wish and long to make resort,
There to repair the joys that it hath lost,
And, sitting safe, to sing in Cupid's quire
That sweetest bliss is crown of love's desire.

[*Balthazar and Lorenzo above.*

Bal. O sleep, mine eyes, see not my love profan'd;
Be deaf, my ears, hear not my discontent;
Die, heart: another joys what thou deserv'st.
Lor. Watch still, mine eyes, to see this love disjoin'd;
Hear still, mine ears, to hear them both lament; 160
Live, heart, to joy at fond Horatio's fall.
Bel. Why stands Horatio speechless all this while?
Hor. The less I speak, the more I meditate.
Bel. But whereon dost thou chiefly meditate?
Hor. On dangers past, and pleasures to ensue.
Bal. On pleasures past, and dangers to ensue.
Bel. What dangers and what pleasures dost thou mean?
Hor. Dangers of war, and pleasures of our love.
Lor. Dangers of death, but pleasures none at all.
Bel. Let dangers go, thy war shall be with me: 170
But such a war, as breaks no bond of peace.
Speak thou fair words, I'll cross them with fair words;
Send thou sweet looks, I'll meet them with sweet looks;
Write loving lines, I'll answer loving lines;
Give me a kiss, I'll countercheck thy kiss:
Be this our warring peace, or peaceful war.
Hor. But, gracious madam, then appoint the field,
Where trial of this war shall first be made.
Bal. Ambitious villain, how his boldness grows!
Bel. Then be thy father's pleasant bow'r the field, 180
Where first we vow'd a mutual amity;
The court were dangerous, that place is safe.
Our hour shall be, when Vesper 'gins to rise,
That summons home distressful travellers:
There none shall hear us but the harmless birds;
Haply the gentle nightingale

Shall carol us asleep, ere we be ware,
And, singing with the prickle at her breast,
Tell our delight and mirthful dalliance:
Till then each hour will seem a year and more.   190
Hor. But, honey sweet and honourable love,
Return we now into your father's sight:
Dang'rous suspicion waits on our delight.
Lor. Ay, danger mixed with jealous despite
Shall send thy soul into eternal night.   [*Exeunt.*

SCENE III

Enter KING OF SPAIN, Portingal Ambassador,
DON CYPRIAN, *etc.*

King. Brother of Castile, to the prince's love
What says your daughter Bellimperia?
Cyp. Although she coy it, as becomes her kind,
And yet dissemble that she loves the prince,
I doubt not, I, but she will stoop in time.   200
And were she froward, which she will not be,
Yet herein shall she follow my advice,
Which is to love him, or forgo my love.
King. Then, lord Ambassador of Portingal,
Advise thy king to make this marriage up,
For strength'ning of our late-confirmèd league;
I know no better means to make us friends.
Her dowry shall be large and liberal:
Besides that she is daughter and half-heir
Unto our brother here, Don Cyprian,   210
And shall enjoy the moiety of his land,
I'll grace her marriage with an uncle's gift,
And this it is—in case the match go forward—:
The tribute which you pay, shall be releas'd;
And if by Balthazar she have a son,
He shall enjoy the kingdom after us.
Amb. I'll make the motion to my sovereign liege,
And work it, if my counsel may prevail.
King. Do so, my lord, and if he give consent,
I hope his presence here will honour us,   220
In celebration of the nuptial day;
And let himself determine of the time.

Amb. Will't please your grace command me ought beside?
King. Commend me to the king, and so farewell.
    But where's Prince Balthazar to take his leave?
Amb. That is perform'd already, my good lord.
King. Amongst the rest of what you have in charge,
    The prince's ransom must not be forgot:
    That's none of mine, but his that took him prisoner;
    And well his forwardness deserves reward:
    It was Horatio, our knight marshal's son.
Amb. Between us there's a price already pitch'd,
    And shall be sent with all convenient speed.
King. Then once again farewell, my lord.
Amb. Farewell, my lord of Castile, and the rest.   *[Exit.*
King. Now, brother, you must take some little pains
    To win fair Bellimperia from her will:
    Young virgins must be rulèd by their friends.
    The prince is amiable, and loves her well;
    If she neglect him and forgo his love,
    She both will wrong her own estate and ours.
    Therefore, whiles I do entertain the prince
    With greatest pleasure that our court affords,
    Endeavour you to win your daughter's thought:
    If she give back, all this will come to naught.   *[Exeunt.*

SCENE IV

Enter HORATIO, BELLIMPERIA, *and* PEDRINGANO.

Hor. Now that the night begins with sable wings
    To overcloud the brightness of the sun,
    And that in darkness pleasures may be done:
    Come, Bellimperia, let us to the bow'r,
    And there in safety pass a pleasant hour.
Bel. I follow thee, my love, and will not back,
    Although my fainting heart controls my soul.
Hor. Why, make you doubt of Pedringano's faith?
Bel. No, he is as trusty as my second self.—
    Go, Pedringano, watch without the gate,
    And let us know if any make approach.
Ped. [*aside.*] Instead of watching, I'll deserve more gold
    By fetching Don Lorenzo to this match. [*Exit Pedringano.*
Hor. What means my love?

Bel.   I know not what myself;
    And yet my heart foretells me some mischance.   260
Hor. Sweet, say not so; fair fortune is our friend,
    And heav'ns have shut up day to pleasure us.
    The stars, thou see'st, hold back their twinkling shine,
    And Luna hides herself to pleasure us.
Bel. Thou hast prevail'd; I'll conquer my misdoubt,
    And in thy love and counsel drown my fear.
    I fear no more; love now is all my thoughts.
    Why sit we not? for pleasure asketh ease.
Hor. The more thou sitt'st within these leafy bowers,
    The more will Flora deck it with her flowers.   270
Bel. Ay, but if Flora spy Horatio here,
    Her jealous eye will think I sit too near.
Hor. Hark, madam, how the birds record by night,
    For joy that Bellimperia sits in sight.
Bel. No, Cupid counterfeits the nightingale,
    To frame sweet music to Horatio's tale.
Hor. If Cupid sing, then Venus is not far:
    Ay, thou art Venus, or some fairer star.
Bel. If I be Venus, thou must needs be Mars;
    And where Mars reigneth, there must needs be wars.   280
Hor. Then thus begin our wars: put forth thy hand,
    That it may combat with my ruder hand.
Bel. Set forth thy foot to try the push of mine.
Hor. But first my looks shall combat against thine.
Bel. Then ward thyself: I dart this kiss at thee.
Hor. Thus I retort the dart thou threw'st at me.
Bel. Nay, then to gain the glory of the field,
    My twining arms shall yoke and make thee yield.
Hor. Nay, then my arms are large and strong withal:
    Thus elms by vines are compass'd, till they fall.   290
Bel. O, let me go; for in my troubled eyes
    Now may'st thou read that life in passion dies.
Hor. O, stay a while, and I will die with thee;
    So shalt thou yield, and yet have conquer'd me.
Bel. Who's there? Pedringano! we are betray'd!

Enter LORENZO, BALTHAZAR, SERBERINE, PEDRINGANO,
    disguised.

Lor. My lord, away with her, take her aside.—
    O, sir, forbear: your valour is already tried.

Quickly despatch, my masters.
[*They hang him in the arbour.*
Hor. What, will you murder me?
Lor. Ay, thus, and thus: these are the fruits of love.
[*They stab him.*
Bel. O, save his life, and let me die for him! 300
O, save him, brother; save him, Balthazar:
I lov'd Horatio; but he lov'd not me.
Bal. But Balthazar loves Bellimperia.
Lor. Although his life were still ambitious-proud,
Yet is he at the highest now he is dead.
Bel. Murder! murder! Help, Hieronimo, help!
Lor. Come, stop her mouth; away with her. [*Exeunt.*

SCENE V

Enter HIERONIMO *in his shirt, etc.*

Hier. What outcries pluck me from my naked bed,
And chill my throbbing heart with trembling fear,
Which never danger yet could daunt before? 310
Who calls Hieronimo? speak, here I am.
I did not slumber; therefore 'twas no dream.
No, no, it was some woman cried for help;
And here within this garden did she cry;
And in this garden must I rescue her.—
But stay, what murd'rous spectacle is this?
A man hang'd up and all the murd'rers gone!
And in my bower, to lay the guilt on me!
This place was made for pleasure, not for death.
[*He cuts him down.*
Those garments that he wears I oft have seen—: 320
Alas, it is Horatio, my sweet son!
O no, but he that whilom was my son!
O, was it thou that call'dst me from my bed?
O speak, if any spark of life remain:
I am thy father; who hath slain my son?
What savage monster, not of human kind,
Hath here been glutted with thy harmless blood,
And left thy bloody corpse dishonour'd here,
For me, amidst these dark and deathful shades,

>   To drown thee with an ocean of my tears? 330
>   O heav'ns, why made you night to cover sin?
>   By day this deed of darkness had not been.
>   O earth, why didst thou not in time devour
>   The vild profaner of this sacred bow'r?
>   O poor Horatio, what hadst thou misdone,
>   To leese thy life, ere life was new begun?
>   O wicked butcher, whatsoe'er thou wert,
>   How could thou strangle virtue and desert?
>   Ay me most wretched, that have lost my joy,
>   In leesing my Horatio, my sweet boy! 340

Enter ISABELLA.

Isab. My husband's absence makes my heart to throb:—
    Hieronimo!
Hier. Here, Isabella, help me to lament;
    For sighs are stopp'd, and all my tears are spent.
Isab. What world of grief! my son Horatio!
    O, where's the author of this endless woe?
Hier. To know the author were some ease of grief;
    For in revenge my heart would find relief.
Isab. Then is he gone? and is my son gone too?
    O, gush out, tears, fountains and floods of tears; 350
    Blow, sighs, and raise an everlasting storm;
    For outrage fits our cursèd wretchedness.
    [*Ay me, Hieronimo, sweet husband, speak!*
Hier. *He supp'd with us to-night, frolic and merry,*
    And said he would go visit Balthazar
    At the duke's palace: there the prince doth lodge.
    He had no custom to stay out so late:
    He may be in his chamber; some go see.
    Roderigo, ho!

Enter PEDRO and JAQUES.

Isab. *Ay me, he raves! sweet Hieronimo.* 360
Hier. *True, all Spain takes note of it.*
    Besides, he is so generally belov'd;
    His majesty the other day did grace him
    With waiting on his cup: these be favours,
    Which do assure me he cannot be short-liv'd.

Isab. *Sweet Hieronimo!*
Hier. *I wonder how this fellow got his clothes!—*
Sirrah, sirrah, I'll know the truth of all:
Jaques, run to the Duke of Castile's presently,
And bid my son Horatio to come home:
I and his mother have had strange dreams to-night.
Do ye hear me, sir?
Jaques. *Ay, sir.*
Hier. *Well, sir, be gone.*
Pedro, come hither; know'st thou who this is?
Ped. *Too well, sir.*
Hier. *Too well! who, who is it? Peace, Isabella!*
Nay, blush not, man.
Ped. *It is my lord Horatio.*
Hier. *Ha, ha, St. James! but this doth make me laugh,*
That there are more deluded than myself.
Ped. *Deluded?*
Hier. *Ay:*
I would have sworn myself, within this hour,
That this had been my son Horatio:
His garments are so like.
Ha! are they not great persuasions?
Isab. *O, would to God it were not so!*
Hier. *Were not, Isabella? dost thou dream it is?*
Can thy soft bosom entertain a thought,
That such a black deed of mischief should be done
On one so pure and spotless as our son?
Away, I am ashamed.
Isab. *Dear Hieronimo,*
Cast a more serious eye upon thy grief:
Weak apprehension gives but weak relief.
Hier. *It was a man, sure, that was hang'd up here;*
A youth, as I remember: I cut him down.
If it should prove my son now after all—
Say you? say you?—Light! lend me a taper;
Let me look again.—O God!
Confusion, mischief, torment, death and hell,
Drop all your stings at once in my cold bosom,
That now is stiff with horror: kill me quickly!
Be gracious to me, thou infective night,
And drop this deed of murder down on me;
Gird in my waste of grief with thy large darkness,

   And let me not survive to see the light
   May put me in the mind I had a son.
Isab. *O sweet Horatio ! O my dearest son !*
Hier. *How strangely had I lost my way to grief !*]
   Sweet, lovely rose, ill-pluck'd before thy time,
   Fair, worthy son, not conquer'd, but betray'd,
   I'll kiss thee now, for words with tears are stay'd.
Isab. And I'll close up the glasses of his sight,
   For once these eyes were only my delight.   410
Hier. See'st thou this handkercher besmear'd with blood?
   It shall not from me, till I take revenge.
   See'st thou those wounds that yet are bleeding fresh?
   I'll not entomb them, till I have revenge.
   Then will I joy amidst my discontent;
   Till then my sorrow never shall be spent.
Isab. The heav'ns are just; murder cannot be hid:
   Time is the author both of truth and right,
   And time will bring this treachery to light.
Hier. Meanwhile, good Isabella, cease thy plaints,   420
   Or, at the least, dissemble them awhile:
   So shall we sooner find the practice out,
   And learn by whom all this was brought about.
   Come, Isabel, now let us take him up, [*They take him up.*
   And bear him in from out this cursèd place.
   I'll say his dirge; singing fits not this case.

   O aliquis mihi quas pulchrum ver educat herbas,
       [*Hieronimo sets his breast unto his sword.*
   Misceat, et nostro detur medicina dolori ;
   Aut, si qui faciunt annorum oblivia, succos
   Praebeat ; ipse metam magnum quaecunque per orbem 430
   Gramina Sol pulchras effert in luminis oras ;
   Ipse bibam quicquid meditatur saga veneni,
   Quicquid et herbarum vi caeca nenia nectit :
   Omnia perpetiar, lethum quoque, dum semel omnis
   Noster in extincto moriatur pectore sensus.—
   Ergo tuos oculos nunquam, mea vita, videbo,
   Et tua perpetuus sepelivit lumina somnus ?
   Emoriar tecum : sic, sic juvat ire sub umbras.—
   Attamen absistam properato cedere letho,
   Ne mortem vindicta tuam tam nulla sequatur.   440
    [*Here he throws it from him and bears the body away.*

SCENE VI

Ghost of Andrea, Revenge.

Andrea. Brought'st thou me hither to increase my pain?
　　I look'd that Balthazar should have been slain:
　　But 'tis my friend Horatio that is slain,
　　And they abuse fair Bellimperia,
　　On whom I doted more than all the world,
　　Because she lov'd me more than all the world.
Revenge. Thou talk'st of harvest, when the corn is green:
　　The end is crown of every work well done;
　　The sickle comes not, till the corn be ripe.
　　Be still; and ere I lead thee from this place, 450
　　I'll show thee Balthazar in heavy case.

ACT III

SCENE I.—*The Court of Portugal.*

Enter Viceroy of Portingal, Nobles, Alexandro, Villuppo.

Vic. Infortunate condition of kings,
　　Seated amidst so many helpless doubts!
　　First we are plac'd upon extremest height,
　　And oft supplanted with exceeding hate,
　　But ever subject to the wheel of chance;
　　And at our highest never joy we so,
　　As we both doubt and dread our overthrow.
　　So striveth not the waves with sundry winds,
　　As fortune toileth in the affairs of kings,
　　That would be fear'd, yet fear to be belov'd,　　　　10
　　Sith fear or love to kings is flattery.
　　For instance, lordings, look upon your king,
　　By hate deprivèd of his dearest son,
　　The only hope of our successive line.
Nob. I had not thought that Alexandro's heart
　　Had been envenom'd with such extreme hate;
　　But now I see that words have several works,
　　And there's no credit in the countenance.
Vil. No; for, my lord, had you beheld the train,
　　That feignèd love had colour'd in his looks,　　　　20
　　When he in camp consorted Balthazar,
　　Far more inconstant had you thought the sun,
　　That hourly coasts the centre of the earth,
　　Than Alexandro's purpose to the prince.
Vic. No more, Villuppo, thou hast said enough,
　　And with thy words thou slay'st our wounded thoughts.
　　Nor shall I longer dally with the world,
　　Procrastinating Alexandro's death:
　　Go some of you, and fetch the traitor forth,
　　That, as he is condemnèd, he may die.　　　　　　30

Enter ALEXANDRO, *with a* Nobleman *and halberts.*

Nob. In such extremes will nought but patience serve.
Alex. But in extremes what patience shall I use?
  Nor discontents it me to leave the world,
  With whom there nothing can prevail but wrong.
Nob. Yet hope the best.
Alex.   'Tis heaven is my hope:
  As for the earth, it is too much infect
  To yield me hope of any of her mould.
Vic. Why linger ye? bring forth that daring fiend,
  And let him die for his accursèd deed.
Alex. Not that I fear the extremity of death   40
  (For nobles cannot stoop to servile fear)
  Do I, O king, thus discontented live.
  But this, O this, torments my labouring soul,
  That thus I die suspected of a sin,
  Whereof, as heav'ns have known my secret thoughts,
  So am I free from this suggestion.
Vic. No more, I say! to the tortures! when?
  Bind him, and burn his body in those flames,
        [*They bind him to the stake.*
  That shall prefigure those unquenchèd fires
  Of Phlegethon, preparèd for his soul.   50
Alex. My guiltless death will be aveng'd on thee,
  On thee, Villuppo, that hath malic'd thus,
  Or for thy meed hast falsely me accus'd.
Vil. Nay, Alexandro, if thou menace me,
  I'll lend a hand to send thee to the lake,
  Where those thy words shall perish with thy works:
  Injurious traitor! monstrous homicide!

Enter Ambassador.

Amb. Stay, hold a while;
  And here—with pardon of his majesty—
  Lay hands upon Villuppo.
Vic.   Ambassador,   60
  What news hath urg'd this sudden enterance?
Amb. Know, sovereign lord, that Balthazar doth live.
Vic. What say'st thou? liveth Balthazar our son?

Amb. Your highness' son, Lord Balthazar, doth live;
And, well entreated in the court of Spain,
Humbly commends him to your majesty.
These eyes beheld—and these my followers—;
With these, the letters of the king's commends
        [*Gives him letters.*
Are happy witnesses of his highness' health.
        [*The King looks on the letters, and proceeds.*
Vic. " Thy son doth live, your tribute is receiv'd;   70
Thy peace is made, and we are satisfied.
The rest resolve upon as things propos'd
For both our honours and thy benefit."
Amb. These are his highness' farther articles.
        [*He gives him more letters.*
Vic. Accursèd wretch, to intimate these ills
Against the life and reputation
Of noble Alexandro! Come, my lord, unbind him:
Let him unbind thee, that is bound to death,
To make a quital for thy discontent.   [*They unbind him.*
Alex. Dread lord, in kindness you could do no less,   80
Upon report of such a damnèd fact;
But thus we see our innocence hath sav'd
The hopeless life which thou, Villuppo, sought
By thy suggestions to have massacred.
Vic. Say, false Villuppo, wherefore didst thou thus
Falsely betray Lord Alexandro's life?
Him, whom thou know'st that no unkindness else,
But ev'n the slaughter of our dearest son,
Could once have mov'd us to have misconceiv'd.
Alex. Say, treacherous Villuppo, tell the king: 90
Wherein hath Alexandro us'd thee ill?
Vil. Rent with remembrance of so foul a deed,
My guilty soul submits me to thy doom:
For not for Alexandro's injuries,
But for reward and hope to be preferr'd,
Thus have I shamelessly hazarded his life.
Vic. Which, villain, shall be ransom'd with thy death—:
And not so mean a torment as we here
Devis'd for him who, thou said'st, slew our son,
But with the bitt'rest torments and extremes   100
That may be yet invented for thine end.
        [*Alexandro seems to entreat.*

Entreat me not! go, take the traitor hence:
[*Exit Villuppo.*

And, Alexandro, let us honour thee
With public notice of thy loyalty.—
To end those things articulated here
By our great lord, the mighty King of Spain,
We with our council will deliberate.
Come, Alexandro, keep us company. [*Exeunt.*

SCENE II

Enter HIERONIMO.

Hier. O eyes! no eyes, but fountains fraught with tears;
  O life! no life, but lively form of death; 110
  O world! no world, but mass of public wrongs,
Confus'd and fill'd with murder and misdeeds!
O sacred heav'ns! if this unhallow'd deed,
If this inhuman and barbarous attempt,
If this incomparable murder thus
Of mine, but now no more my son,
Shall unreveal'd and unrevengèd pass,
How should we term your dealings to be just,
If you unjustly deal with those that in your justice trust?
The night, sad secretary to my moans, 120
With direful visions wakes my vexèd soul,
And with the wounds of my distressful son
Solicits me for notice of his death.
The ugly fiends do sally forth of hell,
And frame my steps to unfrequented paths,
And fear my heart with fierce inflamèd thoughts.
The cloudy day my discontents records,
Early begins to register my dreams,
And drive me forth to seek the murtherer.
Eyes, life, world, heav'ns, hell, night, and day, 130
See, search, shew, send some man, some mean, that may—
[*A letter falleth.*
What's here? a letter? tush! it is not so!—
A letter written to Hieronimo! [*Red ink.*
" For want of ink, receive this bloody writ:
Me hath my hapless brother hid from thee;
Revenge thyself on Balthazar and him:

> For these were they that murderèd thy son.
> Hieronimo, revenge Horatio's death,
> And better fare than Bellimperia doth."
> What means this unexpected miracle? 140
> My son slain by Lorenzo and the prince!
> What cause had they Horatio to malign?
> Or what might move thee, Bellimperia,
> To accuse thy brother, had he been the mean?
> Hieronimo, beware!—thou art betray'd,
> And to entrap thy life this train is laid.
> Advise thee therefore, be not credulous:
> This is devisèd to endanger thee,
> That thou, by this, Lorenzo shouldst accuse;
> And he, for thy dishonour done, should draw 150
> Thy life in question and thy name in hate.
> Dear was the life of my belovèd son,
> And of his death behoves me be reveng'd:
> Then hazard not thine own, Hieronimo,
> But live t' effect thy resolution.
> I therefore will by circumstances try,
> What I can gather to confirm this writ;
> And, heark'ning near the Duke of Castile's house,
> Close, if I can, with Bellimperia,
> To listen more, but nothing to bewray. 160

Enter PEDRINGANO.

Now, Pedringano!
Ped. Now, Hieronimo!
Hier. Where's thy lady?
Ped. I know not; here's my lord.

Enter LORENZO.

Lor. How now, who's this? Hieronimo?
Hier. My lord——
Ped. He asketh for my lady Bellimperia.
Lor. What to do, Hieronimo? The duke, my father, hath,
Upon some disgrace, awhile remov'd her hence;
But if it be ought I may inform her of,
Tell me, Hieronimo, and I'll let her know it.
Hier. Nay, nay, my lord, I thank you; it shall not need.

    I had a suit unto her, but too late,   170
    And her disgrace makes me unfortunate.
Lor. Why so, Hieronimo? use me.
Hier. Oh no, my lord; I dare not; it must not be;
    I humbly thank your lordship.[1]
Lor.   Why then, farewell.
Hier. My grief no heart, my thoughts no tongue can tell. [*Exit.*
Lor. Come hither, Pedringano, see'st thou this?
Ped. My lord, I see it, and suspect it too.
Lor. This is that damnèd villain Serberine,
    That hath, I fear, reveal'd Horatio's death.
Ped. My lord, he could not, 'twas so lately done;   180
    And since he hath not left my company.
Lor. Admit he have not, his condition's such,
    As fear or flatt'ring words may make him false.
    I know his humour, and therewith repent
    That e'er I us'd him in this enterprise.
    But, Pedringano, to prevent the worst,
    And 'cause I know thee secret as my soul,
    Here, for thy further satisfaction, take thou this,
                      [*Gives him more gold.*
    And hearken to me—thus it is devis'd:
    This night thou must (and, prithee, so resolve)   190
    Meet Serberine at Saint Luigi's Park—
    Thou know'st 'tis here hard by behind the house—
    There take thy stand, and see thou strike him sure:
    For die he must, if we do mean to live.
Ped. But how shall Serberine be there, my lord?
Lor. Let me alone; I'll send to him to meet
    The prince and me, where thou must do this deed.
Ped. It shall be done, my lord, it shall be done;
    And I'll go arm myself to meet him there.

---

[1] Line 173 and first part of 174 (O no . . . lordship) are replaced, in all the Qq. from 1602 onwards, by the following lines:

    Hier. *Who? you, my lord?*
        I reserve your favour for a greater honour;
        This is a very toy, my lord, a toy.
    Lor. *All's one, Hieronimo, acquaint me with it.*
    Hier. *I' faith, my lord, it is an idle thing;*
        I must confess I ha' been too slack, too tardy,
        Too remiss unto your honour.
    Lor.   *How now, Hieronimo?*
    Hier. *In troth, my lord, it is a thing of nothing:*
        The murder of a son, or so——
        A thing of nothing, my lord!

Lor. When things shall alter, as I hope they will,   200
   Then shalt thou mount for this; thou know'st my mind.
                              [*Exit Pedringano.*

   Che le Ieron!

                   Enter Page.

Page.   My lord?
Lor.   Go, sirrah,
   To Serberine, and bid him forthwith meet
   The prince and me at Saint Luigi's Park,
   Behind the house; this evening, boy!
Page.   I go, my lord.
Lor. But, sirrah, let the hour be eight o'clock:
   Bid him not fail.
Page.   I fly, my lord.   [*Exit.*
Lor. Now to confirm the complot thou hast cast
   Of all these practices, I'll spread the watch,
   Upon precise commandment from the king,   210
   Strongly to guard the place where Pedringano
   This night shall murder hapless Serberine.
   Thus must we work that will avoid distrust;
   Thus must we practise to prevent mishap,
   And thus one ill another must expulse.
   This sly enquiry of Hieronimo
   For Bellimperia breeds suspicion,
   And this suspicion bodes a further ill.
   As for myself, I know my secret fault,
   And so do they; but I have dealt for them: 220
   They that for coin their souls endangerèd,
   To save my life, for coin shall venture theirs;
   And better it's that base companions die,
   Than by their life to hazard our good haps.
   Nor shall they live, for me to fear their faith:
   I'll trust myself, myself shall be my friend;
   For die they shall, slaves are ordain'd to no other end.
                                                    [*Exit.*

SCENE III

Enter PEDRINGANO, *with a pistol.*

Ped. Now, Pedringano, bid thy pistol hold,
And hold on, Fortune! once more favour me;
Give but success to mine attempting spirit, 230
And let me shift for taking of mine aim.
Here is the gold: this is the gold propos'd;
It is no dream that I adventure for,
But Pedringano is possess'd thereof.
And he that would not strain his conscience
For him that thus his liberal purse hath stretch'd,
Unworthy such a favour, may he fail,
And, wishing, want, when such as I prevail.
As for the fear of apprehension,
I know, if need should be, my noble lord 240
Will stand between me and ensuing harms;
Besides, this place is free from all suspect:
Here therefore will I stay and take my stand.

Enter the Watch.

1. I wonder much to what intent it is
   That we are thus expressly charg'd to watch.
2. 'Tis by commandment in the king's own name.
3. But we were never wont to watch and ward
   So near the duke, his brother's, house before.
2. Content yourself, stand close, there's somewhat in't.

Enter SERBERINE.

Ser. Here, Serberine, attend and stay thy pace; 250
For here did Don Lorenzo's page appoint
That thou by his command shouldst meet with him.
How fit a place—if one were so dispos'd—
Methinks this corner is to close with one.
Ped. Here comes the bird that I must seize upon:
Now, Pedringano, or never, play the man!
Ser. I wonder that his lordship stays so long,
Or wherefore should he send for me so late?

Ped. For this, Serberine!—and thou shalt ha't. [*Shoots the dag.*
    So, there he lies; my promise is perform'd.   260

The Watch.

1. Hark, gentlemen, this is a pistol shot.
2. And here's one slain;—stay the murderer.

Ped. Now by the sorrows of the souls in hell,
                          [*He strives with the watch.*
    Who first lays hand on me, I'll be his priest.

3. Sirrah, confess, and therein play the priest,
    Why hast thou thus unkindly kill'd the man?

Ped. Why? because he walk'd abroad so late.

3. Come, sir, you had been better kept your bed,
    Than have committed this misdeed so late.
2. Come, to the marshal's with the murderer!   270
1. On to Hieronimo's! help me here
    To bring the murder'd body with us too.

Ped. Hieronimo? carry me before whom you will:
    Whate'er he be, I'll answer him and you;
    And do your worst, for I defy you all.   *Exeunt.*

SCENE IV

Enter LORENZO *and* BALTHAZAR.

Bal. How now, my lord, what makes you rise so soon?
Lor. Fear of preventing our mishaps too late.
Bal. What mischief is it that we not mistrust?
Lor. Our greatest ills we least mistrust, my lord,
    And inexpected harms do hurt us most.   280
Bal. Why, tell me, Don Lorenzo, tell me, man,
    If ought concerns our honour and your own.
Lor. Nor you, nor me, my lord, but both in one:
    For I suspect—and the presumption's great—
    That by those base confed'rates in our fault
    Touching the death of Don Horatio,
    We are betray'd to old Hieronimo.
Bal. Betray'd, Lorenzo? tush! it cannot be.
Lor. A guilty conscience, urgèd with the thought
    Of former evils, easily cannot err: 290
    I am persuaded—and dissuade me not—

That all's revealed to Hieronimo.
And therefore know that I have cast it thus:—

Enter Page.

But here's the page. How now? what news with thee?
Page. My lord, Serberine is slain.
Bal.   Who? Serberine, my man?
Page. Your highness' man, my lord.
Lor.   Speak, page, who murder'd him?
Page. He that is apprehended for the fact.
Lor. Who?
Page.   Pedringano.
Bal. Is Serberine slain, that lov'd his lord so well?
Injurious villain, murd'rer of his friend!   300
Lor. Hath Pedringano murder'd Serberine?
My lord, let me entreat you to take the pains
To exasperate and hasten his revenge
With your complaints unto my lord the king.
This their dissension breeds a greater doubt.
Bal. Assure thee, Don Lorenzo, he shall die,
Or else his highness hardly shall deny.
Meanwhile I'll haste the marshal-sessions:
For die he shall for this his damnèd deed. [*Exit Balthazar.*
Lor. Why so, this fits our former policy,   310
And thus experience bids the wise to deal.
I lay the plot: he prosecutes the point;
I set the trap: he breaks the worthless twigs,
And sees not that wherewith the bird was lim'd.
Thus hopeful men, that mean to hold their own,
Must look like fowlers to their dearest friends.
He runs to kill whom I have holp to catch,
And no man knows it was my reaching fetch.
'Tis hard to trust unto a multitude,
Or any one, in mine opinion,   320
When men themselves their secrets will reveal.

Enter a Messenger *with a letter.*

    Boy——
Page.   My lord?
Lor. What's he?
Mes.   I have a letter to your lordship.

Lor. From whence?
Mes. From Pedringano that's imprison'd.
Lor. So he is in prison then?
Mes. Ay, my good lord.
Lor. What would he with us?—He writes us here,
To stand good lord, and help him in distress.—
Tell him I have his letters, know his mind;
And what we may, let him assure him of.
Fellow, begone: my boy shall follow thee. 330
[*Exit Messenger.*

This works like wax; yet once more try thy wits.
Boy, go, convey this purse to Pedringano;
Thou know'st the prison, closely give it him,
And be advis'd that none be there about:
Bid him be merry still, but secret;
And though the marshal-sessions be to-day,
Bid him not doubt of his delivery.
Tell him his pardon is already sign'd,
And thereon bid him boldly be resolv'd:
For, were he ready to be turnèd off— 340
As 'tis my will the uttermost be tried—
Thou with his pardon shalt attend him still.
Show him this box, tell him his pardon's in't;
But open't not, and if thou lov'st thy life;
But let him wisely keep his hopes unknown:
He shall not want while Don Lorenzo lives.
Away!
Page. I go, my lord, I run.
Lor. But, sirrah, see that this be cleanly done. [*Exit Page.*
Now stands our fortune on a tickle point,
And now or never ends Lorenzo's doubts. 350
One only thing is uneffected yet,
And that's to see the executioner.
But to what end? I list not trust the air
With utterance of our pretence therein,
For fear the privy whisp'ring of the wind
Convey our words amongst unfriendly ears,
That lie too open to advantages.
E quel che voglio io, nessun lo sa;
Intendo io: quel mi basterà. [*Exit.*

SCENE V

Enter Boy, *with the box.*

Boy. My master hath forbidden me to look in this box; and, by
   my troth, 'tis likely, if he had not warned me, I should not
   have had so much idle time; for we men's-kind, in our
   minority, are like women in their uncertainty: that they
   are most forbidden, they will soonest attempt: so I now.
   ——By my bare honesty, here's nothing but the bare
   empty box: were it not sin against secrecy, I would say it
   were a piece of gentlemanlike knavery. I must go to
   Pedringano, and tell him his pardon is in this box; nay, I
   would have sworn it, had I not seen the contrary.—I cannot
   choose but smile to think how the villain will flout the
   gallows, scorn the audience, and descant on the hangman,
   and all presuming of his pardon from hence. Will't not be
   an odd jest for me to stand and grace every jest he makes,
   pointing my finger at this box, as who would say: "Mock
   on, here's thy warrant." Is't not a scurvy jest that a man
   should jest himself to death? Alas! poor Pedringano, I
   am in a sort sorry for thee; but if I should be hanged with
   thee, I cannot weep. [*Exit.*

SCENE VI

Enter HIERONIMO *and the* Deputy.

Hier. Thus must we toil in other men's extremes,
   That know not how to remedy our own; 380
   And do them justice, when unjustly we,
   For all our wrongs, can compass no redress.
   But shall I never live to see the day,
   That I may come, by justice of the heavens,
   To know the cause that may my cares allay?
   This toils my body, this consumeth age,
   That only I to all men just must be,
   And neither gods nor men be just to me.
Dep. Worthy Hieronimo, your office asks
   A care to punish such as do transgress. 390

Hier. So is't my duty to regard his death
   Who, when he liv'd, deserv'd my dearest blood.
   But come, for that we came for: let's begin;
   For here lies that which bids me to be gone.

Enter Officers, Boy, *and* Pedringano, *with a letter in his hand, bound.*

Dep. Bring forth the prisoner, for the court is set.
Ped. Gramercy, boy, but it was time to come;
   For I had written to my lord anew
   A nearer matter that concerneth him,
   For fear his lordship had forgotten me.
   But sith he hath remember'd me so well— 400
   Come, come, come on, when shall we to this gear?
Hier. Stand forth, thou monster, murderer of men,
   And here, for satisfaction of the world,
   Confess thy folly, and repent thy fault;
   For there's thy place of execution.
Ped. This is short work: well, to your marshalship
   First I confess—nor fear I death therefore—:
   I am the man, 'twas I slew Serberine.
   But, sir, then you think this shall be the place,
   Where we shall satisfy you for this gear? 410
Dep. Ay, Pedringano.
Ped.   Now I think not so.
Hier. Peace, impudent; for thou shalt find it so:
   For blood with blood shall, while I sit as judge,
   Be satisfièd, and the law discharg'd.
   And though myself cannot receive the like,
   Yet will I see that others have their right.
   Despatch: the fault's approvèd and confess'd,
   And by our law he is condemn'd to die.
Hangm. Come on, sir, are you ready?
Ped. To do what, my fine, officious knave? 420
Hangm. To go to this gear.
Ped. O sir, you are too forward: thou wouldst fain furnish me with a halter, to disfurnish me of my habit. So I should go out of this gear, my raiment, into that gear, the rope. But, hangman, now I spy your knavery, I'll not change without boot, that's flat.
Hangm. Come, sir.

Ped. So, then, I must up?

Hangm. No remedy.

Ped. Yes, but there shall be for my coming down.

Hangm. Indeed, here's a remedy for that.

Ped. How? be turned off?

Hangm. Ay, truly; come, are you ready? I pray, sir, despatch; the day goes away.

Ped. What, do you hang by the hour? if you do, I may chance to break your old custom.

Hangm. Faith, you have reason; for I am like to break your young neck.

Ped. Dost thou mock me, hangman? pray God, I be not preserved to break your knave's pate for this.

Hangm. Alas, sir! you are a foot too low to reach it, and I hope you will never grow so high while I am in the office.

Ped. Sirrah, dost see yonder boy with the box in his hand?

Hangm. What, he that points to it with his finger?

Ped. Ay, that companion.

Hangm. I know him not; but what of him?

Ped. Dost thou think to live till his old doublet will make thee a new truss?

Hangm. Ay, and many a fair year after, to truss up many a honester man than either thou or he.

Ped. What hath he in his box, as thou thinkest?

Hangm. Faith, I cannot tell, nor I care not greatly; methinks you should rather hearken to your soul's health.

Ped. Why, sirrah hangman, I take it that that is good for the body is likewise good for the soul: and it may be, in that box is balm for both.

Hangm. Well, thou art even the merriest piece of man's flesh that e'er groaned at my office door!

Ped. Is your roguery become an office with a knave's name?

Hangm. Ay, and that shall all they witness that see you seal it with a thief's name.

Ped. I prithee, request this good company to pray with me.

Hangm. Ay, marry, sir, this is a good motion: my masters, you see here's a good fellow.

Ped. Nay, nay, now I remember me, let them alone till some other time; for now I have no great need.

Hier. I have not seen a wretch so impudent.
O monstrous times, where murder's set so light,
And where the soul, that should be shrin'd in heaven,

>   Solely delights in interdicted things, 470
>   Still wand'ring in the thorny passages,
>   That intercepts itself of happiness.
>   Murder! O bloody monster! God forbid
>   A fault so foul should 'scape unpunishèd.
>   Despatch, and see this execution done!—
>   This makes me to remember thee, my son.
>
>   [*Exit Hieronimo.*
>
> *Ped.* Nay, soft, no haste.
> *Dep.* Why, wherefore stay you? Have you hope of life?
> *Ped.* Why, ay!
> *Hangm.*   As how?
> *Ped.* Why, rascal, by my pardon from the king. 480
> *Hangm.* Stand you on that? then you shall off with this.
>   [*He turns him off.*
> *Dep.* So, executioner;—convey him hence;
>   But let his body be unburièd:
>   Let not the earth be chokèd or infect
>   With that which heav'n contemns, and men neglect.
>   [*Exeunt.*

SCENE VII

Enter HIERONIMO.

> *Hier.* Where shall I run to breathe abroad my woes,
>   My woes, whose weight hath wearièd the earth?
>   Or mine exclaims, that have surcharg'd the air
>   With ceaseless plaints for my deceasèd son?
>   The blust'ring winds, conspiring with my words, 490
>   At my lament have mov'd the leafless trees,
>   Disrob'd the meadows of their flower'd green,
>   Made mountains marsh with spring-tides of my tears,
>   And broken through the brazen gates of hell.
>   Yet still tormented is my tortur'd soul
>   With broken sighs and restless passions,
>   That wingèd mount; and, hov'ring in the air,
>   Beat at the windows of the brightest heavens,
>   Soliciting for justice and revenge:
>   But they are plac'd in those empyreal heights, 500
>   Where, countermur'd with walls of diamond,
>   I find the place impregnable; and they
>   Resist my woes, and give my words no way.

Enter Hangman *with a letter.*

Hangm. O lord, sir! God bless you, sir! the man, sir, Petergade,
    sir, he that was so full of merry conceits—
Hier. Well, what of him?
Hangm. O lord, sir, he went the wrong way; the fellow had a
    fair commission to the contrary. Sir, here is his passport;
    I pray you, sir, we have done him wrong.   510
Hier. I warrant thee, give it me.
Hangm. You will stand between the gallows and me?
Hier. Ay, ay.
Hangm. I thank your lord worship.   [*Exit Hangman.*
Hier. And yet, though somewhat nearer me concerns,
    I will, to ease the grief that I sustain,
    Take truce with sorrow while I read on this.
    " My lord, I write, as mine extremes requir'd,
    That you would labour my delivery:
    If you neglect, my life is desperate,   520
    And in my death I shall reveal the troth.
    You know, my lord, I slew him for your sake,
    And was confed'rate with the prince and you;
    Won by rewards and hopeful promises,
    I holp to murder Don Horatio too."—
    Holp he to murder mine Horatio?
    And actors in th' accursèd tragedy
    Wast thou, Lorenzo, Balthazar and thou,
    Of whom my son, my son deserv'd so well?
    What have I heard, what have mine eyes beheld?   530
    O sacred heavens, may it come to pass
    That such a monstrous and detested deed,
    So closely smother'd, and so long conceal'd,
    Shall thus by this be vengèd or reveal'd?
    Now see I what I durst not then suspect,
    That Bellimperia's letter was not feign'd.
    Nor feignèd she, though falsely they have wrong'd
    Both her, myself, Horatio, and themselves.
    Now may I make compare 'twixt hers and this,
    Of every accident I ne'er could find   540
    Till now, and now I feelingly perceive
    They did what heav'n unpunish'd would not leave.
    O false Lorenzo! are these thy flatt'ring looks?

Is this the honour that thou didst my son?
And Balthazar—bane to thy soul and me!—
Was this the ransom he reserv'd thee for?
Woe to the cause of these constrainèd wars!
Woe to thy baseness and captivity,
Woe to thy birth, thy body and thy soul,
Thy cursèd father, and thy conquer'd self! 550
And bann'd with bitter execrations be
The day and place where he did pity thee!
But wherefore waste I mine unfruitful words,
When naught but blood will satisfy my woes?
I will go plain me to my lord the king,
And cry aloud for justice through the court,
Wearing the flints with these my wither'd feet,
And either purchase justice by entreats,
Or tire them all with my revenging threats.   [*Exit.*

SCENE VIII

Enter ISABELLA *and her* Maid.

Isab. So that, you say, this herb, will purge the eye, 560
    And this, the head?—
    Ah!—but none of them will purge the heart!
    No, there's no medicine left for my disease,
    Nor any physic to recure the dead.   [*She runs lunatic.*
    Horatio! O, where's Horatio?
Maid. Good madam, affright not thus yourself
    With outrage for your son Horatio:
    He sleeps in quiet in the Elysian fields.
Isab. Why, did I not give you gowns and goodly things,
    Bought you a whistle and a whipstalk too, 570
    To be revengèd on their villanies?
Maid. Madam, these humours do torment my soul.
Isab. My soul—poor soul! thou talk'st of things—
    Thou know'st not what: my soul hath silver wings,
    That mounts me up unto the highest heavens;
    To heav'n: ay, there sits my Horatio,
    Back'd with a troop of fiery Cherubins,
    Dancing about his newly healèd wounds,
    Singing sweet hymns and chanting heav'nly notes:
    Rare harmony to greet his innocence, 580

That died, ay died, a mirror in our days.
But say, where shall I find the men, the murderers,
That slew Horatio?   Whither shall I run
To find them out that murderèd my son?   [*Exeunt.*

SCENE IX

BELLIMPERIA *at a window.*

Bel. What means this outrage that is offer'd me?
Why am I thus sequester'd from the court?
No notice!   Shall I not know the cause
Of these my secret and suspicious ills?
Accursèd brother, unkind murderer,
Why bend'st thou thus thy mind to martyr me?   590
Hieronimo, why writ I of thy wrongs,
Or why art thou so slack in thy revenge?
Andrea, O Andrea! that thou saw'st
Me for thy friend Horatio handled thus,
And him for me thus causeless murderèd!—
Well, force perforce, I must constrain myself
To patience, and apply me to the time,
Till heav'n, as I have hop'd, shall set me free.

Enter CHRISTOPHIL.

Chris. Come, madam Bellimperia, this may not be.   [*Exeunt.*

SCENE X

Enter LORENZO, BALTHAZAR, *and the* Page.

Lor. Boy, talk no further; thus far things go well.   600
   Thou art assurèd that thou saw'st him dead?
Page. Or else, my lord, I live not.
Lor.   That's enough.
   As for his resolution in his end,
   Leave that to him with whom he sojourns now.—
   Here, take my ring and give it Christophil,
   And bid him let my sister be enlarg'd,
   And bring her hither straight.—   [*Exit Page.*

  This that I did was for a policy,
  To smooth and keep the murder secret,
  Which, as a nine-days' wonder, being o'erblown,   610
  My gentle sister will I now enlarge.
Bal. And time, Lorenzo: for my lord the duke,
  You heard, enquirèd for her yester-night.
Lor. Why, and my lord, I hope you heard me say
  Sufficient reason why she kept away;
  But that's all one. My lord, you love her?
Bal.   Ay.
Lor. Then in your love beware; deal cunningly:
  Salve all suspicions, only soothe me up;
  And if she hap to stand on terms with us—
  As for her sweetheart and concealment so—   620
  Jest with her gently: under feignèd jest
  Are things conceal'd that else would breed unrest.—
  But here she comes.

Enter BELLIMPERIA.

        Now, sister?
Bel.   Sister?—No!
  Thou art no brother, but an enemy;
  Else wouldst thou not have us'd thy sister so:
  First, to affright me with thy weapons drawn,
  And with extremes abuse my company;
  And then to hurry me, like whirlwind's rage,
  Amidst a crew of thy confederates,
  And clap me up, where none might come at me,   630
  Nor I at any, to reveal my wrongs.
  What madding fury did possess thy wits?
  Or wherein is't that I offended thee?
Lor. Advise you better, Bellimperia,
  For I have done you no disparagement;
  Unless, by more discretion than deserv'd,
  I sought to save your honour and mine own.
Bel. Mine honour? why, Lorenzo, wherein is't
  That I neglect my reputation so,
  As you, or any, need to rescue it?   640
Lor. His highness and my father were resolv'd
  To come confer with old Hieronimo,
  Concerning certain matters of estate,

   That by the viceroy was determinèd.
Bel. And wherein was mine honour touch'd in that?
Bal. Have patience, Bellimperia; hear the rest.
Lor. Me (next in sight) as messenger they sent,
 To give him notice that they were so nigh:
 Now when I came, consorted with the prince,
 And unexpected, in an arbour there,   650
 Found Bellimperia with Horatio—
Bel. How then?
Lor. Why, then, remembering that old disgrace,
 Which you for Don Andrea had endur'd,
 And now were likely longer to sustain,
 By being found so meanly accompanied,
 Thought rather—for I knew no readier mean—
 To thrust Horatio forth my father's way.
Bal. And carry you obscurely somewhere else,
 Lest that his highness should have found you there. 660
Bel. Ev'n so, my lord? And you are witness
 That this is true which he entreateth of?
 You, gentle brother, forg'd this for my sake,
 And you, my lord, were made his instrument?
 A work of worth, worthy the noting too!
 But what's the cause that you conceal'd me since?
Lor. Your melancholy, sister, since the news
 Of your first favourite Don Andrea's death,
 My father's old wrath hath exasperate.
Bal. And better was't for you, being in disgrace,   670
 To absent yourself, and give his fury place.
Bel. But why had I no notice of his ire?
Lor. That were to add more fuel to your fire,
 Who burnt like Ætna for Andrea's loss.
Bel. Hath not my father then enquir'd for me?
Lor. Sister, he hath, and thus excus'd I thee.
          [He whispereth in her ear.
 But, Bellimperia, see the gentle prince;
 Look on thy love, behold young Balthazar,
 Whose passions by thy presence are increas'd;
 And in whose melancholy thou may'st see   680
 Thy hate, his love; thy flight, his following thee.
Bel. Brother, you are become an orator—
 I know not, I, by what experience—
 Too politic for me, past all compare,

Since last I saw you; but content yourself:
The prince is meditating higher things.
Bal. 'Tis of thy beauty then that conquers kings;
  Of those thy tresses, Ariadne's twines,
  Wherewith my liberty thou hast surpris'd;
  Of that thine ivory front, my sorrow's map, 690
  Wherein I see no hav'n to rest my hope.
Bel. To love and fear, and both at once, my lord,
  In my conceit, are things of more import
  Than women's wits are to be busied with.
Bal. 'Tis I that love.
Bel.   Whom?
Bal.   Bellimperia.
Bel. But I that fear.
Bal.   Whom?
Bel.   Bellimperia.
Lor. Fear yourself?
Bel.   Ay, brother.
Lor.   How?
Bel.   As those
That, what they love, are loath and fear to lose.
Bal. Then, fair, let Balthazar your keeper be.
Bel. No, Balthazar doth fear as well as we: 700
  Et tremulo metui pavidum junxere timorem—
  Est vanum stolidae proditionis opus.
Lor. Nay, and you argue things so cunningly,
  We'll go continue this discourse at court.
Bal. Led by the loadstar of her heav'nly looks,
  Wends poor, oppressèd Balthazar,
  As o'er the mountains walks the wanderer,
  Incertain to effect his pilgrimage. [*Exeunt.*

SCENE XI

Enter two Portingals, *and* Hieronimo *meets them.*

1. By your leave, sir.
Hier. [*'Tis neither as you think, nor as you think,* 710
  Nor as you think; you're wide all:
  These slippers are not mine, they were my son Horatio's.
  My son! and what's a son? A thing begot
  Within a pair of minutes—thereabout;

A lump bred up in darkness, and doth serve
To ballace these light creatures we call women ;
And, at nine months' end, creeps forth to light.
What is there yet in a son,
To make a father dote, rave, or run mad ?
Being born, it pouts, cries, and breeds teeth. 720
What is there yet in a son ? He must be fed,
Be taught to go, and speak. Ay, or yet
Why might not a man love a calf as well ?
Or melt in passion o'er a frisking kid,
As for a son ? Methinks, a young bacon,
Or a fine little smooth horse colt,
Should move a man as much as doth a son :
For one of these, in very little time,
Will grow to some good use ; whereas a son,
The more he grows in stature and in years, 730
The more unsquar'd, unbevell'd, he appears,
Reckons his parents among the rank of fools,
Strikes care upon their heads with his mad riots ;
Makes them look old, before they meet with age.
This is a son !—And what a loss were this,
Consider'd truly ?——O, but my Horatio
Grew out of reach of these insatiate humours :
He lov'd his loving parents ;
He was my comfort, and his mother's joy,
The very arm that did hold up our house : 740
Our hopes were storèd up in him,
None but a damnèd murderer could hate him.
He had not seen the back of nineteen year,
When his strong arm unhors'd
The proud Prince Balthazar, and his great mind,
Too full of honour, took him to his mercy—
That valiant, but ignoble Portingal !
Well, heaven is heaven still !
And there is Nemesis, and Furies,
And things call'd whips, 750
And they sometimes do meet with murderers :
They do not always 'scape, that is some comfort.
Ay, ay, ay ; and then time steals on,
And steals, and steals, till violence leaps forth
Like thunder wrapped in a ball of fire,
And so doth bring confusion to them all.]

   Good leave have you: nay, I pray you go,
   For I'll leave you, if you can leave me so.
 2. Pray you, which is the next way to my lord the duke's?
Hier. The next way from me.
 1.   To his house, we mean. 760
Hier. O, hard by: 'tis yon house that you see.
 2. You could not tell us if his son were there?
Hier. Who, my Lord Lorenzo?
 1.   Ay, sir.
   [*He goeth in at one door and comes out at another.*
Hier.   O, forbear!
   For other talk for us far fitter were.
   But if you be importunate to know
   The way to him, and where to find him out,
   Then list to me, and I'll resolve your doubt.
   There is a path upon your left-hand side,
   That leadeth from a guilty conscience
   Unto a forest of distrust and fear— 770
   A darksome place, and dangerous to pass:
   There shall you meet with melancholy thoughts,
   Whose baleful humours if you but uphold,
   It will conduct you to Despair and Death—
   Whose rocky cliffs when you have once beheld,
   Within a hugy dale of lasting night,
   That, kindled with the world's iniquities,
   Doth cast up filthy and detested fumes—:
   Not far from thence, where murderers have built
   A habitation for their cursèd souls, 780
   There, in a brazen cauldron, fix'd by Jove,
   In his fell wrath, upon a sulphur flame,
   Yourselves shall find Lorenzo bathing him
   In boiling lead and blood of innocents.
 1. Ha, ha, ha!
Hier. Ha, ha, ha! Why, ha, ha, ha! Farewell, good ha, ha, ha!
               [*Exit.*
 2. Doubtless this man is passing lunatic,
   Or imperfection of his age doth make him dote.
   Come, let's away to seek my lord the duke. [*Exeunt.*

SCENE XII

Enter HIERONIMO, *with a poniard in one hand and a rope in the other.*

Hier. Now, sir, perhaps I come and see the king; 790
  The king sees me, and fain would hear my suit:
  Why, is not this a strange and seld-seen thing,
  That standers-by with toys should strike me mute?—
  Go to, I see their shifts, and say no more.——
  Hieronimo, 'tis time for thee to trudge:
  Down by the dale that flows with purple gore,
  Standeth a fiery tower: there sits a judge
  Upon a seat of steel and molten brass,
  And 'twixt his teeth he holds a fire-brand,
  That leads unto the lake where hell doth stand. 800
  Away, Hieronimo! to him be gone:
  He'll do thee justice for Horatio's death.
  Turn down this path: thou shalt be with him straight;
  Or this, and then thou need'st not take thy breath:
  This way or that way!——Soft and fair, not so:
  For if I hang or kill myself, let's know
  Who will revenge Horatio's murther then?
  No, no! fie, no! pardon me, I'll none of that.
      [*He flings away the dagger and halter.*
  This way I'll take, and this way comes the king:
      [*He takes them up again.*
  And here I'll have a fling at him, that's flat; 810
  And, Balthazar, I'll be with thee to bring,
  And thee, Lorenzo! Here's the king—nay, stay;
  And here, ay here—there goes the hare away.

Enter KING, Ambassador, CASTILE, *and* LORENZO.

King. Now show, ambassador, what our viceroy saith:
  Hath he receiv'd the articles we sent?
Hier. Justice, O, justice to Hieronimo.
Lor. Back! see'st thou not the king is busy?
Hier.   O, is he so?
King. Who is he that interrupts our business?
Hier. Not I. Hieronimo, beware! go by, go by!

Amb. Renownèd King, he hath receiv'd and read
     Thy kingly proffers, and thy promis'd league;
     And, as a man extremely over-joy'd
     To hear his son so princely entertain'd,
     Whose death he had so solemnly bewail'd,
     This for thy further satisfaction,
     And kingly love, he kindly lets thee know:
     First, for the marriage of his princely son
     With Bellimperia, thy belovèd niece,
     The news are more delightful to his soul,
     Than myrrh or incense to the offended heavens.
     In person, therefore, will he come himself,
     To see the marriage rites solemnisèd,
     And, in the presence of the court of Spain,
     To knit a sure inextricable band
     Of kingly love and everlasting league
     Betwixt the crowns of Spain and Portingal.
     There will he give his crown to Balthazar,
     And make a queen of Bellimperia.
King. Brother, how like you this our viceroy's love?
Cast. No doubt, my lord, it is an argument
     Of honourable care to keep his friend,
     And wondrous zeal to Balthazar his son;
     Nor am I least indebted to his grace,
     That bends his liking to my daughter thus.
Amb. Now last, dread lord, here hath his highness sent
     (Although he send not that his son return)
     His ransom due to Don Horatio.
Hier. Horatio! who calls Horatio?
King. And well remember'd: thank his majesty.
     Here, see it given to Horatio.
Hier. Justice, O, justice, justice, gentle king!
King. Who is that? Hieronimo?
Hier. Justice, O, justice! O my son, my son!
     My son, whom naught can ransom or redeem!
Lor. Hieronimo, you are not well-advis'd.
Hier. Away, Lorenzo, hinder me no more;
     For thou hast made me bankrupt of my bliss.
     Give me my son! you shall not ransom him!
     Away! I'll rip the bowels of the earth,
               [*He diggeth with his dagger.*
     And ferry over to th' Elysian plains,

  And bring my son to show his deadly wounds.
  Stand from about me!
  I'll make a pickaxe of my poniard,
  And here surrender up my marshalship;
  For I'll go marshal up the fiends in hell,
  To be avengèd on you all for this.
King. What means this outrage?
  Will none of you restrain his fury?
Hier. Nay, soft and fair! you shall not need to strive:
  For needs must he go that the devils drive.   870
              [*Exit.*

King. What accident hath happ'd Hieronimo?
  I have not seen him to demean him so.
Lor. My gracious lord, he is with extreme pride,
  Conceiv'd of young Horatio his son—
  And covetous of having to himself
  The ransom of the young prince Balthazar—
  Distract, and in a manner lunatic.
King. Believe me, nephew, we are sorry for't:
  This is the love that fathers bear their sons.
  But, gentle brother, go give to him this gold,   880
  The prince's ransom; let him have his due.
  For what he hath, Horatio shall not want;
  Haply Hieronimo hath need thereof.
Lor. But if he be thus helplessly distract,
  'Tis requisite his office be resign'd,
  And giv'n to one of more discretion.
King. We shall increase his melancholy so.
  'Tis best that we see further in it first,
  Till when ourself will hold exempt the place.
  And, brother, now bring in the ambassador,   890
  That he may be a witness of the match
  'Twixt Balthazar and Bellimperia,
  And that we may prefix a certain time,
  Wherein the marriage shall be solemnis'd,
  That we may have thy lord, the viceroy, here.
Amb. Therein your highness highly shall content
  His majesty, that longs to hear from hence.
King. On, then, and hear you, lord ambassador——   [*Exeunt.*

SCENE XIIa

Enter JAQUES and PEDRO.

Jaq. *I wonder, Pedro, why our master thus*
 At midnight sends us with our torches light,   900
 When man, and bird, and beast, are all at rest,
 Save those that watch for rape and bloody murder.
Ped. *O Jaques, know thou that our master's mind*
 Is much distraught, since his Horatio died,
 And—now his agèd years should sleep in rest,
 His heart in quiet—like a desp'rate man,
 Grows lunatic and childish for his son.
 Sometimes, as he doth at his table sit,
 He speaks as if Horatio stood by him;
 Then starting in a rage, falls on the earth,   910
 Cries out "Horatio, where is my Horatio?"
 So that with extreme grief and cutting sorrow
 There is not left in him one inch of man:
 See, where he comes.

Enter HIERONIMO.

Hier. *I pry through every crevice of each wall,*
 Look on each tree, and search through every brake,
 Beat at the bushes, stamp our grandam earth,
 Dive in the water, and stare up to heaven:
 Yet cannot I behold my son Horatio.—
 How now, who's there? spirits, spirits?   920
Ped. *We are your servants that attend you, sir.*
Hier. *What make you with your torches in the dark?*
Ped. *You bid us light them, and attend you here.*
Hier. *No, no, you are deceiv'd! not I;—you are deceiv'd!*
 Was I so mad to bid you light your torches now?
 Light me your torches at the mid of noon,
 When-as the sun-god rides in all his glory;
 Light me your torches then.
Ped.   *Then we burn daylight.*
Hier. *Let it be burnt; Night is a murd'rous slut,*
 That would not have her treasons to be seen;   930
 And yonder pale-fac'd Hecate there, the moon,

> *Doth give consent to that is done in darkness,*
> *And all those stars that gaze upon her face,*
> *Are aglets on her sleeve, pins on her train;*
> *And those that should be powerful and divine,*
> *Do sleep in darkness, when they most should shine.*

Ped. *Provoke them not, fair sir, with tempting words:*
> *The heav'ns are gracious, and your miseries*
> *And sorrow makes you speak, you know not what.*

Hier. *Villain, thou liest! and thou dost nought*   940
> *But tell me I am mad: thou liest, I am not mad!*
> *I know thee to be Pedro, and he Jaques.*
> *I'll prove it to thee; and were I mad, how could I?*
> *Where was she that same night,*
> *When my Horatio was murder'd?*
> *She should have shone: search thou the book.—Had the moon shone,*
> *In my boy's face there was a kind of grace,*
> *That I know—nay, I do know—had the murd'rer seen him,*
> *His weapon would have fall'n and cut the earth,*
> *Had he been fram'd of naught but blood and death.*   950
> *Alack! when mischief doth it knows not what,*
> *What shall we say to mischief?*

Enter ISABELLA.

Isab. *Dear Hieronimo, come in a-doors;*
> *O, seek not means so to increase thy sorrow.*

Hier. *Indeed, Isabella, we do nothing here;*
> *I do not cry: ask Pedro, and ask Jaques;*
> *Not I indeed; we are very merry, very merry.*

Isab. *How? be merry here, be merry here?*
> *Is not this the place, and this the very tree,*
> *Where my Horatio died, where he was murder'd?*   960

Hier. *Was—do not say what: let her weep it out.*
> *This was the tree; I set it of a kernel:*
> *And when our hot Spain could not let it grow,*
> *But that the infant and the human sap*
> *Began to wither, duly twice a morning*
> *Would I be sprinkling it with fountain-water.*
> *At last it grew and grew, and bore and bore,*
> *Till at the length*
> *It grew a gallows, and did bear our son:*

It bore thy fruit and mine—O wicked, wicked plant! 970
          [*One knocks within at the door.*
  See, who knock there.
Ped.   *It is a painter, sir.*
Hier. *Bid him come in, and paint some comfort,*
  For surely there's none lives but painted comfort.
  Let him come in!—One knows not what may chance:
  God's will that I should set this tree!—but even so
  Masters ungrateful servants rear from nought,
  And then they hate them that did bring them up.

             Enter the Painter.

Paint. *God bless you, sir.*
Hier.   *Wherefore? why, thou scornful villain?*
  How, where, or by what means should I be bless'd?
Isab. *What wouldst thou have, good fellow?*
Paint.   *Justice, madam.*   980
Hier. *O ambitious beggar!*
  Wouldst thou have that that lives not in the world?
  Why, all the undelved mines cannot buy
  An ounce of justice!
  'Tis a jewel so inestimable.   I tell thee,
  God hath engross'd all justice in his hands,
  And there is none but what comes from him.
Paint.   *O, then I see*
  That God must right me for my murder'd son.
Hier. *How, was thy son murder'd?*
Paint. *Ay, sir; no man did hold a son so dear.*   990
Hier. *What, not as thine? that's a lie,*
  As massy as the earth: I had a son,
  Whose least unvalu'd hair did weigh
  A thousand of thy sons: and he was murder'd.
Paint. *Alas, sir, I had no more but he.*
Hier. *Nor I, nor I: but this same one of mine*
  Was worth a legion.   But all is one.
  Pedro, Jaques, go in a-doors; Isabella, go,
  And this good fellow here and I
  Will range this hideous orchard up and down,   1000
  Like to two lions rear'd of their young.
  Go in a-doors, I say.
          [*Exeunt.   The painter and he sits down.*

> *Come, let's talk wisely now.*
> *Was thy son murder'd?*

Paint. *Ay, sir.*
Hier. *So was mine.*
> *How dost take it? art thou not sometimes mad?*
> *Is there no tricks that comes before thine eyes?*

Paint. *O Lord, yes, sir.*
Hier. *Art a painter? canst paint me a tear, or a wound, a groan, or a sigh? canst paint me such a tree as this?*
Paint. *Sir, I am sure you have heard of my painting: my name's Bazardo.* 1010
Hier. *Bazardo! afore God, an excellent fellow. Look you, sir, do you see, I'd have you paint me for my gallery, in your oil-colours matted, and draw me five years younger than I am—do ye see, sir, let five years go; let them go like the marshal of Spain—my wife Isabella standing by me, with a speaking look to my son Horatio, which should intend to this or some such-like purpose: "God bless thee, my sweet son;" and my hand leaning upon his head, thus, sir; do you see?—may it be done?*
Paint. *Very well, sir.* 1020
Hier. *Nay, I pray, mark me, sir: then, sir, would I have you paint me this tree, this very tree. Canst paint a doleful cry?*
Paint. *Seemingly, sir.*
Hier. *Nay, it should cry; but all is one. Well, sir, paint me a youth run through and through with villains' swords, hanging upon this tree. Canst thou draw a murderer?*
Paint. *I'll warrant you, sir; I have the pattern of the most notorious villains that ever lived in all Spain.*
Hier. *O, let them be worse, worse: stretch thine art, and let their beards be of Judas his own colour; and let their eye-brows jutty over: in any case observe that. Then, sir, after some violent noise, bring me forth in my shirt, and my gown under mine arm, with my torch in my hand, and my sword reared up thus:—and with these words:* 1034

> *"What noise is this? who calls Hieronimo?"*

> *May it be done?*

Paint. *Yea, sir.*
Hier. *Well, sir; then bring me forth, bring me through alley and alley, still with a distracted countenance going along, and let my hair heave up my night-cap. Let the clouds scowl, make*

the moon dark, the stars extinct, the winds blowing, the bells tolling, the owls shrieking, the toads croaking, the minutes jarring, and the clock striking twelve. And then at last, sir, starting, behold a man hanging, and tottering, as you know the wind will wave a man, and I with a trice to cut him down. And looking upon him by the advantage of my torch, find it to be my son Horatio. There you may show a passion, there you may show a passion! Draw me like old Priam of Troy, crying: " The house is a-fire, the house is a-fire, as the torch over my head! " Make me curse, make me rave, make me cry, make me mad, make me well again, make me curse hell, invocate heaven, and in the end leave me in a trance—and so forth. 1053

Paint. *And is this the end?*

Hier. *O no, there is no end: the end is death and madness! As I am never better than when I am mad: then methinks I am a brave fellow; then I do wonders: but reason abuseth me, and there's the torment, there's the hell. At the last, sir, bring me to one of the murderers; were he as strong as Hector, thus would I tear and drag him up and down.* 1060

> [He beats the painter in, then comes out again, with a book in his hand.

SCENE XIII

Enter HIERONIMO, *with a book in his hand.*

Vindicta mihi!
Ay, heav'n will be reveng'd of every ill;
Nor will they suffer murder unrepaid.
Then stay, Hieronimo, attend their will:
For mortal men may not appoint their time!—
" *Per scelus semper tutum est sceleribus iter.*"
Strike, and strike home, where wrong is offer'd thee;
For evils unto ills conductors be,
And death's the worst of resolution.
For he that thinks with patience to contend   1070
To quiet life, his life shall easily end.—
" *Fata si miseros juvant, habes salutem;
Fata si vitam negant, habes sepulchrum:* "
If destiny thy miseries do ease,

Then hast thou health, and happy shalt thou be;
If destiny deny thee life, Hieronimo,
Yet shalt thou be assurèd of a tomb—:
If neither, yet let this thy comfort be:
Heav'n cov'reth him that hath no burial.
And to conclude, I will revenge his death! 1080
But how? not as the vulgar wits of men,
With open, but inevitable ills,
As by a secret, yet a certain mean,
Which under kindship will be cloakèd best.
Wise men will take their opportunity
Closely and safely, fitting things to time.—
But in extremes advantage hath no time;
And therefore all times fit not for revenge.
Thus therefore will I rest me in unrest,
Dissembling quiet in unquietness, 1090
Not seeming that I know their villanies,
That my simplicity may make them think,
That ignorantly I will let all slip;
For ignorance, I wot, and well they know,
Remedium malorum iners est.
Nor ought avails it me to menace them
Who, as a wintry storm upon a plain,
Will bear me down with their nobility.
No, no, Hieronimo, thou must enjoin
Thine eyes to observation, and thy tongue 1100
To milder speeches than thy spirit affords,
Thy heart to patience, and thy hands to rest,
Thy cap to courtesy, and thy knee to bow,
Till to revenge thou know, when, where and how.
[*A noise within.*
How now, what noise? what coil is that you keep?

Enter a Servant.

Serv. Here are a sort of poor petitioners,
   That are importunate, and it shall please you, sir,
   That you should plead their cases to the king.
Hier. That I should plead their several actions?
   Why, let them enter, and let me see them.

Enter three Citizens *and an* Old Man.

1.   So,   1110
   I tell you this: for learning and for law,
   There is not any advocate in Spain
   That can prevail, or will take half the pain
   That he will, in pursuit of equity.
Hier. Come near, you men, that thus importune me.—
   [*Aside.*] Now must I bear a face of gravity;
   For thus I us'd, before my marshalship,
   To plead in causes as corregidor.—
   Come on, sirs, what's the matter?
2.   Sir, an action.
Hier. Of battery?
1.   Mine of debt.
Hier.   Give place.   1120
2. No, sir, mine is an action of the case.
3. Mine an *ejectione firmae* by a lease.
Hier. Content you, sirs; are you determinèd
   That I should plead your several actions?
1. Ay, sir, and here's my declaration.
2. And here's my band.
3.   And here's my lease.
                                   [*They give him papers.*
Hier. But wherefore stands yon silly man so mute,
   With mournful eyes and hands to heav'n uprear'd?
   Come hither, father, let me know thy cause.
Senex. O worthy sir, my cause, but slightly known,   1130
   May move the hearts of warlike Myrmidons,
   And melt the Corsic rocks with ruthful tears.
Hier. Say, father, tell me what's thy suit?
Senex.   No, sir, could my woes
   Give way unto my most distressful words,
   Then should I not in paper, as you see,
   With ink bewray what blood began in me.
Hier. What's here? "The humble supplication
   Of Don Bazulto for his murder'd son."
Senex. Ay, sir.
Hier.   No, sir, it was my murder'd son:
   O my son, my son, O my son Horatio!   1140
   But mine, or thine, Bazulto, be content.
   Here, take my handkercher, and wipe thine eyes,

Whiles wretched I in thy mishaps may see
The lively portrait of my dying self.
[He draweth out a bloody napkin.
O no, not this; Horatio, this was thine;
And when I dy'd it in thy dearest blood,
This was a token 'twixt thy soul and me,
That of thy death revengèd I should be.
But here, take this, and this—what, my purse?—
Ay, this, and that, and all of them are thine;   1150
For all as one are our extremities.
1. O, see the kindness of Hieronimo!
2. This gentleness shows him a gentleman.
Hier. See, see, O see thy shame, Hieronimo;
See here a loving father to his son!
Behold the sorrows and the sad laments,
That he deliv'reth for his son's decease!
If love's effects so strive in lesser things,
If love enforce such moods in meaner wits,
If love express such power in poor estates: 1160
Hieronimo, when as a raging sea,
Toss'd with the wind and tide, o'erturnest then
The upper billows course of waves to keep,
Whilst lesser waters labour in the deep:
Then sham'st thou not, Hieronimo, to neglect
The sweet revenge of thy Horatio?
Though on this earth justice will not be found,
I'll down to hell, and in this passion
Knock at the dismal gates of Pluto's court,
Getting by force, as once Alcides did,   1170
A troop of Furies and tormenting hags
To torture Don Lorenzo and the rest.
Yet lest the triple-headed porter should
Deny my passage to the slimy strand,
The Thracian poet thou shalt counterfeit:
Come on, old father, be my Orpheus,
And if thou canst no notes upon the harp,
Then sound the burden of thy sore heart's-grief,
Till we do gain that Proserpine may grant
Revenge on them that murderèd my son.   1180
Then will I rent and tear them, thus and thus,
Shiv'ring their limbs in pieces with my teeth.
[Tears the papers.

1. O sir, my declaration! [*Exit Hieronimo, and they after.*
2. Save my bond!

Enter HIERONIMO.

2. Save my bond!
3. Alas, my lease! it cost me ten pound,
   And you, my lord, have torn the same.
Hier. That cannot be, I gave it never a wound;
   Show me one drop of blood fall from the same:
   How is it possible I should slay it then?
   Tush, no; run after, catch me if you can.   1190
   [*Exeunt all but the Old Man. Bazulto remains till Hieronimo enters again, who, staring him in the face, speaks.*
Hier. And art thou come, Horatio, from the depth,
   To ask for justice in this upper earth,
   To tell thy father thou art unreveng'd,
   To wring more tears from Isabella's eyes,
   Whose lights are dimm'd with over-long laments?
   Go back, my son, complain to Aeacus,
   For here's no justice; gentle boy, be gone,
   For justice is exilèd from the earth:
   Hieronimo will bear thee company.
   Thy mother cries on righteous Rhadamanth   1200
   For just revenge against the murderers.
Senex. Alas, my lord, whence springs this troubled speech?
Hier. But let me look on my Horatio.
   Sweet boy, how art thou chang'd in death's black shade!
   Had Proserpine no pity on thy youth,
   But suffer'd thy fair crimson-colour'd spring
   With wither'd winter to be blasted thus?
   Horatio, thou art older than thy father:
   Ah, ruthless fate, that favour thus transforms!
Baz. Ay, my good lord, I am not your young son.   1210
Hier. What, not my son? thou then a Fury art,
   Sent from the empty kingdom of black night
   To summon me to make appearance
   Before grim Minos and just Rhadamanth,
   To plague Hieronimo that is remiss,
   And seeks not vengeance for Horatio's death.
Baz. I am a grievèd man, and not a ghost,
   That came for justice for my murder'd son.

Hier. Ay, now I know thee, now thou nam'st thy son:
    Thou art the lively image of my grief;   1220
    Within thy face, my sorrows I may see.
    Thy eyes are gumm'd with tears, they cheeks are wan,
    Thy forehead troubled, and thy mutt'ring lips
    Murmur sad words abruptly broken off;
    By force of windy sighs thy spirit breathes,
    And all this sorrow riseth for thy son:
    And selfsame sorrow feel I for my son.
    Come in, old man, thou shalt to Isabel;
    Lean on my arm: I thee, thou me, shalt stay,
    And thou, and I, and she will sing a song,   1230
    Three parts in one, but all of discords fram'd—:
    Talk not of chords, but let us now be gone,
    For with a cord Horatio was slain.   [*Exeunt.*

SCENE XIV

Enter KING OF SPAIN, *the* DUKE, VICEROY, *and* LORENZO,
    BALTHAZAR, DON PEDRO, *and* BELLIMPERIA.

King. Go, brother, 'tis the Duke of Castile's cause;
    Salute the Viceroy in our name.
Cast.   I go.
Vic. Go forth, Don Pedro, for thy nephew's sake,
    And greet the Duke of Castile.
Ped.   It shall be so.
King. And now to meet these Portuguese:
    For as we now are, so sometimes were these,
    Kings and commanders of the western Indies.   1240
    Welcome, brave Viceroy, to the court of Spain,
    And welcome all his honourable train!
    'Tis not unknown to us for why you come,
    Or have so kingly cross'd the seas:
    Sufficeth it, in this we note the troth
    And more than common love you lend to us.
    So is it that mine honourable niece
    (For it beseems us now that it be known)
    Already is betroth'd to Balthazar:
    And by appointment and our condescent   1250
    To-morrow are they to be marrièd.

>   To this intent we entertain thyself,
>   Thy followers, their pleasure, and our peace.
>   Speak, men of Portingal, shall it be so?
>   If ay, say so; if not, say flatly no.
> *Vic.* Renownèd King, I come not, as thou think'st,
>   With doubtful followers, unresolvèd men,
>   But such as have upon thine articles
>   Confirm'd thy motion, and contented me.
>   Know, sovereign, I come to solemnise   1260
>   The marriàge of thy belovèd niece,
>   Fair Bellimperia, with my Balthazar,
>   With thee, my son; whom sith I live to see,
>   Here take my crown, I give it her and thee;
>   And let me live a solitary life,
>   In ceaseless prayers,
>   To think how strangely heav'n hath thee preserv'd.
> *King.* See, brother, see, how nature strives in him!
>   Come, worthy Viceroy, and accompany
>   Thy friend with thine extremities: 1270
>   A place more private fits this princely mood.
> *Vic.* Or here, or where your highness thinks it good.
>   [*Exeunt all but Castile and Lorenzo.*

SCENE XV

Castile, Lorenzo.

Cast. Nay, stay, Lorenzo, let me talk with you.
    See'st thou this entertainment of these kings?
Lor. I do, my lord, and joy to see the same.
Cast. And know'st thou why this meeting is?
Lor. For her, my lord, whom Balthazar doth love,
    And to confirm their promis'd marriàge.
Cast. She is thy sister?
Lor.   Who, Bellimperia? ay,
    My gracious lord, and this is the day,   1280
    That I have long'd so happily to see.
Cast. Thou wouldst be loath that any fault of thine
    Should intercept her in her happiness?
Lor. Heav'ns will not let Lorenzo err so much.
Cast. Why then, Lorenzo, listen to my words:

> It is suspected, and reported too,
> That thou, Lorenzo, wrong'st Hieronimo,
> And in his suits towards his majesty
> Still keep'st him back, and seek'st to cross his suit.

Lor. That I, my lord——?

Cast. I tell thee, son, myself have heard it said,
> When (to my sorrow) I have been asham'd
> To answer for thee, though thou art my son.
> Lorenzo, know'st thou not the common love
> And kindness that Hieronimo hath won
> By his deserts within the court of Spain?
> Or see'st thou not the king my brother's care
> In his behalf, and to procure his health?
> Lorenzo, shouldst thou thwart his passions,
> And he exclaim against thee to the king,
> What honour were't in this assembly,
> Or what a scandal were 't among the kings
> To hear Hieronimo exclaim on thee?
> Tell me—and look thou tell me truly too—
> Whence grows the ground of this report in court?

Lor. My lord, it lies not in Lorenzo's power
> To stop the vulgar, liberal of their tongues:
> A small advantage makes a water-breach,
> And no man lives that long contenteth all.

Cast. Myself have seen thee busy to keep back
> Him and his supplications from the king.

Lor. Yourself, my lord, hath seen his passions,
> That ill beseem'd the presence of a king:
> And for I pitied him in his distress,
> I held him thence with kind and courteous words,
> As free from malice to Hieronimo
> As to my soul, my lord.

Cast. Hieronimo, my son, mistakes thee then.

Lor. My gracious father, believe me, so he doth.
> But what's a silly man, distract in mind
> To think upon the murder of his son?
> Alas! how easy is it for him to err!
> But for his satisfaction and the world's,
> 'Twere good, my lord, that Hieronimo and I
> Were reconcil'd, if he misconster me.

Cast. Lorenzo, thou hast said; it shall be so.
> Go one of you, and call Hieronimo.

Enter BALTHAZAR *and* BELLIMPERIA.

Bal. Come, Bellimperia, Balthazar's content,
    My sorrow's ease and sovereign of my bliss,
    Sith heaven hath ordain'd thee to be mine: 1330
    Disperse those clouds and melancholy looks,
    And clear them up with those thy sun-bright eyes,
    Wherein my hope and heaven's fair beauty lies.
Bel. My looks, my lord, are fitting for my love,
    Which, new-begun, can show no brighter yet.
Bal. New-kindled flames should burn as morning sun.
Bel. But not too fast, lest heat and all be done.
    I see my lord my father.
Bal.   Truce, my love;
    I'll go salute him.
Cast.   Welcome, Balthazar,
    Welcome, brave prince, the pledge of Castile's peace! 1340
    And welcome, Bellimperia!—How now, girl?
    Why com'st thou sadly to salute us thus?
    Content thyself, for I am satisfied:
    It is not now as when Andrea liv'd;
    We have forgotten and forgiven that,
    And thou art gracèd with a happier love.—
    But, Balthazar, here comes Hieronimo;
    I'll have a word with him.

Enter HIERONIMO *and a* Servant.

Hier. And where's the duke?
Serv.   Yonder.
Hier.   Ev'n so.—
    What new device have they devisèd, trow?   1350
    Pocas palabras! mild as the lamb!
    Is't I will be reveng'd? No, I am not the man.—
Cast. Welcome, Hieronimo.
Lor. Welcome, Hieronimo.
Bal. Welcome, Hieronimo.
Hier. My lords, I thank you for Horatio.
Cast. Hieronimo, the reason that I sent
    To speak with you, is this.
Hier.   What, so short?

Then I'll be gone, I thank you for 't.
Cast. Nay, stay, Hieronimo!—go call him, son.
Lor. Hieronimo, my father craves a word with you.
Hier. With me, sir? why, my lord, I thought you had done.
Lor. No; [*Aside*] would he had!
Cast. Hieronimo, I hear
You find yourself aggrievèd at my son,
Because you have not access unto the king;
And say 'tis he that intercepts your suits.
Hier. Why, is not this a miserable thing, my lord?
Cast. Hieronimo, I hope you have no cause,
And would be loath that one of your deserts
Should once have reason to suspect my son,
Consid'ring how I think of you myself.
Hier. Your son Lorenzo! whom, my noble lord?
The hope of Spain, mine honourable friend?
Grant me the combat of them, if they dare:
[*Draws out his sword.*
I'll meet him face to face, to tell me so!
These be the scandalous reports of such
As love not me, and hate my lord too much:
Should I suspect Lorenzo would prevent
Or cross my suit, that lov'd my son so well?
My lord, I am asham'd it should be said.
Lor. Hieronimo, I never gave you cause.
Hier. My good lord, I know you did not.
Cast. There then pause;
And for the satisfaction of the world,
Hieronimo, frequent my homely house,
The Duke of Castile, Cyprian's ancient seat;
And when thou wilt, use me, my son, and it:
But here, before Prince Balthazar and me,
Embrace each other, and be perfect friends.
Hier. Ay, marry, my lord, and shall.
Friends, quoth he? see, I'll be friends with you all:
Especially with you, my lovely lord;
For divers causes it is fit for us
That we be friends: the world's suspicious,
And men may think what we imagine not.
Bal. Why, this is friendly done, Hieronimo.
Lor. And that I hope: old grudges are forgot?
Hier. What else? it were a shame it should not be so.

Cast. Come on, Hieronimo, at my request;
  Let us entreat your company to-day. [*Exeunt.*
Hier. Your lordship's to command.—Pah! keep your way:
  Chi mi fa più carezze che non suole, 1401
  Tradito mi ha, o tradir mi voule.
  [*Exit.*

SCENE XVI

Enter Ghost *and* Revenge.

Ghost. Awake, Erichtho! Cerberus, awake!
  Solicit Pluto, gentle Proserpine!
  To combat, Acheron and Erebus!
  For ne'er, by Styx and Phlegethon in hell,
  O'er-ferried Charon to the fiery lakes
  Such fearful sights, as poor Andrea sees.
  Revenge, awake!
Revenge.   Awake? for why?
Ghost. Awake, Revenge; for thou art ill-advis'd 1410
  To sleep—awake! what, thou art warn'd to watch!
Revenge. Content thyself, and do not trouble me.
Ghost. Awake, Revenge, if love—as love hath had—
  Have yet the power or prevalence in hell!
  Hieronimo with Lorenzo is join'd in league,
  And intercepts our passage to revenge:
  Awake, Revenge, or we are woe-begone!
Revenge. Thus worldlings ground, what they have dream'd, upon.
  Content thyself, Andrea: though I sleep,
  Yet is my mood soliciting their souls. 1420
  Sufficeth thee that poor Hieronimo
  Cannot forget his son Horatio.
  Nor dies Revenge, although he sleep awhile;
  For in unquiet quietness is feign'd,
  And slumb'ring is a common worldly wile.—
  Behold, Andrea, for an instance, how
  Revenge hath slept, and then imagine thou,
  What 'tis to be subject to destiny.

Enter a Dumb-Show.

Ghost. Awake, Revenge; reveal this mystery.
Revenge. Lo! the two first the nuptial torches bore 1430

>   As brightly burning as the mid-day's sun;
>   But after them doth Hymen hie as fast,
>   Clothèd in sable and a saffron robe,
>   And blows them out, and quencheth them with blood,
>   As discontent that things continue so.
> *Ghost.* Sufficeth me; thy meaning's understood,
>   And thanks to thee and those infernal powers,
>   That will not tolerate a lover's woe.—
>   Rest thee, for I will sit to see the rest.
> *Revenge.* Then argue not, for thou hast thy request. 1440
> [*Exeunt.*

ACT IV

SCENE I

Enter BELLIMPERIA *and* HIERONIMO.

Bel. Is this the love thou bear'st Horatio?
    Is this the kindness that thou counterfeit'st?
    Are these the fruits of thine incessant tears?
    Hieronimo, are these thy passions,
    Thy protestations and thy deep laments,
    That thou wert wont to weary men withal?
    O unkind father! O deceitful world!
    With what excuses canst thou show thyself
    From this dishonour and the hate of men?
    Thus to neglect the loss and life of him 10
    Whom both my letters and thine own belief
    Assures thee to be causeless slaughterèd!
    Hieronimo, for shame, Hieronimo,
    Be not a history to after-times
    Of such ingratitude unto thy son:
    Unhappy mothers of such children then,
    But monstrous fathers to forget so soon
    The death of those, whom they with care and cost
    Have tender'd so, thus careless should be lost.
    Myself, a stranger in respect of thee, 20
    So lov'd his life, as still I wish their deaths.
    Nor shall his death be unreveng'd by me,
    Although I bear it out for fashion's sake:
    For here I swear, in sight of heav'n and earth,
    Shouldst thou neglect the love thou shouldst retain,
    And give it over, and devise no more,
    Myself should send their hateful souls to hell,
    That wrought his downfall with extremest death.

Hier. But may it be that Bellimperia
    Vows such revenge as she hath deign'd to say? 30
    Why, then I see that heav'n applies our drift,
    And all the saints do sit soliciting

For vengeance on those cursèd murtherers.
Madam, 'tis true, and now I find it so:
I found a letter, written in your name,
And in that letter, how Horatio died.
Pardon, O pardon, Bellimperia,
My fear and care in not believing it;
Nor think I thoughtless think upon a mean
To let his death be unreveng'd at full. 40
And here I vow—so you but give consent,
And will conceal my resolution—:
I will ere long determine of their deaths
That causeless thus have murderèd my son.
Bel. Hieronimo, I will consent, conceal,
And ought that may effect for thine avail,
Join with thee to revenge Horatio's death.
Hier. On, then; and whatsoever I devise,
Let me entreat you, grace my practices,
For why the plot's already in mine head. 50
Here they are.

Enter BALTHAZAR *and* LORENZO.

Bal. How now, Hieronimo?
What, courting Bellimperia?
Hier. Ay, my lord;
Such courting as (I promise you):
She hath my heart, but you, my lord, have hers.
Lor. But now, Hieronimo, or never,
We are to entreat your help.
Hier. My help?
Why, my good lords, assure yourselves of me;
For you have giv'n me cause—:
Ay, by my faith have you!
Bal. It pleased you,
At the entertainment of the ambassador, 60
To grace the king so much as with a show.
Now, were your study so well furnishèd,
As for the passing of the first night's sport
To entertain my father with the like,
Or any such-like pleasing motion,
Assure yourself, it would content them well.
Hier. Is this all?
Bal. Ay, this is all.

Hier. Why then, I'll fit you: say no more.
    When I was young, I gave my mind
    And plied myself to fruitless poetry;   70
    Which though it profit the professor naught,
    Yet is it passing pleasing to the world.
Lor. And how for that?
Hier.   Marry, my good lord, thus:
    (And yet, methinks, you are too quick with us)—:
    When in Toledo there I studièd,
    It was my chance to write a tragedy:
    See here, my lords—   [*He shows them a book.*
    Which, long forgot, I found this other day.
    Now would your lordships favour me so much
    As but to grace me with your acting it—   80
    I mean each one of you to play a part—
    Assure you it will prove most passing strange,
    And wondrous plausible to that assembly.
Bal. What, would you have us play a tragedy?
Hier. Why, Nero thought it no disparagement,
    And kings and emperors have ta'en delight
    To make experience of their wits in plays.
Lor. Nay, be not angry, good Hieronimo;
    The prince but ask'd a question.
Bal. In faith, Hieronimo, and you be in earnest,   90
    I'll make one.
Lor.   And I another.
Hier. Now, my good lord, could you entreat
    Your sister Bellimperia to make one?
    For what's a play without a woman in it.
Bel. Little entreaty shall serve me, Hieronimo;
    For I must needs be employèd in your play.
Hier. Why, this is well: I tell you, lordings,
    It was determinèd to have been acted,
    By gentlemen and scholars too,
    Such as could tell what to speak.
Bal.   And now   100
    It shall be play'd by princes and courtiers,
    Such as can tell how to speak:
    If, as it is our country manner,
    You will but let us know the argument.
Hier. That shall I roundly.   The chronicles of Spain
    Record this written of a knight of Rhodes:

> He was betroth'd, and wedded at the length,
> To one Perseda, an Italian dame,
> Whose beauty ravish'd all that her beheld,
> Especially the soul of Soliman,
> Who at the marriage was the chiefest guest.
> By sundry means sought Soliman to win
> Perseda's love, and could not gain the same.
> Then 'gan he break his passions to a friend,
> One of his bashaws, whom he held full dear;
> Her had this bashaw long solicited,
> And saw she was not otherwise to be won,
> But by her husband's death, this knight of Rhodes,
> Whom presently by treachery he slew.
> She, stirr'd with an exceeding hate therefore,
> As cause of this slew Soliman,
> And, to escape the bashaw's tyranny,
> Did stab herself: and this the tragedy.

Lor. O excellent!
Bel. But say, Hieronimo, what then became
  Of him that was the bashaw?
Hier.   Marry, thus:
> Mov'd with remorse of his misdeeds,
> Ran to a mountain-top, and hung himself.

Bal. But which of us is to perform that part?
Hier. O, that will I, my lords; make no doubt of it:
> I'll play the murderer, I warrant you;
> For I already have conceited that.

Bal. And what shall I?
Hier. Great Soliman, the Turkish emperor.
Lor. And I?
Hier.   Erastus, the knight of Rhodes.
Bel. And I?
Hier.   Perseda, chaste and resolute.—
> And here, my lords, are several abstracts drawn,
> For each of you to note your parts,
> And act it, as occasion's offer'd you.
> You must provide a Turkish cap,
> A black mustachio and a falchion;
>   [*Gives a paper to Balthazar.*
> You with a cross, like to a knight of Rhodes;
>   [*Gives another to Lorenzo.*

And, madam, you must attire yourself
  [He giveth Bellimperia another.
Like Phœbe, Flora, or the huntress,
Which to your discretion shall seem best.
And as for me, my lords, I'll look to one,
And, with the ransom that the viceroy sent,
So furnish and perform this tragedy,
As all the world shall say, Hieronimo
Was liberal in gracing of it so.   150
Bal. Hieronimo, methinks a comedy were better.
Hier. A comedy?
Fie! comedies are fit for common wits:
But to present a kingly troop withal,
Give me a stately-written tragedy;
Tragœdia cothurnata, fitting kings,
Containing matter, and not common things.
My lords, all this must be perform'd,
As fitting for the first night's revelling.
The Italian tragedians were so sharp of wit,   160
That in one hour's meditation
They would perform anything in action.
Lor. And well it may; for I have seen the like
In Paris 'mongst the French tragedians.
Hier. In Paris? mass! and well rememberèd!
There's one thing more that rests for us to do.
Bal. What's that, Hieronimo? forget not anything.
Hier. Each one of us
Must act his part in unknown languages,
That it may breed the more variety: 170
As you, my lord, in Latin, I in Greek,
You in Italian, and for because I know
That Bellimperia hath practised the French,
In courtly French shall all her phrases be.
Bel. You mean to try my cunning then, Hieronimo?
Bal. But this will be a mere confusion,
And hardly shall we all be understood.
Hier. It must be so; for the conclusion
Shall prove the invention and all was good:
And I myself in an oration,   180
And with a strange and wondrous show besides,
That I will have there behind a curtain,
Assure yourself, shall make the matter known:

  And all shall be concluded in one scene,
  For there's no pleasure ta'en in tediousness.
Bal. How like you this?
Lor.   Why, thus my lord:
  We must resolve to soothe his humours up.
Bal. On then, Hieronimo; farewell till soon.
Hier. You'll ply this gear?
Lor.   I warrant you.
        [*Exeunt all but Hieronimo.*
Hier.   Why so:
  Now shall I see the fall of Babylon,   190
  Wrought by the heav'ns in this confusion.
  And if the world like not this tragedy,
  Hard is the hap of old Hieronimo.   [*Exit.*

SCENE II.

Enter ISABELLA *with a weapon.*

Isab. Tell me no more!—O monstrous homicides!
  Since neither piety nor pity moves
  The king to justice or compassion,
  I will revenge myself upon this place,
  Where thus they murder'd my belovèd son.
        [*She cuts down the arbour.*
  Down with these branches and these loathsome boughs
  Of this unfortunate and fatal pine: 200
  Down with them, Isabella; rent them up,
  And burn the roots from whence the rest is sprung.
  I will not leave a root, a stalk, a tree,
  A bough, a branch, a blossom, nor a leaf,
  No, not an herb within this garden-plot—:
  Accursèd complot of my misery!
  Fruitless for ever may this garden be,
  Barren the earth, and blissless whosoe'er
  Imagines not to keep it unmanur'd!
  An eastern wind, commix'd with noisome airs,   210
  Shall blast the plants and the young saplings;
  The earth with serpents shall be pesterèd,
  And passengers, for fear to be infect,
  Shall stand aloof, and, looking at it, tell:

"There, murder'd, died the son of Isabel."
Ay, here he died, and here I him embrace:
See, where his ghost solicits, with his wounds,
Revenge on her that should revenge his death.
Hieronimo, make haste to see thy son;
For sorrow and despair hath cited me   220
To hear Horatio plead with Rhadamanth:
Make haste, Hieronimo, to hold excus'd
Thy negligence in pursuit of their deaths
Whose hateful wrath bereav'd him of his breath.—
Ah, nay, thou dost delay their deaths,
Forgiv'st the murd'rers of thy noble son,
And none but I bestir me—to no end!
And as I curse this tree from further fruit,
So shall my womb be cursèd for his sake;
And with this weapon will I wound the breast,   230
The hapless breast, that gave Horatio suck.
                              [*She stabs herself.*

SCENE III.

Enter HIERONIMO; *he knocks up the curtain.*
Enter the Duke *of* CASTILE.

Cast. How now, Hieronimo, where's your fellows,
  That you take all this pain?
Hier. O sir, it is for the author's credit,
  To look that all things may go well.
  But, good my lord, let me entreat your grace,
  To give the king the copy of the play:
  This is the argument of what we show.
Cast. I will, Hieronimo.
Hier.   One thing more, my good lord.
Cast. What's that?
Hier.   Let me entreat your grace   240
  That, when the train are pass'd into the gallery,
  You would vouchsafe to throw me down the key.
Cast. I will, Hieronimo.   [*Exit Castile.*
Hier.   What, are you ready, Balthazar?
  Bring a chair and a cushion for the king.

Enter BALTHAZAR, *with a chair.*

Well done, Balthazar! hang up the title:
Our scene is Rhodes;—what, is your beard on?
Bal. Half on; the other is in my hand.
Hier. Despatch for shame; are you so long?   [*Exit Balthazar.*
   Bethink thyself, Hieronimo,
   Recall thy wits, recount thy former wrongs   250
   Thou hast receiv'd by murder of thy son,
   And lastly—not least!—how Isabel,
   Once his mother and thy dearest wife,
   All woe-begone for him, hath slain herself.
   Behoves thee then, Hieronimo, to be reveng'd!
   The plot is laid of dire revenge:
   On, then, Hieronimo, pursue revenge;
   For nothing wants but acting of revenge!
                                      [*Exit Hieronimo.*

SCENE IV.

Enter SPANISH KING, VICEROY, *the* DUKE OF CASTILE,
and their train.

King. Now, Viceroy, shall we see the tragedy
   Of Soliman, the Turkish emperor,   260
   Perform'd—of pleasure—by your son the prince,
   My nephew Don Lorenzo, and my niece.
Vic. Who? Bellimperia?
King.   Ay, and Hieronimo, our marshal,
   At whose request they deign to do't themselves:
   These be our pastimes in the court of Spain.
   Here, brother, you shall be the bookkeeper:
   This is the argument of that they show.
                              [*He giveth him a book.*
   *Gentlemen, this play of Hieronimo, in sundry languages, was
   thought good to be set down in English more largely, for the
   easier understanding to every public reader.*

Enter BALTHAZAR, BELLIMPERIA, *and* HIERONIMO.

*Bal. Bashaw, that Rhodes is ours, yield heav'ns the honour,
   And holy Mahomet, our sacred prophet!*

> *And be thou grac'd with every excellence* 270
> *That Soliman can give, or thou desire.*
> *But thy desert in conquering Rhodes is less*
> *Than in reserving this fair Christian nymph,*
> *Perseda, blissful lamp of excellence,*
> *Whose eyes compel, like powerful adamant,*
> *The warlike heart of Soliman to wait.*

King. See, Viceroy, that is Balthazar, your son,
  That represents the emperor Soliman:
  How well he acts his amorous passion!
Vic. Ay, Bellimperia hath taught him that. 280
Cast. That's because his mind runs all on Bellimperia.
Hier. *Whatever joy earth yields, betide your majesty.*
Bal. *Earth yields no joy without Perseda's love.*
Hier. *Let then Perseda on your grace attend.*
Bal. *She shall not wait on me, but I on her :*
  Drawn by the influence of her lights, I yield.
  But let my friend, the Rhodian knight, come forth,
  Erasto, dearer than my life to me,
  That he may see Perseda, my belov'd.

Enter ERASTO.

King. Here comes Lorenzo: look upon the plot, 290
  And tell me, brother, what part plays he?
Bel. *Ah, my Erasto, welcome to Perseda.*
Lor. *Thrice happy is Erasto that thou liv'st ;*
  Rhodes' loss is nothing to Erasto's joy :
  Sith his Perseda lives, his life survives.
Bal. *Ah, bashaw, here is love between Erasto*
  And fair Perseda, sovereign of my soul.
Hier. *Remove Erasto, mighty Soliman,*
  And then Perseda will be quickly won.
Bal. *Erasto is my friend ; and while he lives,* 300
  Perseda never will remove her love.
Hier. *Let not Erasto live to grieve great Soliman.*
Bal. *Dear is Erasto in our princely eye.*
Hier. *But if he be your rival, let him die.*
Bal. *Why, let him die !—so love commandeth me.*
  Yet grieve I that Erasto should so die.
Hier. *Erasto, Soliman saluteth thee,*

SCENE IV. *The Spanish Tragedy* 265

  And lets thee wit by me his highness' will,
  Which is, thou shouldst be thus employ'd.   [*Stabs him.*
Bel.   *Ay me!*
  Erasto! see, Soliman, Erasto's slain!   310
Bal. *Yet liveth Soliman to comfort thee.*
  Fair queen of beauty, let not favour die,
  But with a gracious eye behold his grief,
  That with Perseda's beauty is increas'd,
  If by Perseda his grief be not releas'd.
Bel. *Tyrant, desist soliciting vain suits;*
  Relentless are mine ears to thy laments,
  As thy butcher is pitiless and base,
  Which seiz'd on my Erasto, harmless knight.
  Yet by thy power thou thinkest to command,   320
  And to thy power Perseda doth obey:
  But, were she able, thus she would revenge
  Thy treacheries on thee, ignoble prince: [*Stabs him.*
  And on herself she would be thus reveng'd.   [*Stabs herself.*
King. Well said!—Old marshal, this was bravely done!
Hier. But Bellimperia plays Perseda well!
Vic. Were this in earnest, Bellimperia,
  You would be better to my son than so.
King. But now what follows for Hieronimo?
Hier. Marry, this follows for Hieronimo: 330
  Here break we off our sundry languages,
  And thus conclude I in our vulgar tongue.
  Haply you think—but bootless are your thoughts—
  That this is fabulously counterfeit,
  And that we do as all tragedians do:
  To die to-day (for fashioning our scene)
  The death of Ajax or some Roman peer,
  And in a minute starting up again,
  Revive to please to-morrow's audience.
  No, princes; know I am Hieronimo,   340
  The hopeless father of a hapless son,
  Whose tongue is tun'd to tell his latest tale,
  Not to excuse gross errors in the play.
  I see, your looks urge instance of these words;
  Behold the reason urging me to this: [*Shows his dead son.*
  See here my show, look on this spectacle,
  Here lay my hope, and here my hope hath end;
  Here lay my heart, and here my heart was slain;

Here lay my treasure, here my treasure lost;
Here lay my bliss, and here my bliss bereft: 350
But hope, heart, treasure, joy, and bliss,
All fled, fail'd, died, yea, all decay'd with this.
From forth these wounds came breath that gave me life;
They murder'd me that made these fatal marks.
The cause was love, whence grew this mortal hate;
The hate: Lorenzo and young Balthazar;
The love: my son to Bellimperia.
But night, the cov'rer of accursèd crimes,
With pitchy silence hush'd these traitors' harms,
And lent them leave, for they had sorted leisure 360
To take advantage in my garden-plot
Upon my son, my dear Horatio:
There merciless they butcher'd up my boy,
In black, dark night, to pale, dim, cruel death.
He shrieks: I heard (and yet, methinks, I hear)
His dismal outcry echo in the air.
With soonest speed I hasted to the noise,
Where hanging on a tree I found my son,
Through-girt with wounds, and slaughter'd as you see.
And griev'd I, think you, at this spectacle? 370
Speak, Portuguese, whose loss resembles mine:
If thou canst weep upon thy Balthazar,
'Tis like I wail'd for my Horatio.
And you, my lord, whose reconcilèd son
March'd in a net, and thought himself unseen,
And rated me for brainsick lunacy,
With "God amend that mad Hieronimo!"—
How can you brook our play's catastrophe?
And here behold this bloody handkercher,
Which at Horatio's death I weeping dipp'd 380
Within the river of his bleeding wounds:
It as propitious, see, I have reserv'd,
And never hath it left my bloody heart,
Soliciting remembrance of my vow
With these, O, these accursèd murderers:
Which now perform'd my heart is satisfied.
And to this end the bashaw I became
That might revenge me on Lorenzo's life,
Who therefore was appointed to the part,
And was to represent the knight of Rhodes, 390

That I might kill him more conveniently.
So, Viceroy, was this Balthazar, thy son,
That Soliman which Bellimperia,
In person of Perseda, murderèd:
Solely appointed to that tragic part
That she might slay him that offended her.
Poor Bellimperia miss'd her part in this:
For though the story saith she should have died,
Yet I of kindness, and of care to her,
Did otherwise determine of her end;   400
But love of him whom they did hate too much
Did urge her resolution to be such.—
And, princes, now behold Hieronimo,
Author and actor in this tragedy,
Bearing his latest fortune in his fist;
And will as resolute conclude his part,
As any of the actors gone before.
And, gentles, thus I end my play;
Urge no more words: I have no more to say.
                                      [*He runs to hang himself.*
King. O hearken, Viceroy! Hold, Hieronimo!   410
    Brother, my nephew and thy son are slain!
Vic. We are betray'd; my Balthazar is slain!
    Break ope the doors; run, save Hieronimo.
                          [*They break in and hold Hieronimo.*
                          Hieronimo,
Do but inform the king of these events;
Upon mine honour, thou shalt have no harm.
Hier. Viceroy, I will not trust thee with my life,
    Which I this day have offer'd to my son.
    Accursèd wretch!
    Why stay'st thou him that was resolv'd to die?
King. Speak, traitor! damnèd, bloody murd'rer, speak!   420
    For now I have thee, I will make thee speak.
    Why hast thou done this undeserving deed?
Vic. Why hast thou murderèd my Balthazar?
Cast. Why hast thou butcher'd both my children thus?
Hier. [*But are you sure they are dead ?*
Cast.   *Ay, slave, too sure.*
Hier. *What, and yours too ?*
Vic. *Ay, all are dead ; not one of them survive.*
Hier. *Nay, then I care not ; come, and we shall be friends :*

> *Let us lay our heads together:*
> *See, here's a goodly noose will hold them all.* 430

Vic. *O damnèd devil, how secure he is!*

Hier. *Secure? why, dost thou wonder at it?*
> *I tell thee, Viceroy, this day I have seen revenge,*
> *And in that sight am grown a prouder monarch,*
> *Than ever sat under the crown of Spain.*
> *Had I as many lives as there be stars,*
> *As many heav'ns to go to, as those lives,*
> *I'd give them all, ay, and my soul to boot,*
> *But I would see thee ride in this red pool.*]
> O, good words! 440
> As dear to me was my Horatio,
> As yours, or yours, or yours, my lord, to you.
> My guiltless son was by Lorenzo slain,
> And by Lorenzo and that Balthazar
> Am I at last revengèd thoroughly,
> Upon whose souls may heav'ns be yet aveng'd
> With greater far than these afflictions.

Cast. But who were thy confederates in this?

Vic. That was thy daughter Bellimperia;
> For by her hand my Balthazar was slain: 450
> I saw her stab him.

King.   Why speak'st thou not?[1]

---

[1] Instead of ll. 451 (second half: "Why speak'st thou not") to 462, the Qq. from 1602 onwards have the following passage (they have also put ll. 448-451, first half, before l. 440):

[Hier.] *Methinks, since I grew inward with revenge,*
> *I cannot look with scorn enough on death.*

King. *What, dost thou mock us, slave? bring tortures forth.*

Hier. *Do, do, do: and meantime I'll torture you.*
> *You had a son, as I take it; and your son*
> *Should ha' been married to your daughter:*
> *Ha, was it not so?—You had a son too,*
> *He was my liege's nephew; he was proud*
> *And politic; had he liv'd, he might have come*
> *To wear the crown of Spain (I think 'twas so)—:*
> *'Twas I that kill'd him; look you, this same hand,*
> *'Twas it that stabb'd his heart—do ye see this hand?*
> *For one Horatio, if you ever knew him: a youth,*
> *One that they hang'd up in his father's garden;*
> *One that did force your valiant son to yield,*
> *While your more valiant son did take him prisoner.*

Vic. *Be deaf, my senses; I can hear no more.*

King. *Fall, heav'n, and cover us with thy sad ruins.*

Cast. *Roll all the world within thy pitchy cloud.*

Hier. *Now do I applaud what I have acted.*
> *Nunc iners cadat manus!*
> *Now to express the rapture of my part—*

Hier. What lesser liberty can kings afford
  Than harmless silence? then afford it me.
  Sufficeth, I may not, nor I will not tell thee.
King. Fetch forth the tortures: traitor as thou art,
  I'll make thee tell.
Hier.   Indeed,
  Thou may'st torment me, as his wretched son
  Hath done in murd'ring my Horatio:
  But never shalt thou force me to reveal
  The thing which I have vow'd inviolate.   460
  And therefore, in despite of all thy threats,
  Pleas'd with their deaths, and eas'd with their revenge,
  First take my tongue, and afterwards my heart.

      [*He bites out his tongue.*

King. O monstrous resolution of a wretch!
  See, Viceroy, he hath bitten forth his tongue,
  Rather than to reveal what we requir'd.
Cast. Yet can he write.
King. And if in this he satisfy us not,
  We will devise th' extremest kind of death
  That ever was invented for a wretch.   470

      [*Then he makes signs for a knife to mend his pen.*

Cast. O, he would have a knife to mend his pen.
Vic. Here, and advise thee that thou write the troth.—
  Look to my brother! save Hieronimo!

      [*He with a knife stabs the duke and himself.*

King. What age hath ever heard such monstrous deeds?
  My brother, and the whole succeeding hope
  That Spain expected after my decease!—
  Go, bear his body hence, that we may mourn
  The loss of our belovèd brother's death—:
  That he may be entomb'd!—Whate'er befall,
  I am the next, the nearest, last of all.   480
Vic. And thou, Don Pedro, do the like for us:
  Take up our hapless son, untimely slain;
  Set me with him, and he with woeful me,
  Upon the main-mast of a ship unmann'd,
  And let the wind and tide haul me along
  To Scylla's barking and untamèd gulf,
  Or to the loathsome pool of Acheron,

To weep my want for my sweet Balthazar:
Spain hath no refuge for a Portingal.

[*The trumpets sound a dead march; the King of Spain mourning after his brother's body, and the King of Portingal bearing the body of his son.*

SCENE V.

Enter Ghost *and* Revenge.

Ghost. Ay, now my hopes have end in their effects, 490
When blood and sorrow finish my desires:
Horatio murder'd in his father's bower;
Vild Serberine by Pedringano slain;
False Pedringano hang'd by quaint device;
Fair Isabella by herself misdone;
Prince Balthazar by Bellimperia stabb'd;
The Duke of Castile and his wicked son
Both done to death by old Hieronimo;
My Bellimperia fall'n, as Dido fell,
And good Hieronimo slain by himself: 500
Ay, these were spectacles to please my soul!—
Now will I beg at lovely Proserpine
That, by the virtue of her princely doom,
I may consort my friends in pleasing sort,
And on my foes work just and sharp revenge.
I'll lead my friend Horatio through those fields,
Where never-dying wars are still inur'd;
I'll lead fair Isabella to that train,
Where pity weeps, but never feeleth pain;
I'll lead my Bellimperia to those joys, 510
That vestal virgins and fair queens possess;
I'll lead Hieronimo where Orpheus plays,
Adding sweet pleasure to eternal days.
But say, Revenge—for thou must help, or none—
Against the rest how shall my hate be shown?
Rev. This hand shall hale them down to deepest hell,
Where none but Furies, bugs and tortures dwell.
Ghost. Then, sweet Revenge, do this at my request:
Let me be judge, and doom them to unrest.
Let loose poor Tityus from the vulture's gripe, 520

  And let Don Cyprian supply his room;
  Place Don Lorenzo on Ixion's wheel,
  And let the lover's endless pains surcease
  (Juno forgets old wrath, and grants him ease);
  Hang Balthazar about Chimæra's neck,
  And let him there bewail his bloody love,
  Repining at our joys that are above;
  Let Serberine go roll the fatal stone,
  And take from Sisyphus his endless moan;
  False Pedringano, for his treachery,   530
  Let him be dragg'd through boiling Acheron,
  And there live, dying still in endless flames,
  Blasheming gods and all their holy names.
Rev. Then haste we down to meet thy friends and foes:
  To place thy friends in ease, the rest in woes;
  For here though death hath end their misery,
  I'll there begin their endless tragedy.   [*Exeunt.*

CAMBYSES, KING OF PERSIA

THE DIVISION OF THE PARTS

COUNSEL
HUF
PRAXASPES
MURDER
LOB
THE THIRD LORD
} *For one Man.*

LORD
RUF
COMMONS' CRY
COMMONS' COMPLAINT
LORD SMERDIS
VENUS
} *For one Man.*

KNIGHT
SNUF
SMALL HABILITY
PROOF
EXECUTION
ATTENDANCE
SECOND LORD
} *For one Man.*

CAMBYSES
EPILOGUE
} *For one Man.*

PROLOGUE
SISAMNES
DILIGENCE
CRUELTY
HOB
PREPARATION
THE FIRST LORD
} *For one Man.*

AMBIDEXTER
TRIAL
} *For one Man.*

MERETRIX
SHAME
OTIAN
MOTHER
LADY
QUEEN
} *For one Man.*

YOUNG CHILD
CUPID
} *For one Man.*

PROLOGUE

The PROLOGUE *entreth.*

Agathon, he whose counsel wise to prince's weal extended,
By good advice unto a prince three things he hath commended
First is that he hath government and ruleth over men;
Secondly, to rule with laws, eke justice, saith he, then;
Thirdly, that he must well conceive he may not always reign.
Lo, thus the rule unto a prince Agathon squarèd plain.
Tully the wise, whose sapience in volumes great doth tell,
Who in wisdom in that time did many men excel,
"A prince," saith he, "is of himself a plain and speaking law.
The law, a schoolmaster divine,"—this by his rule I draw.   10
The sage and witty Seneca his words thereto did frame:
"The honest exercise of kings, men will ensue the same.
But contrariwise if that a king abuse his kingly seat,
His ignomy and bitter shame in fine shall be more great."
In Persia there reigned a king, who Cyrus hight by name,
Who did deserve, as I do read, the lasting blast of fame.
But he, when Sisters Three had wrought to shear his vital thread,
As heir due to take the crown, Cambyses did proceed.
He in his youth was trainèd up, by trace of virtue's lore;
Yet (being king) did clean forget his perfect race before.   20
Then cleaving more unto his will, such vice did imitate
As one of Icarus his kind: forewarning then did hate,
Thinking that none could him dismay, ne none his fact could see;
Yet at the last a fall he took, like Icarus to be:
Else, as the fish, which oft had take the pleasant bait from hook,
In safe did spring and pierce the streams when fisher fast did look,
To hoist up from the watery waves unto the drièd land,
Then 'scaped, at last by subtle bait come to the fisher's hand;
Even so this King Cambyses here, when he had wrought his will,
Taking delight the innocent his guiltless blood to spill.   30

Then mighty Jove would not permit to prosecute offence,
But what measure the king did mete, the same did Jove commence,
To bring to end with shame his race, two years he did not reign.
His cruelty we will dilate, and make the matter plain.
Craving that this may suffice now your patience to win—
I take my way.   Behold, I see the players coming in.

FINIS

CAMBYSES, KING OF PERSIA

First enter CAMBYSES, *the king*, KNIGHT, *and* COUNSELLOR.

Camb. My Counsel grave and sapient with lords of legal train,
   Attentive ears towards me bend, and mark what shall be sain.
   So you likewise, my valiant knight, whose manly acts doth fly
   By bruit of Fame, that sounding trump doth pierce the azure sky.
   My sapient words I say perpend, and so your skill dilate.
   You know that Mors vanquishèd hath Cyrus, that king of state:
   And I, by due inheritance possess that princely crown,
   Ruling by sword of mighty force in place of great renown.
   You know, and often have heard tell my father's worthy facts,
   A manly Mars's heart he bare appearing by his acts. 10
   And what? shall I to ground let fall my father's golden praise?
   No! no! I mean for to attempt this same more large to raise.
   In that that I, his son, succeed his kingly seat as due,
   Extend your counsel unto me in that I ask of you.
   I am the king of Persia, a large and fertile soil,
   The Egyptians against us repugn, as varlets slave and vile;
   Therefore I mean with Mars's heart, with wars them to frequent;
   Them to subdue as captives mine. This is my heart's intent.
   So shall I win honour's delight, and praise of me shall go.
   My Counsel speak, and, lordings eke:—is it not best do so? 20
Couns. O puissant king, your blissful words deserves abundant praise,
   That you in this do go about your father's fame to raise.

Oh blissful day, that king so young such profit should
  conceive,
His father's praise and his to win, from those that would
  deceive.
Sure, my true and sovereign king, I fall before you prest,
Answer to give as duty mine, in that your Grace request.
If that your heart addicted be, the Egyptians to convince,
Through Mars's aid the conquest won, then deed of happy
  prince
Shall pierce the skies unto the throne of the supernal seat,
And merit there a just reward, of Jupiter the Great.   30
But then your Grace must not turn back from this pre-
  tenced will,
For to proceed in virtuous life, employ endeavour still.
Extinguish vice, and in that cup to drink have no delight.
To martial feats and kingly sport fix all your whole delight.

King. My Counsel grave, a thousand thanks with heart I do you
  render,
That you my case so prosperous entirely do tender!
I will not swerve from those your steps whereto you would
  me train.
But now, my lord and valiant knight, with words give
  answer plain.
Are you content with me to go, the Mars's games to try?

Lord. Yea, peerless prince, to aid your Grace, myself will live
  and die.   40

Knight. And I, for my hability, for fear will not turn back,
But as the ship against the rocks sustain and bide the wrack.

King. O willing hearts, a thousand thanks I render unto you.
Strike up your drums with courage great, we will march
  forth even now!

Couns. Permit, O king, few words to hear, my duty serves no
  less.
Therefore give leave to Counsel thine, his mind for to express.

King. Speak on my Counsel what it be, you shall have favour
  mine.

Couns. Then will I speak unto your Grace, as duty doth me bind.
Your Grace doth mean for to attempt of war the manly art.
Your Grace therein may hap receive with others for your
  part   50

> The dint of death—in those affairs, all persons are alike.
> The heart courageous oftentimes his detriment doth seek.
> It's best therefore to permit a ruler of your land
> To sit and judge with equity when things of right are scanned

King. My Grace doth yield to this your talk; to be thus now it shall.
> My knight, therefore prepare yourself, Sisamnes for to call.
> A judge he is of prudent skill, even he shall bear the sway
> In absence mine, when from the land I do depart my way.

Knight. Your knight before your Grace even here, himself hath, ready prest
> With willing heart for to fulfil as your Grace made request.
> *[Exit.* 60

Couns. Pleaseth your Grace, I judge of him to be a man right fit,
> For he is learned in the Law, having the gift of wit.
> In your Grace's precinct I do not view for it a meeter man.
> His learning is of good effect, bring proof thereof I can.
> I do not know what is his life, his conscience hid from me;
> I doubt not but the fear of God before his eyes to be.

Lord. Report declares he is a man that to himself is nigh,
> One that favoureth much the world and sets too much thereby.
> But this I say of certainty: if he your Grace succeed
> In your absence but for a while, he will be warned indeed 70
> No injustice for to frequent, no partial judge to prove,
> But rule all things with equity, to win your Grace's love.

King. Of that he shall a warning have, my hests for to obey;
> Great punishment for his offence against him will I lay.

Enter SISAMNES.

Couns. Behold, I see him now aggress and enter into place.
Sisam. O puissant prince and mighty king, the gods preserve your Grace!
> Your Grace's message came to me, your will purporting forth;
> With grateful mind I it received, according to mine oath,
> Erecting then myself with speed, before your Grace's eyes,
> The tenor of your princely will, from you for to agnise. 80

King. Sisamnes, this the whole effect the which for you I sent:
> Our mind it is to elevate you to great preferment.

> My Grace and gracious Counsel eke hath chose you for this cause.
> In judgment you do office bear, which have the skill in laws.
> We think that you accordingly by justice rule will deal,
> That for offence none shall have cause, of wrong you to appeal.

Sisam. Abundant thanks unto your Grace for this benignity,
> To you, his Counsel, in like case, with lords of clemency.
> Whatso your Grace to me permits, if I therein offend:
> Such execution then commence, and use it to this end, 90
> That all other, by that my deed, example so may take.
> To admonish them to flee the same by fear it may them make.

King. Then according to your words, if you therein offend,
> I assure you even from my breast correction shall extend.
> From Persia I mean to go into the Egypt land:
> Them to convince by force of arms, and win the upper hand.
> While I therefore absent shall be, I do you full permit,
> As governor in this my right, in that estate to sit;
> For to detect, and eke correct, those that abuse my grace.
> This is the total of my will. Give answers in this case! 100

Sisam. Unworthy much, O prince, am I, and for this gift unfit
> But sith that it hath pleased your Grace, that I in it must sit
> I do avouch unto my death, according to my skill,
> With equity for to observe your Grace's mind and will,
> And nought from it to swerve indeed, but sincerely to stay
> Else let me taste the penalty, as I before did say.

King. Well, then, of this authority I give you full possession.

Sisam. And I will it fulfil also, as I have made profession.

King. My Counsel then let us depart, a small stay [for][1] to make;
> To Egypt land now forth with speed my voyage will I take. 110
> Strike up your drums us to rejoice, to hear the warlike sound.
> Stay you here, Sisamnes, judge, and look well to your bound.

> > [*Exeunt* KING, LORD, *and* COUNSEL.

Sisam. Even now the king hath me extolled and set me up aloft.
> Now may I wear the broidered guard and lie in down-bed soft;

---

[1] Supplied by Manly.

Now may I purchase house and land, and have all at my will;
Now may I build a princely place, my mind for to fulfil;
Now may I abrogate the law, as I shall think it good;
If any one me now offend, I may demand his blood.
According to the proverb old, my mouth I will up-make.
Now it doth lie all in my hand to leave or else to take, 120
To deal with justice to my bound, and so to live in hope.
But oftentimes the birds be gone, while one for nest doth
    grope.
Do well or ill, I dare avouch some evil on me will speak:
No, truly yet I do not mean the king's precepts to break;
To place I mean for to return my duty to fulfil.   [*Exit.*

Enter the VICE [AMBIDEXTER], *with an old capcase on his head, an old pail about his hips for harness, a scummer and a potlid by his side, and a rake on his shoulder.*

Amb.   Stand away, stand away, for the passion of God!
    Harnessed I am, prepared to the field.
      I would have been content at home to have bod,
But I am sent forth with my spear and shield.
    I am appointed to fight against a snail,   130
And Wilken Wren the ancient shall bear:
      I doubt not but against him to prevail,
To be a man my deeds shall declare.
    If I overcome him, then a butterfly takes his part,
His weapon must be a blue-specked hen:
      But you shall see me overthrow him with a fart.
So, without conquest, he shall go home again!
    If I overcome him, I must fight with a fly,
And a black-pudding the fly's weapon must be.
    At the first blow on the ground he shall lie,   140
I will be sure to thrust him through the mouth to the knee,
    To conquest these fellows the man I will play!
Ha, ha, ha! now ye will make me to smile.

    .   .   .   .   .   .[1]

To see if I can all men beguile.
    Ha! my name? My name would you so fain know?

---

[1] A line missing, as Hawkins pointed out.

Yea, iwis, shall ye, and that with all speed:
 I have forgot it, therefore I cannot show.
Ha! ha! now I have it, I have it, indeed.
 My name is Ambidexter: I signify one 150
That with both hands finely can play;
 Now with King Cambyses, and by and by gone,
Thus do I run this way and that way.
 For, while I mean with a soldier to be,
Then give I a leap to Sisamnes the judge,—
 I dare avouch you shall his destruction see!
To all kind of estates I mean for to trudge.
 Ambidexter? Nay, he is a fellow, if ye knew all!
Cease for a while; hereafter hear more ye shall.

Enter three ruffians, HUF, RUF, *and* SNUF, *singing.*

Huf. Gog's flesh and his wounds, these wars rejoice my heart! 160
 By his wounds, I hope to do well, for my part.
By Gog's heart, the world shall go hard if I do not shift:
 At some old carle's budget I mean for to lift.

Ruf. By His flesh, nose, eyes, and ears,
 I will venture void of all cares.
He is not a soldier that doth fear any doubt,
 If that he would bring his purpose about.

Snuf. Fear that fear list, it shall not be I.
 By Gog's wounds, I will make some neck stand awray.
If I lose my share, I swear by Gog's heart, 170
 Then let another take up my part.

Huf. Yet I hope to come the richest soldier away.

Ruf. If a man ask ye, ye may hap to say nay.

Snuf. Let all men get what they can, not to leese, I hope;
 Wheresoever I go, in each corner I will grope.

Amb. What and ye run in the corner of some pretty maid?

Snuf. To grope there, good fellow, I will not be afraid.

Huf. Gog's wounds, what art thou that with us dost mell?
 Thou seemest to be a soldier, the truth to tell;
Thou seemest to be harnessed, I cannot tell how. 180
 I think he came lately from riding some cow:
Such a deformed slave did I never see.
 Ruf, dost thou know him? I pray thee tell me.

Cambyses, King of Persia

Ruf. No, by my troth, fellow Huf, I never see him before.
Snuf. As for me, I care not if I never see him more.
　　Come, let us run his arse against the post!
Amb. Ah, ye slaves, I will be with you at host!
　　Ah, ye knaves, I will teach ye how ye shall me deride!

　　　　　　　　　　　[*Here let him swinge them about.*

　　Out of my sight! I can ye not abide!
　　Now, goodman pouchmouth, I am a slave with you?　190
　　Now have at ye afresh again even now.
　　Mine arse against the post you will run?
　　But I will make you from that saying to turn.
Huf. I beseech ye heartily to be content.
Ruf. I ensure you, by mine honesty, no hurt we meant.
　　Beside that, again, we do not know what ye are:
　　Ye know that soldiers their stoutness will declare,—
　　Therefore if we have anything offended,
　　Pardon our rudeness and it shall be amended.
Amb. Yea, God's pity, begin ye to entreat me?　200
　　Have at ye once again! by the mass, I will beat ye.

　　　　　　　　　　　　　　　[*Fight again.*

Huf. Gog's heart, let us kill him! Suffer no longer!

　　　　　　　　　　　　　　　[*Draw their swords.*

Snuf. Thou slave, we will see if thou be the stronger.
Ruf. Strike off his head at one blow!
　　That we be soldiers, Gog's heart, let him know!
Amb. Oh the passion of God, I have done, by mine honesty!
　　I will take your part hereafter, verily.
All. Then come, let us agree.
Amb. Shake hands with me, I shake hands with thee.
　　Ye are full of courtesy, that is the best.　210
　　And you take great pain, ye are a mannerly guest.
　　Why, masters, do you not know me? the truth to me tell.
All. No, trust us; not very well.
Amb. Why, I am Ambidexter, whom many soldiers do love.
Huf. Gog's heart, to have thy company needs we must prove.
　　We must play with both hands, with our hostess and host,

Play with both hands, and score on the post,
Now and then, with our captain, for many a delay,
We will not stick with both hands to play.

Amb. The honester man, ye may me trust! 220

Enter MERETRIX, *with a staff on her shoulder.*

Mer. What? is there no lads here that hath a lust
To have a passing trull to help at their need?
Huf. Gog's heart, she is come indeed!
What, Mistress Meretrix, by his wounds, welcome to me.
Mer. What will ye give me? I pray you, let me see.
Ruf. By his heart, she looks for gifts by and by!
Mer. What? Master Ruf? I cry you mercy.
The last time I was with you, I got a broken head:
And lay in the street all night for want of a bed.
Snuf. Gog's wounds, kiss me, my trull so white. 230
In thee, I swear, is all my delight.
If thou shouldst have had a broken head for my sake,
I would have made his head to ache!
Mer. What? Master Ambidexter? Who looked for you?
Amb. Mistress Meretrix, I thought not to see you here now.
There is no remedy,—at meeting I must have a kiss.
Mer. What! man! I will not stick for that, by Gis!

[*Kiss.*

Amb. So now, gramercy, I pray thee be gone.
Mer. Nay, soft, my friend, I mean to have one.
Nay, soft! I swear, and if ye were my brother, 240
Before I let go, I will have another.

[*Kiss, kiss, kiss.*

Ruf. Gog's heart, the whore would not kiss me yet.
Mer. If I be a whore, thou art a knave, then it is quit!
Huf. But hear'st thou, Meretrix? With who this night wilt thou lie?
Mer. With him that giveth the most money.
Huf. Gog's heart, I have no money in purse, ne yet in clout!
Mer. Then get thee hence and pack, like a lout!
Huf. Adieu, like a whore! [*Exit* HUF.

Mer.   Farewell, like a knave![1]

Ruf. Gog's nails, Mistress Meretrix, now he is gone,
    A match ye shall make straight with me: 250
    I will give thee sixpence to lie one night with thee.

Mer. Gog's heart, slave, dost think I am a sixpenny jug?
    No, wis ye, Jack, I look a little more smug.

Snuf. I will give her eightpence to serve me first.

Mer. Gramercy, Snuf, thou art not the worst.

Ruf. By Gog's heart, she were better be hanged, to forsake me
    and take thee!

Snuf. Were she so? that shall we see!

Ruf. By Gog's heart, my dagger into her I will thrust!

Snuf. Ah, ye boy, ye would do it and ye durst!

Amb. Peace, my masters; ye shall not fight.   260
    He that draws first, I will him smite.

Ruf. Gog's wounds, Master Snuf, are ye so lusty?

Snuf. Gog's sides, Master Ruf, are ye so crusty?

Ruf. You may happen to see!

Snuf. Do what thou darest to me!

> [*Here draw and fight. Here she must lay on and coil
> them both; the* VICE *must run his way for fear;*
> SNUF *fling down his sword and buckler and run
> his way.*]

Mer. Gog's sides, knaves! seeing to fight ye be so rough,
    Defend yourselves, for I will give ye both enough.
    I will teach ye how ye shall fall out for me!
    Yea, thou slave, Snuf! no more blows wilt thou bide?
    To take thy heels a time hast thou spied?   270
    Thou villain, seeing Snuf has gone away,
    A little better I mean thee to pay!

> [*He falleth down; she falleth upon him, and beats him,
> and taketh away his weapon.*]

Ruf. Alas, good Mistress Meretrix, no more!
    My legs, sides and arms with beating be sore

Mer. Thou a soldier, and lose thy weapon!
    Go hence, sir boy. Say a woman hath thee beaten!

---

[1] The rhyme seems to demand some such word as "whoreson."

Ruf. Good Mistress Meretrix, let me my weapon have;
    Take pity on me, mine honesty to save!
    If it be known this repulse I sustain,
    It will redound to my ignomy and shame.   280

Mer. If thou wilt be my man, and wait upon me,
    This sword and buckler I will give thee.

Ruf. I will do all at your commandment;
    As servant to you I will be obedient.

Mer. Then let me see how before me you can go.
    When I speak to you, you shall do so.
    Off with your cap at place and at board,
    "Forsooth, Mistress Meretrix," at every word.
    Tut! tut! in the camp such soldiers there be:
    One good woman would beat away two or three.   290
    Well, I am sure customers tarry at home:
    Mannerly before, and let us be gone.   [*Exeunt.*

Enter AMBIDEXTER.

Amb. Oh the passion of God, be they here still or no?
    I durst not abide to see her beat them so!
    I may say to you I was in such a flight,[1]
    Body of me, I see the hair of my head stand upright
    When I saw her so hard upon them lay on,
    Oh the passion of God, thought I, she will be with me anon!
    I made no more ado, but avoided the thrust,
    And to my legs began for to trust;   300
    And fell a-laughing to myself, when I was once gone.
    'It is wisdom', quoth I, 'by the mass, to save one.'
    Then into this place I intended to trudge,
    Thinking to meet Sisamnes the judge.
    Behold where he cometh! I will him meet,
    And like a gentleman I mean him to greet.

Enter SISAMNES.

Sisam. Since that the King's Grace's Majesty in office did me set,
    What abundance of wealth to me might I get.

---

[1] Other editions have "fright."

> Now and then some vantage I achieve; much more yet may I take,
> But that I fear unto the king that some complaint will make. 310

Amb. Jesu, Master Sisamnes, you are unwise!

Sisam. Why so? I pray thee, let me agnise.
> What, Master Ambidexter, is it you?
> Now welcome to me, I make God a vow!

Amb. Jesu, Master Sisamnes, with me you are well acquainted!
> By me rulers may be trimly painted.
> Ye are unwise if ye take not time while ye may:
> If ye will not now, when ye would ye shall have nay.
> What is he that of you dare make exclamation,
> Of your wrong-dealing to make explication? 320
> Can you not play with both hands, and turn with the wind?

Sisam. Believe me, your words draw deep in my mind.
> In colour wise unto this day to bribes I have inclined.
> More the same for to frequent, of truth I am now minded.
> Behold, even now unto me suitors do proceed.

Enter SMALL HABILITY.

Sm. Hab. I beseech you here, good Master Judge, a poor man's cause to tender.
> Condemn me not in wrongful wise that never was offender!
> You know right well my right it is. I have not for to give.
> You take away from me my due, that should my corpse relieve.
> The commons of you do complain; from them you devocate, 330
> With anguish great and grievous words their hearts do penetrate.
> The right you sell unto the wrong, your private gain to win;
> You violate the simple man, and count it for no sin.

Sisam. Hold thy tongue, thou prattling knave, and give to me reward,
> Else, in this wise, I tell thee truth, thy tale will not be heard.
> Ambidexter, let us go hence, and let the knave alone.

Amb. Farewell, Small Hability, for help now get you none;
> Bribes hath corrupt him good laws to pollute. [*Exeunt.*

Sm. Hab. A naughty man that will not obey the king's constitute!
    With heavy heart I will return, till God redress my pain.   340
                                                      [*Exit.*

Enter SHAME, *with a trump black.*

Shame. From among the grisly ghosts I come, from tyrant's testy train.
    Unseemly Shame, of sooth, I am, procured to make plain
    The odious facts and shameless deeds[1] Cambyses king doth use.
All piety and virtuous life he doth it clean refuse;
Lechery and drunkenness he doth it much frequent;
The tiger's kind to imitate he hath given full consent.
He nought esteems his Counsel grave, ne virtuous bringing-up,
But daily still receives the drink of damned Vice's cup.
He can bide no instruction, he takes so great delight
In working of iniquity for to frequent his spite.   350
As Fame doth sound the royal trump of worthy men and trim,
So Shame doth blow with strained blast the trump of shame on him.   [*Exit.*[2]

Enter the KING, LORD, PRAXASPES, *and* SISAMNES.

King. My judge, since my departure hence, have you used judgment right?
    If faithful steward I ye find, the same I will requite.
Sisam. No doubt your Grace shall not once hear that I have done amiss.
Prax. I much rejoice to hear so good news as this.

Enter COMMONS' CRY *running in; speak this verse; and go out again hastily.*

Com. Cry. Alas, alas, how are the commons oppressed
    By that vile judge, Sisamnes by name!
        I do not know how it should be redressed.
    To amend his life no whit he doth frame.   360

---

[1] "that" omitted.   [2] Presumably, with a blast on his trumpet.

> We are undone and thrown out of door.
> His damnable dealing doth us so torment.
> At his hand we can find no relief nor succour.
> God grant him grace for to repent!
>
> [*Run away crying.*

King. What doleful cries be these, my lord, that sound do in mine ear?
Intelligence if you can give, unto your king declare.
To me it seemeth my commons all they do lament and cry
Out on Sisamnes, judge most chief, even now standing us by.

Prax. Even so, O king, it seemed to me, as you rehearsal made;
I doubt the judge culpable be in some respect or trade.   370

Sisam. Redoubted king, have no mistrust, no whit your mind dismay;
There is not one that can me charge or aught against me lay.

Enter COMMONS' COMPLAINT, *with* PROOF *and* TRIAL.

Com. Comp. Commons' Complaint I represent, with thrall of doleful state.
My urgent cause erected forth, my grief for to dilate,
Unto the king I will prepare my misery to tell,
To have relief of this my grief, and fettered feet so fell.
Redoubted prince and mighty king, myself I prostrate here!
Vouchsafe, O king, with me to bear, for this that I appear!
With humble suit I pardon crave of your Most Royal Grace,
To give me leave my mind to break, before you in this place.

King. Commons' Complaint, keep nothing back, fear not thy tale to tell.   381
Whate're he be within this land that hath not used thee well,
As prince's mouth shall sentence give, he shall receive the same.
Unfold the secrets of thy breast, for I extinguish blame.

Com. Comp. God preserve your Royal Grace, and send you blissful days,
That all your deeds might still accord, to give the gods the praise!
My complaint is, O mighty king, against that judge you by,
Whose careless deeds, gain to receive, hath made the commons cry.

> He, by taking bribes and gifts, the poor he doth oppress,
> Taking relief from infants young, widows and fatherless. 390

King. Untrustful traitor and corrupt judge, how likest thou this complaint?
> Forewarning I to thee did give, of this to make restraint.
> And hast thou done this devilish deed mine ire for to augment?
> I sentence give, thou Judas judge; thou shalt thy deed repent.

Sisam. O puissant prince, it is not so! his complaint I deny.

Com. Comp. If it be not so, most mighty king, in place then let me die!
> Behold that I have brought with me both Proof and Trial true,
> To stand even here, and sentence give, what by him did ensue.

Proof. I, Proof, do him in this appeal: he did the commons wrong.
> Unjustly he with them hath dealt, his greedy was so strong;
> His heart did covet in to get, he carèd not which way. 401
> The poor did leese their due and right, because they want to pay
> Unto him for bribes, indeed,—this was his wonted use.
> Whereas your Grace good laws did make, he did the same abuse.

Trial. I, Trial, here to verify what Proof doth now unfold,
> To stand against him in his wrong as now I dare be bold.

King. How likest thou this, thou caitiff vile? Canst thou the same deny?

Sisam. O noble king, forgive my fact! I yield to thy mercy.

King. Complaint and Proof, redress will I all this your misery.
> Depart with speed, from whence you came, and straight command by me 410
> The execution-man to come before my Grace with haste.

All. For to fulfil this your request, no time we mean to waste.

[Exeunt they three.

King. My lord, before my Grace go call Otian, this judge's son,
> And he shall hear and also see what his father hath done.
> The father he shall suffer death, the son his room succeed,
> And, if that he no better prove, so likewise shall he speed.

Prax. As your Grace hath commandment given, I mean for to fulfil.
   [Step aside and fetch him.
King. Accursed judge, couldst thou consent to do this cursed ill?
   According unto thy demand, thou shalt, for this thy guilt,
   Receive thy death before mine eyes,—thy blood it shall be spilt. 420

Enter PRAXASPES *with* OTIAN.

Prax. Behold, O king, Sisamnes' son before you doth appear.
King. Otian, this is my mind, therefore to me come near.
   Thy father here for judgment wrong procured hath his death,
   And thou, his son, shalt him succeed when he hath lost his breath;
   And, if that thou dost once offend, as thou seest thy father have,
   In like wise thou shalt suffer death, no mercy shall thee save.
Otian. O mighty king, vouchsafe your grace my father to remit.
   Forgive his fault, his pardon I do ask of you as yet.
   Alas! although my father hath your princely heart offended,
   Amends for miss he will now make, and faults shall be amended. 430
   Instead of his requested life, pleaseth your grace take mine!
   This offer I as tender child, so duty doth me bind.
King. Do not entreat my grace no more, for he shall die the death.
   Where is the execution-man, him to bereave of breath?

Enter EXECUTION.

Exec. At hand, and if it like your Grace, my duty to dispatch,
   In hope that I, when deed is done, a good reward shall catch.
King. Dispatch with sword this judge's life; extinguish fear and cares.
   So done, draw thou his cursed skin straight over both his ears.
   I will see the office done, and that before mine eyes.
Exec. To do the thing my king commands I give the enterprise.
Sisam. Otian, my son, the king to death by law hath me condemned, 441

And you in room and office mine, his Grace's will hath placed;
Use justice, therefore, in this case, and yield unto no wrong,
Lest thou do purchase the like death ere ever it be long.[1]

Otian. O father dear, these words to hear,—that you must die by force—
Bedews my cheeks with stilled tears; the king hath no remorse.
The grievous griefs and strained sighs my heart doth break in twain,
And I deplore, most woeful child, that I should see you slain.
O false and fickle frowning dame, that turneth as the wind,
Is this the joy in father's age, thou me assignest to find? 450
O doleful day, unhappy hour, that loving child should see
His father dear before his face thus put to death should be!
Yet, father, give me blessing thine, and let me once embrace
Thy comely corpse in folded arms, and kiss thy ancient face!

Sisam. O child, thou makes my eyes to run, as rivers do, by stream.
My leave I take of thee, my son; beware of this my beam!

King. Dispatch even now, thou man of death; no longer seem to stay!

Exec. Come, Master Sisamnes, come on your way!
My office I must pay; forgive therefore my deed.

Sisam. I do forgive it thee, my friend; dispatch therefore with speed! 460

[*Smite him in the neck with a sword to signify his death.*

Prax. Behold, O king, how he doth bleed, being of life bereft!

King. In this wise he shall not yet be left.
Pull his skin over his ears to make his death more vile.
A wretch he was, a cruel thief, my commons to beguile!

[*Flays him with a false skin.*

Otian. What child is he of nature's mould could bide the same to see,
His father flayed in this wise? Oh, how it grieveth me!

King. Otian, thou seest thy father dead, and thou art in his room.
If thou beest proud, as he hath been, even thereto shalt thou come.

---

[1] This line is missing from E. Allde's edition.

Cambyses, King of Persia

Otian. O king, to me this is a glass: with grief in it I view
   Example that unto your Grace I do not prove untrue. 470
Prax. Otian, convey your father hence to tomb where he shall lie.
Otian. And if it please your lordship, it shall be done by and by.
   Good execution-man, for need, help me with him away.
Exec. I will fulfil, as you to me did say.

 [They take him away.

King. My lord, now that my Grace hath seen that finished is this deed,
   To question mine give tentive ear, and answer make with speed:
   Have not I done a gracious deed, to redress my commons' woe?
Prax. Yea, truly, if it please your Grace, ye have indeed done so.
   But now, O king, in friendly wise, I counsel you in this
   Certain vices for to leave that in you placed is;— 480
   The vice of drunkenness, O king, which doth you sore infect,
   With other great abuses, which I wish you to detect.
King. Peace, my lord! what needeth this? Of this I will not hear!
   To palace now I will return, and thereto make good cheer.
   God Bacchus he bestows his gifts, we have good store of wine;
   And also that the ladies be both passing brave and fine.
   But stay! I see a lord now come, and eke a valiant knight.
   What news, my lord? To see you here my heart it doth delight.

Enter LORD *and* KNIGHT *to meet the* KING.

Lord. No news, O king; but of duty come, to wait upon your Grace.
King. I thank you, my lord and loving knight; I pray you with me trace. 490
   My lords and knight, I pray ye tell—I will not be offended—
   Am I worthy of any crime once to be reprehended?
Prax. The Persians much do praise your Grace, but one thing discommend,
   In that to wine subject you be, wherein you do offend,

Sith that the might of wine's effect, doth oft subdue your brain.
My counsel is, to please their hearts, from it you would refrain.

Lord. No, no, my lord, it is not so; for of this prince they tell,
For virtuous proof and princely facts Cyrus he doth excel.
By that his Grace by conquest great the Egyptians did convince,
Of him report abroad doth pass to be a worthy prince. 500

Knight. In person of Crœsus I answer make, we may not his Grace compare
In whole respect for to be like Cyrus, the king's father,
Insomuch your Grace hath yet no child as Cyrus left behind,
Even you I mean, Cambyses king, in whom I favour find.

King. Crœsus said well in saying so; but, Praxaspes, tell me why
That to my mouth in such a sort thou should avouch a lie,
Of drunkenness me thus to charge. But thou with speed shalt see
Whether that I a sober king or else a drunkard be.
I know thou hast a blissful babe, wherein thou dost delight,—
Me to revenge of these thy words I will go wreak this spite:
When I the most have tasted wine, my bow it shall be bent,
At heart of him even then to shoot is now my whole intent;
And, if that I his heart can hit, the king no drunkard is; 513
If heart of his I do not kill, I yield to thee in this.
Therefore, Praxaspes, fetch to me thy youngest son with speed.
There is no way, I tell thee plain, but I will do this deed.

Prax. Redoubted prince, spare my sweet child, he is mine only joy.
I trust your Grace to infant's heart no such thing will employ.
If that his mother hear of this, she is so nigh her flight,
In clay her corpse will soon be shrined, to pass from world's delight. 520

King. No more ado! Go fetch me him; it shall be as I say.
And if that I do speak the word, how dare ye once say nay?

Prax. I will go fetch him to your Grace; but so, I trust, it shall not be!

King. For fear of my displeasure great, go fetch him unto me.

[*Exit* PRAXASPES.

Is he gone? Now, by the gods, I will do as I say!
My lord, therefore fill me some wine, I heartily you pray,
For I must drink to make my brain somewhat intoxicate.
When that the wine is in my head, oh, trimly I can prate.

Lord. Here is the cup, with filled wine, thereof to take repast.

King. Give it me, to drink it off, and see no wine be waste. 530
[Drink.

Once again enlarge this cup, for I must taste it still. *[Drink.*
By the gods, I think of pleasant wine I cannot take my fill!
Now drink is in, give me my bow and arrows from sir knight;
At heart of child I mean to shoot, hoping to cleave it right.

Knight. Behold, O king, where he doth come, his infant young
    in hand.

Enter PRAXASTES, *with the* CHILD.

Prax. O mighty king, your Grace 'behest with sorrow I have
    scanned,
And brought my child from mother's knee, before you to
    appear,
And she thereof no whit doth know that he in place is here.

King. Set him up, my mark to be; I will shoot at his heart.

Prax. I beseech your Grace not so to do! set this pretence
    apart! 540
Farewell, my dear and loving babe! come, kiss thy father
    dear!
A grievous sight to me it is to see thee slain even here.
Is this the gain now from the king for giving counsel good,—
Before my face with such despite to spill my son's heart-
    blood?
Oh heavy day to me this is, and mother in like case!

Young Child. O father, father, wipe your face,
    I see the tears run from your eye.
    My mother is at home sewing of a band.
    Alas! dear father, why do you cry?

King. Before me as a mark now let him stand, 550
    I will shoot at him my mind to fulfil.

Young Child. Alas, alas! father, will you me kill?
    Good Master King, do not shoot at me, my mother loves
    me best of all.
[Shoot.

King. I have dispatched him, down he doth fall!
    As right as a line his heart I have hit.
    Nay, thou shalt see, Praxaspes, stranger news yet.
    My knight, with speed his heart cut out and give it unto me.
Knight. It shall be done, O mighty king, with all celerity.
Lord. My lord Praxaspes, this had not been but your tongue must be walking;
    To the king of correction you must needs be talking! 560
Prax. No correction, my lord; but counsel for the best.
Knight. Here is the heart, according to your Grace's behest.
King. Behold, Praxaspes, thy son's own heart! Oh, how well the same was hit!
    After this wine to do this deed I thought it very fit.
    Esteem thou mayst right well thereby no drunkard is the king,
    That in the midst of all his cups could do this valiant thing.
    My lord and knight, on me attend; to palace we will go,
    And leave him here to take his son when we are gone him fro.
All. With all our hearts we give consent to wait upon your Grace.
            [*Exeunt.*
Prax. A woeful man, O lord, am I, to see him in this case.   570
    My days, I deem, desires their end; this deed will help me hence.
    To have the blossoms of my field destroyed by violence!

Enter MOTHER.

Mother. Alas, alas! I do hear tell the king hath killed my son!
    If it be so, woe worth the deed, that ever it was done.
    It is even so; my lord I see, how by him he doth weep.
    What meant I, that from hands of him this child I did not keep?
    Alas! husband and lord, what did you mean, to fetch this child away?
Prax. O lady wife, I little thought for to have seen this day.
Mother. O blissful babe, O joy of womb, heart's comfort and delight!
    For counsel given unto the king is this thy just requite?   580
    Oh heavy day and doleful time, these mourning tunes to make!

With blubbered eyes, into mine arms from earth I will thee take,
And wrap thee in mine apron white!—But, oh my heavy heart,
The spiteful pangs that it sustains would make it in two to part,
The death of this my son to see! O heavy mother now,
That from thy sweet and sugared joy to sorrow so shouldst bow!
What grief in womb did I retain before I did thee see!
Yet at the last, when smart was gone, what joy wert thou to me!
How tender was I of thy food, for to preserve thy state!
How stilled I thy tender heart, at times early and late! 590
With velvet paps I gave thee suck, with issue from my breast,
And danced thee upon my knee, to bring thee unto rest.
Is this the joy of thee I reap? O king, of tiger's brood!
O tiger's whelp, hadst thou the heart to see this child's heart-blood?
Nature enforceth me, alas! in this wise to deplore,
To wring my hands,—Oh, wellaway, that I should see this hour!
Thy mother yet will kiss thy lips, silk-soft and pleasant white,
With wringing hands, lamenting for to see thee in this plight!
My lording dear, let us go home our mourning to augment.
Prax. My lady dear, with heavy heart to it I do consent, 600
Between us both the child to bear unto our lordly place.
            [*Exeunt.*

Enter AMBIDEXTER.

Amb. Indeed, as ye say, I have been absent a long space.
But is not my cousin Cutpurse with you in the meantime?
To it! to it, cousin, and do your office fine!
How like you Sisamnes for using of me?
He played with both hands, but he sped ill-favouredly!
The king himself was godly uptrained.
He professed virtue, but I think it was feigned.
He plays with both hands, good deeds and ill;
But it was no good deed Praxaspes' son for to kill. 610
As he for the good deed on the judge was commended,

For all his deeds else he is reprehended.
The most evil-disposed person that ever was,
All the state of his life he would not let pass;
Some good deeds he will do, though they be but few.
The like things this tyrant Cambyses doth shew.
No goodness from him to none is exhibited,
But still malediction abroad is distributed;
And yet ye shall see in the rest of his race
What infamy he will work against his own grace. 620
Whist! no more words! here comes the king's brother.

Enter LORD SMERDIS, *with* ATTENDANCE *and* DILIGENCE.

Smer. The king's brother by birth am I, issued from Cyrus' loins.
A grief to me it is to hear of this the king repines.
I like not well of those his deeds that he doth still frequent.
I wish to God that other ways his mind he could content.
Young I am, and next to him; no more of us there be.
I would be glad a quiet realm in this his reign to see.

Att. My lord, your good and willing heart the gods will recompense,
In that your mind so pensive is, for those his great offence.
My lord, his Grace shall have a time to 'pair and to amend.
Happy is he that can escape and not his Grace offend. 631

Dil. If that wicked vice he could refrain, from wasting wine forbear,
A moderate life he would frequent, amending this his square.

Amb. My lord, and if your Honour it shall please,
I can inform you what is best for your ease.
Let him alone, of his deeds do not talk,
Then by his side ye may quietly walk;
After his death you shall be king,
Then may you reform each kind of thing;
In the meantime live quietly, do not with him deal. 640
So shall it redound much to your weal.

Smer. Thou sayest true, my friend; that is the best;
I do not know whether he love me, or do me detest.

Att. Learn from his company all that you may.
I, faithful Attendance, will your Honour obey;
If against your Honour he take any ire,

> His Grace is as like to kindle his fire
> To your Honour's destruction as otherwise.
Dil. Therefore, my lord, take good advise,
> And I, Diligence, your case will so tender 650
> That to his Grace your Honour shall be none offender.
Smer. I thank you both, entire friends; with my Honour still remain.
Amb. Behold where the king doth come with his train!

Enter KING *and a* LORD.

King. O lording dear and brother mine, I joy your state to see,
> Surmising much what is the cause you absent thus from me.
Smer. Pleaseth your Grace, no absence I, but ready to fulfil,
> At all assays, my prince and king, in that your Grace me will.
> What I can do in true defence to you, my prince, aright,
> In readiness I always am to offer forth my might.
King. And I the like to you again do here avouch the same. 660
All. For this your good agreement here, now praised be God's name!
Amb. But hear ye, noble prince; hark in your ear:
> It is best to do as I did declare.
King. My lord and brother Smerdis, now this is my mind and will:
> That you to court of mine return, and there to tarry still
> Till my return within short space, your Honour for to greet.
Smer. At your behest so will I do till time again we meet.
> My leave I take from you, O king; even now I do depart.
> [*Exeunt* SMERDIS, ATTENDANCE, *and* DILIGENCE.
King. Farewell, lord and brother mine! farewell with all my heart!
> My lord, my brother Smerdis is of youth and manly might, 670
> And in his sweet and pleasant face my heart doth take delight.
Lord. Yea, noble prince, if that your Grace before his Honour die,
> He will succeed, a virtuous king, and rule with equity.
King. As you have said, my lord, he is chief heir next my Grace;
> And, if I die to-morrow, next he shall succeed my place.
Amb. And if it please your Grace, O king, I heard him say:

For your death unto the gods day and night he did pray;
He would live so virtuously and get him such a praise
That Fame by trump his due deserts in honour should
    upraise.
He said your Grace deserved had the cursing of all men,   680
That ye should never after him get any praise again.

King. Did he speak thus of my Grace, in such despiteful wise?
Or else dost thou presume to fill my princely ears with lies?

Lord. I cannot think it in my heart that he would report so.

King. How sayest thou? speak the truth: was it so or no?

Amb. I think so, if it please your Grace, but I cannot tell.

King. Thou playest with both hands, now I perceive well!
But, for to put all doubts aside and to make him leese his
    hope,
He shall die by dint of sword or else by choking rope.
Shall he succeed when I am gone, to have more praise
    than I?   690
Were he father as brother mine, I swear that he shall die.
To palace mine I will therefore, his death for to pursue.
                                                        [*Exit.*

Amb. Are ye gone? Straightway I will follow you.
How like ye now, my masters? Doth not this gear cotton?[1]
The proverb old is verified: soon ripe, and soon rotten!
He will not be quiet till his brother be killed.
His delight is wholly to have his blood spilled.
Marry, sir, I told him a notable lie;
If it were to do again, I durst not do it, I!
Marry, when I had done, to it I durst not stand;   700
Thereby you may perceive I use to play with each hand.
But how now, cousin Cutpurse, with whom play you?
Take heed, for his hand is groping even now!
Cousin, take heed, if you do secretly grope.
If ye be taken, cousin, ye must look through a rope.
                                                        [*Exit.*

Enter LORD SMERDIS *alone.*

Smer. I am wandering alone, here and there to walk.
The Court is so unquiet, in it I take no joy.
Solitary to myself now I may talk.
If I could rule, I wist what to say.

---

[1] i.e. Does not this affair prosper?

Enter CRUELTY *and* MURDER *with bloody hands.*

Cruel. My coequal partner, Murder, come away;   710
  From me long thou mayest not stay.
Murd. Yes, from thee I may stay, but not thou from me:
  Therefore I have a prerogative above thee.
Cruel. But in this case we must together abide.
  Come, come! Lord Smerdis I have spied:
  Lay hands on him with all festination,
  That on him we may work our indignation!
      [*They lay hands on him.*
Smer. How now, my friends? what have you to do with me?
Murd. King Cambyses hath sent us unto thee,
  Commanding us straitly, without mercy or favour,   720
  Upon thee to bestow our behaviour,
  With cruelty to murder you and make you away.
      [*Strike him in divers places.*
Smer. Yet pardon me, I heartily you pray!
  Consider, the king is a tyrant tyrannious,
  And all his doings be damnable and pernicious:
  Favour me therefore; I did him never offend.
      [*A little bladder of vinegar pricked.*
Cruel. No favour at all; your life is at an end.
  Even now I strike, his body to wound.
  Behold, now his blood springs out on the ground!
Murd. Now he is dead, let us present him to the king.   730
Cruel. Lay to your hand, away him to bring.   [*Exeunt.*

Enter AMBIDEXTER.

Amb. Oh the passion of God, yonder is a heavy Court:
  Some weep, some wail, and some make great sport.
  Lord Smerdis by Cruelty and Murder is slain;
  But, Jesus! for want of him how some do complain!
  If I should have had a thousand pound, I could not forbear
      weeping.
  Now Jesus have his blessed soul in keeping!
  Ah good lord! to think on him, how it doth me grieve!
  I cannot forbear weeping, ye may me believe.   [*Weep.*

Oh, my heart! how my pulses do beat, 740
With sorrowful lamentations I am in such a heat!
Ah, my heart, how for him it doth sorrow!
Nay, I have done, in faith, now, and God give ye good
   morrow!
Ha! ha! Weep? Nay, laugh, with both hands to play!
The king through his cruelty hath made him away.
But hath not he wrought a most wicked deed,
Because king after him he should not proceed,
His own natural brother, and having no more,
To procure his death by violence sore?
In spite, because his brother should never be king, 750
His heart being wicked, consented to this thing.
Now hath he no more brothers nor kindred alive.
If the king use this gear still, he cannot long thrive.

Enter HOB *and* LOB.

Hob. God's hat, neighbour, come away! it's time to market to go!
Lob. God's vast, naybor, zay ye zo?
   The clock hath stricken vive, ich think by Lakin.
   Bum vay, vrom sleep cham not very well waken.
   But, naybor Hob, naybor Hob, what have ye to zel?
Hob. Bum troth, naybor Lob, to you I chill tell:
   Chave two goslings and a chine of [good] pork,— 760
   There is no vatter between this and York.
   Chave a pot of strawberries and a calve's head,—
   A zennight zince, to-morrow, it hath been dead.
Lob. Chave a score of eggs and of butter a pound;
   Yesterday a nest of goodly young rabbits I vound.
   Chave vorty things mo, of more and of less,—
   My brain is not very good them to express.
   But, God's hat, naybor, wotst what?
Hob. No, not well, naybor; what's that?
Lob. Bum vay, naybor, master king is a zhrode lad! 770
   Zo God help me, and holidam, I think the vool be mad!
   Zome zay he deal cruelly: his brother he did kill,
   And also a goodly young lad's heart-blood he did spill.
Hob. Vorbod of God, naybor! has he played zuch a volish deed?
Amb. Goodman Hob and goodman Lob, God be your speed!

As you two towards market do walk,
Of the king's cruelty I did hear you talk;
I ensure you he is a king most vile and pernicious.
His doings and life are odious and vicious.

Lob. It were a good deed zomebody would break his head. 780

Hob. Bum vay, naybor Lob, I chuld he were dead!

Amb. So would I, Lob and Hob, with all my heart!
[*Aside.*] Now with both hands will you see me play my part.
Ah, ye whoreson traitorly knaves,
Hob and Lob, out upon you, slaves!

Lob. And thou call'st me knave, thou art another!
My name is Lob, and Hob my next naybor.

Amb. Hob and Lob! ah, ye country patches!
Ah, ye fools, ye have made wrong matches!
Ye have spoken treason against the king's Grace. 790
For it I will accuse ye before his face.
Then for the same ye shall be martyred,—
At the least ye shall be hanged, drawn and quartered.

Hob. O gentleman, ye shall have two pear-pies, and tell not of me!

Lob. By God, a vat goose chill give thee:
I think no hurt, by my vather's soul I zwear!

Hob. Chave lived well all my life-time, my naybors among;
And now chuld be loth to come to zuch wrong.
To be hanged and quartered the grief would be great!

Lob. A foul evil on thee, Hob! Who bid thee on it treat? 800
Vor it was thou that first did him name.

Hob. Thou liest like a varlet and thou zay'st the zame!
It was zuch a foolish Lob as thou.

Lob. Speak many words, and, by God's nails I vow,
Upon thy pate my staff I will lay!

Amb. [*aside.*] By the mass, I will cause them to make a fray.—
Yea, Lob, thou sayest true: all came through him.

Lob. Bum vay, thou Hob, a little would make me ye trim!
Give thee a zwap on thy nose till thy heart ache!

Hob. If thou darest, do it! Else, man, cry "creak!" 810
I trust, before thou hurt me,
With my staff chill make a Lob of thee!

[*Here let them fight with their staves, not come near*

> *another by three or four yards; the* VICE *set them on as hard as he can; one of their wives come out, and all to beat the* VICE*; he run away.*

Enter MARIAN-MAY-BE-GOOD, HOB'S *wife, running in with a broom, and part them.*

Marian. Oh the body of me, husband Hob, what mean ye to fight?
    For the passion of God, no more blows smite!
    Neighbours and friends so long, and now to fall out?
    What! in your age to seem so stout?
    If I had not parted ye, one had killed another.
Lob. I had not cared, I swear by God's Mother!
Marian. Shake hands again at the request of me;
    As ye have been friends, so friends still be.   820
Hob. Bum troth, cham content and zay'st word, neighbour Lob.
Lob. I am content; agreed, neighbour Hob!

> [*Shake hands and laugh heartily one at another.*

Marian. So, get you to market; no longer stay.
    And with yonder knave let me make a fray.
Hob. Content, wife Marian, chill do as thou dost say;
    But buss me, ich pray thee, at going away!

> [*Exeunt* HOB, LOB.

Marian. Thou whoreson knave, and prickeared boy, why didst thou let them fight?
    If one had killed another here, couldst thou their deaths requite?
    It bears a sign by this thy deed a cowardly knave thou art,
    Else wouldst thou draw that weapon thine, like a knave [1] them to part.   830
Amb. What, Marian-may-be-good, are you come prattling?
    Ye may hap get a box on the ear with your talking.
    If they had killed one another, I had not cared a pease.

> [*Here let her swinge him in her broom; she gets him down, and he her down,—thus one on the top of another make pastime.*

Marian. Ah, villain, myself on thee I must ease!

---

[1] Or "man"?

> Give me a box on the ear? that will I try.
> Who shall be master, thou shalt see by and by!

Amb. Oh, no more, no more, I beseech you heartily!
> Even now I yield, and give you the mastery.

[*Run his way out while she is down.*

Marian. Ah, thou knave, dost thou throw me down and run thy way?
> If he were here again, oh, how I would him pay!   840
> I will after him; and, if I can him meet,
> With these my nails his face I will greet.   [*Exit.*

Enter VENUS *leading out her son,* CUPID, *blind : he must have a bow and two shafts, one headed with gold and th' other with lead.*

Venus. Come forth, my son, unto my words attentive ears resign.
> What I pretend, see you frequent, to force this game of mine.
> The king a kinswoman hath, adorned with beauty store;
> And I wish that Diana's gifts they twain shall keep no more,
> But use my silver sugared game their joys for to augment.
> When I do speak, to wound his heart, Cupid my son, consent!
> And shoot at him the shaft of love, that bears the head of gold,
> To wound his heart in lovers' wise, his grief for to unfold. 850
> Though kin she be unto his Grace, that nature me expel,
> Against the course thereof he may in my game please me well.
> Wherefore, my son, do not forget; forthwith pursue the deed!

Cupid. Mother, I mean for to obey as you have whole decreed.
> But you must tell me, mother dear, when I shall arrow draw,
> Else your request to be attained will not be worth a straw.
> I am blind and cannot see, but still do shoot by guess.
> The poets well, in places store, of my might do express.

Venus. Cupid, my son, when time shall serve that thou shalt do this deed,
> Then warning I to thee will give; but see thou shoot with speed.   860

Enter a LORD, *a* LADY, *and a* WAITING-MAID.

Lord. Lady dear, to king akin, forthwith let us proceed
   To trace abroad the beauty fields, as erst we had decreed.
   The blowing buds, whose savoury scents our sense will much delight;
   The sweet smell of musk white-rose, to please the appetite;
   The chirping birds, whose pleasant tunes therein shall bear record,
   That our great joy we shall it find in field to walk abroad;
   On lute and cittern there to play, a heavenly harmony.
   Our ears shall hear, heart to content, our sports to beautify.
Lady. Unto your words, most comely lord, myself submit do I;
   To trace with you in field so green I mean not to deny. 870
                  [Here trace up and down playing.
Maid. And I, your waiting-maid, at hand with diligence will be,
   For to fulfil with heart and hand, when you shall command me.

Enter KING, LORD, *and* KNIGHT.

King. Come on, my lord and knight; abroad our mirth let us employ.
   Since he is dead, this heart of mine in corpse I feel it joy.
   Should brother mine have reigned king when I had yielded breath?
   A thousand brothers I rather had to put them all to death.
   But, oh, behold, where I do see a lord and lady fair!
   For beauty she most worthy is to sit in prince's chair.
Venus. Shoot forth, my son; now is the time that thou must wound his heart.
Cupid. Content you, mother; I will do my part. 880
                  [Shoot there, and go out VENUS *and* CUPID.
King. Of truth, my lord, in eye of mine all ladies she doth excel.
   Can none report what dame she is, and to my Grace it tell?
Lord. Redoubted prince, pleaseth your Grace, to you she is akin,
   Cousin-german nigh of birth, by mother's side come in.
Knight. And that her waiting-maiden is, attending her upon.
   He is a lord of prince's court, and will be there anon.
   They sport themselves in pleasant field, to former used use.

King. My lord and knight, of truth I speak: my heart it cannot choose
But with my lady I must speak and so express my mind.
My lord and ladies, walking there, if you will favour find, 890
Present yourselves unto my Grace, and by my side come stand.

First Lord. We will fulfil, most mighty king, as your Grace doth command.

King. Lady dear, intelligence my Grace hath got of late,
You issued out of mother's stock and kin unto my state.
According to rule of birth you are cousin-german mine.
Yet do I wish that farther of this kindred I could find,
For Cupid he, that eyeless boy, my heart hath so enflamed
With beauty you me to content the like cannot be named;
For, since I entered in this place and on you fixed mine eyes,
Most burning fits about my heart in ample wise did rise. 900
The heat of them such force doth yield, my corpse they scorch, alas!
And burns the same with wasting heat, as Titan doth the grass.
And, sith this heat is kindled so, and fresh in heart of me,
There is no way but of the same the quencher you must be.
My meaning is that beauty yours my heart with love doth wound;
To give me love mind to content, my heart hath you outfound.
And you are she must be my wife, else shall I end my days.
Consent to this, and be my queen, to wear the crown with praise!

Lady. If it please your Grace, O mighty king, you shall not this request.
It is a thing that Nature's course doth utterly detest, 910
And high it would the gods displease,—of all that is the worst.
To grant your Grace to marry so, it is not that I durst.
Yet humble thanks I render now unto you, mighty king,
That you vouchsafe to great estate so gladly would me bring.
Were it not it were offence, I would it not deny,
But such great honour to achieve my heart I would apply.

>   Therefore, O king, with humble heart in this I pardon crave.
>   My answer is: in this request your mind ye may not have.
>
> *King.* May I not? nay, then, I will, by all the gods I vow!
>   And I will marry thee as wife,—this is mine answer now. 920
>   Who dare say nay what I pretend, who dare the same withstand,
>   Shall lose his head and have report as traitor through my land.
>   There is no nay; I will you have, and you my queen shall be.
>
> *Lady.* Then, mighty king, I crave your Grace to hear the words of me:
>   Your counsel take of lordings' wit, the laws aright peruse.
>   If I with safe may grant this deed, I will it not refuse.
>
> *King.* No, no! what I have said to you, I mean to have it so.
>   For counsel theirs I mean not, I, in this respect to go.
>   But to my palace let us go, the marriage to prepare;
>   For, to avoid my will in this, I can it not forbear. 930
>
> *Lady.* O God, forgive me, if I do amiss!
>   The king by compulsion enforceth me this.
>
> *Maid.* Unto the gods for your estate I will not cease to pray,
>   That you may be a happy queen and see most joyful day.
>
> *King.* Come on, my lords, with gladsome hearts let us rejoice with glee!
>   Your music show to joy this deed at the request of me!
>
> *Both.* For to obey your Grace's words our Honours do agree.
>
>   [*Exeunt.*
>
> ### *Enter* AMBIDEXTER.
>
> *Amb.* Oh the passion of me! marry, as ye say, yonder is a royal court.
>   There is triumphing and sport upon sport,—
>   Such loyal lords, with such lordly exercise, 940
>   Frequenting such pastime as they can devise,
>   Running at tilt, jousting, with running at the ring,
>   Masking and mumming, with each kind of thing,—
>   Such dancing, such singing, with musical harmony,
>   Believe me, I was loth to absent their company.
>   But will you believe? Jesu, what haste they made till they were married!

Not for a million of pounds one day longer they would have
    tarried!
Oh! there was a banquet royal and superexcellent,—
Thousands and thousands at that banquet was spent.
I muse of nothing but how they can be married so soon.   950
I care not if I be married before to-morrow at noon,
If marriage be a thing that so may be had.
How say you, maid? to marry me will ye be glad?
Out of doubt, I believe it is some excellent treasure,—
Else to the same belongs abundant pleasure.
Yet with mine ears I have heard some say:
"That ever I was married, now cursed be the day!"
Those be they that with cursed wives be matched.
That husband for hawk's meat of them is up-snatched,
Head broke with a bedstaff, face all to-bescratched;—   960
"Knave!" "slave!" and "villain!" a coiled coat now and
    then,—
When the wife hath given it, she will say, "Alas, goodman!"
Such were better unmarried, my masters, I trow,
Than all their life after to be matched with a shrow.

Enter PREPARATION.

Prep. With speed I am sent all things to prepare,
    My message to do as the king did declare.
    His Grace doth mean a banquet to make,
    Meaning in this place repast for to take.
    Well, the cloth shall be laid, and all things in readiness,
    To court to return, when done is my business.   970
Amb. A proper man and also fit
    For the king's estate to prepare a banquet!
Prep. What, Ambidexter?   Thou art not unknown!
    A mischief on all good faces, so that I curse not mine own!
    Now, in the knave's name, shake hands with me.
Amb. Well said, goodman pouchmouth; your reverence I see.
    I will teach ye, if your manners no better be!
    Ah, ye slave, the king doth me a gentleman allow;
    Therefore I look that to me ye should bow.   [*Fight.*
Prep. Good Master Ambidexter, pardon my behaviour;   980
    For this your deed you are a knave for your labour!

Amb. Why, ye stale counterly villain, nothing but knave?
  [*Fight*

Prep. I am sorry your mastership offended I have;
  Shake hands, that between us agreement may be.
  I was over-shot with myself, I do see.
  Let me have your help this furniture to provide.
  The king from this place will not long abide.
  [*Set the fruit on the board*

Amb. Content: it is the thing that I would wish;
  I myself will go fetch one dish.
    [*Let the* VICE *fetch a dish of nuts, and let them fall in the bringing of them in.*

Prep. Cleanly, Master Ambidexter; for fair on the ground they lie. 990

Amb. I will have them up again by and by.

Prep. To see all in readiness I will put you in trust;
  There is no nay, to the court needs I must.
  [*Exit* PREPARATION.

Amb. Have ye no doubt, sir, but all shall be well,
  Marry, sir, as you say, this gear doth excel!
  All things is in a readiness, when they come hither,—
  The king's Grace and the queen both together.
  I beseech ye, my masters, tell me, is it not best
  That I be so bold as to bid a guest?
  He is as honest a man as ever spurred cow,— 1000
  My cousin Cutpurse, I mean; I beseech ye, judge you.
  Believe me, cousin, if to be the king's guest ye could be taken,
  I trust that offer will never be forsaken.
  But, cousin, because to that office ye are not like to come,
  Frequent your exercises, a horn on your thumb,
  A quick eye, a sharp knife, at hand a receiver;
  But then take heed, cousin, ye be a cleanly conveyer.
  Content yourself, cousin; for this banquet you are unfit,
  When such as I at the same am unworthy to sit.

Enter KING, QUEEN, *and his train.*

King. My queen and lords, to take repast, let us attempt the same; 1010
  Here is the place; delay no time, but to our purpose frame.

Cambyses, King of Persia

Queen. With willing hearts your whole behest we mind for to obey.

All. And we, the rest of prince's train, will do as you do say.
[*Sit at the banquet.*

King. Methink mine ears doth wish the sound of music's harmony;
Here, for to play before my Grace, in place I would them spy.
[*Play at the banquet.*

Amb. They be at hand, sir, with stick and fiddle;
They can play a new dance, called Hey-diddle-diddle.

King. My queen, perpend; what I pronounce, I will not violate,
But one thing which my heart makes glad I mind to explicate:
You know in court uptrained is a lion very young;   1020
Of one litter two whelps beside, as yet not very strong;
I did request one whelp to see and this young lion fight;
But lion did the whelp convince, by strength of force and might.
His brother whelp, perceiving that the lion was too good,
And he by force was like to see the other whelp his blood,
With force to lion he did run, his brother for to help,—
A wonder great it was to see that friendship in a whelp!—
So then the whelps between them both the lion did convince,
Which thing to see before mine eyes did glad the heart of prince.   [*At this tale told, let the* QUEEN *weep.*

Queen. These words to hear makes stilling tears issue from crystal eyes.   1030

King. What, dost thou mean, my spouse, to weep for loss of any prize?

Queen. No, no, O king, but as you see friendship in brothers whelp,
When one was like to have repulse, the other yielded help.
And was this favour showed in dogs, to shame of royal king?
Alack, I wish these ears of mine had not once heard this thing!
Even so should you, O mighty king, to brother been a stay,
And not, without offence to you, in such wise him to slay.
In all assays it was your part, his cause to have defended,
And, whosoever had him misused, to have them reprehended.

But faithful love was more in dog than it was in your
  Grace.   1040
King. O cursed caitiff vicious and vile, I hate thee in this place!
  This banquet [1] is at an end; take all these things away.
  Before my face thou shalt repent the words that thou dost
    say.
  O wretch most vile, didst thou the cause of brother mine so
    tender,
  The loss of him should grieve thy heart,—he being none
    offender?
  It did me good his death to have, so will it to have thine;
  What friendship he had at my hands, the same even thou
    shalt find.
  I give consent, and make a vow, that thou shalt die the
    death;
  By Cruel's sword and Murder fell even thou shalt lose thy
    breath.
  Ambidexter, see with speed to Cruelty ye go;   1050
  Cause him hither to approach, Murder with him also.
Amb. I am ready for to fulfil, if that it be your Grace's will.
King. Then nought oblight [2] my message given; absent thyself
    away.
Amb. Then in this place I will no longer stay.
  If that I durst, I would mourn your case;
  But, alas! I dare not, for fear of his Grace.

  [*Exit* AMBIDEXTER.

King. Thou cursed Jill, by all the gods I take an oath and swear,
  That flesh of thine these hands of mine in pieces small could
    tear;
  But thou shalt die by dint of sword: there is no friend
    ne fee   1059
  Shall find remorse at prince's hand, to save the life of thee.
Queen. O mighty king and husband mine, vouchsafe to hear
    me speak,
  And licence give to spouse of thine her patient mind to
    break!
  For tender love unto your Grace my words I did so frame;
  For pure love doth heart of king me violate and blame.

---

[1] Qy. insertion of "now" after "banquet." [2] Forget.

Cambyses, King of Persia

And to your Grace is this offence, that I should purchase death?
Then cursed time that I was queen, to shorten this my breath!
Your Grace doth know, by marriage true, I am your wife and spouse,
And one to save another's health at trothplight made our vows;
Therefore, O king, let loving queen at thy hand find remorse,
Let pity be a mean to quench that cruel raging force, 1070
And pardon, plight from prince's mouth, yield grace unto your queen,
That amity with faithful zeal may ever be us between!

King. Ah, caitiff vile, to pity thee my heart it is not bent,
Ne yet to pardon your offence it is not mine intent.

First Lord. Our mighty prince, with humble suit of your Grace this I crave,
That this request it may take place, your favour for to have.
Let mercy yet abundantly the life of queen preserve,
Sith she in most obedient wise your Grace's will doth serve.
As yet your Grace but while with her hath had cohabitation,
And sure this is no desert why to yield her indignation. 1080
Therefore, O king, her life prolong, to joy her days in bliss!

Second Lord. Your Grace shall win immortal fame in granting unto this.
She is a queen whose goodly hue excels the royal rose,
For beauty bright Dame Nature she a large gift did dispose.
For comeliness who may compare? Of all she bears the bell.
This should give cause to move your Grace to love her very well.
Her silver breast in those your arms, to sing the songs of love,—
Fine qualities most excellent to be in her you prove;
A precious pearl of price to prince, a jewel passing all. 1089
Therefore, O king, to beg remorse on both my knees I fall;
To grant her grace to have her life, with heart I do desire.

King. You villains twain, with raging force ye set my heart on fire!
If I consent that she shall die, how dare ye crave her life?

You two to ask this at my hand doth much enlarge my
    strife.
Were it not for shame, you two should die, that for her life
    do sue!
But favour mine from you is gone; my lords, I tell you true.
I sent for Cruelty of late; if he would come away,
I would commit her to his hands his cruel part to play.
Even now I see where he doth come; it doth my heart delight.

Enter CRUELTY *and* MURDER.

Cruel. Come, Murder, come; let us go forth with might;   1100
    Once again the king's commandment we must fulfil.
Murd. I am contented to do it with a good will.
King. Murder and Cruelty, for both of you I sent,
    With all festination your offices to frequent.
    Lay hold on the queen; take her to your power,
    And make her away within this hour!
    Spare for no fear, I do you full permit.
    So I from this place do mean for to flit.
Both. With courageous hearts, O king, we will obey.
King. Then come, my lords, let us depart away.   1110
Both the Lords. With heavy hearts we will do all your Grace
    doth say.   [*Exeunt* KING *and* LORDS.
Cruel. Come, lady and queen, now are you in our handling;
    In faith, with you we will use no dandling.
Murd. With all expedition I, Murder, will take place;
    Though thou be a queen, ye be under my grace.
Queen. With patience I will you both obey.
Cruel. No more words, but go with us away!
Queen. Yet, before I die, some psalm to God let me sing.
Both. We be content to permit you that thing.
Queen [*sings.*] Farewell, you ladies of the court, with all your
    masking hue!   1120
    I do forsake these broidered guards and all the fashions new,
    The court and all the courtly train wherein I had delight;
    I banished am from happy sport, and all by spiteful spite;
    Yet with a joyful heart to God a psalm I mean to sing,
    Forgiving all [men] and the king of each kind of thing.
            [*Sing and exeunt.*

Cambyses, King of Persia

Enter AMBIDEXTER *weeping.*

Amb. Ah, ah, ah, ah! I cannot choose but weep for the queen!
    Nothing but mourning now at the court there is seen.
    Oh, oh, my heart, my heart! Oh, my bum will break!
    Very grief so torments me that scarce I can speak.
    Who could but weep for the loss of such a lady?   1130
    That cannot I do, I swear by mine honesty.
    But, Lord! so the ladies mourn, crying "Alack!"
    Nothing is worn now but only black:
    I believe all [the][1] cloth in Watling Street to make gowns
        would not serve,—
    If I make a lie, the devil let ye starve!
    All ladies mourn, both young and old;
    There is not one that weareth a point's worth of gold.
    There is a sort for fear for the king do pray
    That would have him dead, by the mass, I dare say.
    What a king was he that hath used such tyranny!   1140
    He was akin to Bishop Bonner, I think verily!
    For both their delights was to shed blood,
    But never intended to do any good.
    Cambyses put a judge to death,—that was a good deed,—
    But to kill the young child was worse to proceed,
    To murder his brother and then his own wife,—
    So help me God and holidam, it is pity of his life!
    Hear ye? I will lay twenty thousand pound
    That the king himself doth die by some wound.
    He hath shed so much blood that his will be shed;   1150
    If it come [thus] to pass, in faith, then is he sped.

Enter the KING, *without a gown, a sword thrust up into his side, bleeding.*

King. Out! alas! what shall I do? my life is finished!
    Wounded I am by sudden chance, my blood is minished.
    Gog's heart, what means might I make, my life to preserve?
    Is there nought to be my help? nor is there nought to serve?
    Out upon the court and lords that there remain!
    To help my grief in this my case will none of them take pain?

---

[1] Supplied by Manly.

Who but I in such a wise his death's wound could have got?
As I on horseback up did leap, my sword from scabbard shot,
And ran me thus into the side, as you right well may see,—
A marvel's chance unfortunate that in this wise should be!
I feel myself a-dying now, of life bereft am I, 1162
And Death hath caught me with his dart, for want of blood I spy.
Thus gasping here on ground I lie; for nothing I do care;
A just reward for my misdeeds my death doth plain declare.

[*Here let him quake and stir.*

Amb. How now, noble king? pluck up your heart!
What, will you die, and from us depart?
Speak to me an' ye be alive!
He cannot speak. But behold, now with Death he doth strive.
Alas, good king! alas, he is gone! 1170
The devil take me if for him I make any moan.
I did prognosticate of his end, by the mass;
Like as I did say, so is it come to pass!
I will be gone; if I should be found here,
That I should kill him it would appear.
For fear with his death they do me charge,
Farewell, my masters, I will go take barge;
I mean to be packing; now is the tide;
Farewell, my masters, I will no longer abide!

[*Exit* AMBIDEXTER.

Enter three LORDS.

First Lord. Behold, my lords, it is even so as he to us did tell:
His Grace is dead, upon the ground, by dint of sword most fell. 1181
Second Lord. As he in saddle would have leaped, his sword from sheath did go,
Goring him up into the side,—his life was ended so.
Third Lord. His blood so fast did issue out that nought could him prolong;
Yet, before he yielded up the ghost, his heart was very strong.

First Lord. A just reward for his misdeeds the God above hath wrought,
   For certainly the life he led was to be counted nought.
Second Lord. Yet a princely burial he shall have, according his estate;
   And more of him here at this time we have not to dilate.
Third Lord. My lords, let us take him up, to carry him away.   1190
Both. Content we are with one accord to do as you do say.
                              [*Exeunt all.*

EPILOGUE

Right gentle audience, here have you perused
The tragical history of this wicked king.
According to our duty, we have not refused,
But to our best intent expressed everything.
We trust none is offended for this our doing;
    Our author craves likewise, if he have squared amiss,
    By gentle admonition to know where the fault is.

His good will shall not be neglected to amend the same.
Praying all to bear, therefore, with his simple deed
Until the time serve a better he may frame,—   10
Thus yielding you thanks, to end we decreed
That you so gently have suffered us to proceed,
    In such patient wise as to hear and see,—
    We can but thank ye therefore, we can do no more, we!—

As duty binds us, for our noble Queen let us pray,
And for her Honourable Council, the truth that they may use,
To practise justice and defend her Grace each day;
To maintain God's word they may not refuse,
To correct all those that would her Grace and Grace's laws abuse;
    Beseeching God over us she may reign long,   21
    To be guided by truth and defended from wrong.

"Amen," quoth Thomas Preston.

GLOSSARY

ABHOR (from), to be averse, contrary to
ABIDE, endure, suffer
ABSTRACT, summary
ABUSE, deceive; insult
ACCIDENT, incident
ADRAD, from verb *adread*, fill with fear, dread
ADVISE, consider, bethink
ADVISED, "WELL-," in sound senses
AGLET, tag of a lace, or cord, often ornamented
ALLOW, approve
ALL-TO, entirely, completely
AMBAGE, circumlocution
ANGEL, gold coin worth ten shillings, stamped with figure of the archangel Michael
ANSWER, recompense, repay
APPARENTLY, plainly
APPLY, agree with
APPROVE, prove, testify
APT, ready, willing, fit
ARCHITECT, (?) archetype (Dyce); (?) architecture
ARGUMENT, proof, token
ARTIFICER, artisan

BALLACE, ballast, steady
BASILISK, fabulous reptile, believed to slay with its eye
BATE, flutter with the wings, preparatory to flight (term of falconry)
BATTERY, assault
BEDARE, defy
BEDESMAN, prayer-man, generally one engaged to pray for another
BEHIGHT, promise
BEHOOVE, behove, be necessary, incumbent
BERAY, soil, defile
BEWRAY, betray, reveal
BODE, from the verb *bide*, endure
BOLSTERED, (?) boltered, matted
BOOK-KEEPER, prompter
BOOT, avail, help; something given into the bargain
BOOTLESS, without remedy, of no avail

BOTCHER, mender of old clothes, etc.
Bow, bend
BRABBLE (brabling), brawl
BRAID, start
BRAVERY, bravado, defiance
"BREATHY-SWORDS," words like swords
BROOK, digest; endure, suffer
BRUIT, report
BUG, bugbear
BUSS, kiss
BUTTING, abutting
BYE, aby, atone for

CATES, provisions, dainties
CENSURE, judgment, sentence, opinion
CENSURE, pass sentence
CHARM, exercise magic influence
CHECK, chide
CHEER, countenance, disposition; entertainment
CHEERLY, cheerily
CIVIL, belonging to, employed for, civil war
CLEPE, call, name
CLOSE WITH, come to agreement; come to close quarters
CLOSELY, secretly
CLOY, satisfy, satiate
COCKSHUT, twilight, time when woodcocks were caught in a net, called a "cockshut" (Nares); time when poultry go to roost (?)
COIL, trouble, commotion, "to do"
COISTREL, low varlet
COLT(COWL)STAFF, pole for carrying a cowl, tub
COMPLAT, complot
CONCEIT, idea, fancy, conception, opinion
CONCEIT, conceive, devise
CONCEIVED, possessed
CONSENT, agree
CONSORT, accompany
CONTEMN, despise, disdain
CONTEND, strive, struggle
CONVEYANCE, secret management, artful contrivance
CONVINCE, convict

319

COPESMATE, companion
COR'SIVE, corrosive
COSTARD, head
COUCH (dishonour), uncertain meaning; perhaps to locate, supply details of time and place
COUNTENANCE, be in keeping with
COUNTER, city court prison
COUNTERFEIT, image, portrait
COUNTERMUR'D, with double wall
CREAK, to call out in a harsh tone
CUNNING, skilful, knowing
CURIOUS, elaborate, intricate
CURRENTLY, accordingly
CURST, shrewish

DAG, pistol
DANGERLESS, free from danger
DANK, damp
DAUNT, subdue
DEFEND, forbid, prevent
DELIVERY, deliverance
DEPART, departure, going away
DERIVE, pass, or receive, by inheritance
DESPITE, spite, malicious hate
DESPITEFUL, spiteful, malicious
DETECT, inform against, reveal
DING, fling, dash
DISCOLOURED, of various colours
DISCONTENT, sorrow, displeasure
DISCOVER, reveal, make known
DISTAIN, sully, disgrace
DOOM, sentence
DOTE, act, speak unreasonably
DRIFT, intention, design
DUCAT, gold coin of varying value, current in Europe; Venetian ducat worth about nine shillings
DURING, lasting

EAR, till, plough
EKE, also, likewise
ENGINE, instrument, agent
ENSUE, succeed
ENTREAT, beseech, persuade; treat
ERST, formerly
EXASPERATE, aggravate, provoke
EXCEPT, accept
EXTIRPEN, extirpate

FACT, deed, crime
FAVOUR, comeliness, beauty
FEAR, affright
FEATURE, general appearance
FETCH, stratagem, device
FILED, polished
FLAW, sudden gust or squall of wind

FOND, foolish
FORCE, "HOUSE OF —," fortified house
FORSLOW, delay
FOSTER, forester
FRETFUL, fretting, gnawing
FRIGHT, frighten

GEAR, matter, affair
GIGLOT, wanton
GITE, splendour,
"GIVE BACK," retreat, draw back
GRAVED, entombed
GREE, "MAKE A-," come to an agreement
GRIPE, griffin, vulture
GUERDON, recompense

HAGGARD, wild, untamed (a haggard was a wild female hawk caught in her adult plumage)
HANDSEL, give something as a token of good luck, or as an earnest or pledge
HAP, chance, fortune
HAP, happen, chance
HARQUEBUS, fire-arm in use previous to the musket
HATEFUL, harbouring hate, malignant
HAST, command
HIGHT, called, named
HOLIDAM, an early variant of halidom
HOUGH-MONDAY, Monday in Hocktide (second Monday after Easter). A season of festivity and old ceremonies, said to have been instituted in commemoration of a victory over the Danes. At this season church dues were collected (see Brand "Antiquities")
HOUGHT, hocked, hamstrung
HUMOUROUS, full of whims, capricious

ILL-THEWED, ill-mannered (Oxford Dict.)
IMPETRATE, procure
INCENSE, inflame, kindle
INFECT, tainted, corrupt
INFECTIVE, infecting, infectious
INJURIOUS, insulting, pernicious
INSTANCE, proof, evidence
INSULT, show insolence and contempt, triumph over
INTEND, express, design to express
INTENT, "TO THIS —," to this end
INTENTIVE, intent, eagerly attentive

Glossary

INTERCEPT, prevent, cut off from
INTREAT, treat, use
INURE, accustom, habituate
INURED, practised continually, habitual
IRK, annoy, trouble

JET, strut
JETTY, black
JOY, enjoy

KIND, nature; kindred
KINDLESS, without natural feeling

LADE, load, fill
LAKEN, (Our) Ladykin
LEESE, lose
LET, hinder
LEWD, base, ignorant
LIKE, please
LIME, catch with bird-lime, ensnare
LIST, like, choose, wish; listen
LOATHE, to cause loathing
LORDAINE, clown
LOT, allot

MACE, club, weapon of war
"MAIN BATTLE," main body of an army
MATTED, dull, lustreless
MEAN, measure, method
MELL, meddle
MERELY, entirely, absolutely
MIND, intend
MINDFUL, bearing in remembrance
MISCONSTER, misconstrue
MITHRIDATE, an antidote to poison, so called after the famous King of Pontus who made himself poison-proof
MOTION, proposal, request
MUSCADO, (?) a musket (Oxford Dict.)
MUTCHADO, moustache

NE, nor
NICE(LY), fastidious(ly), scrupulous(ly)
NILL, will not

OLD, hyperbolical expression: "grand," "rare"
ONCE, once for all; used for additional emphasis
ORGANON, organ, instrument
OVERTHROW, to fall over, or down

"PAINTED CLOTH," cloth, or canvas painted with scenes and mottoes, with which rooms were hung
PANTOFLES, slippers, or other light foot-gear
PARBREAK, vomit
PART, apportion
PASSIONATE, melancholy, sorrowful
PATHAIRE, (?) a passionate outburst, (Oxford Dict.); variant of patar, petar, petard (Gollancz, Lamb's specimens, 1893)
PINED, afflicted
PITCH, set; fix, settle
PLAIN, make complaint
PLANCHER, planking, floor
PLAT, plan, plot
PLATFORM, scheme, plot
PLAUSIBLE, pleasing, worthy of applause
PLENISH, be replenished
POPULOUS, popular, belonging to, or befitting, the people
PORTINGAL, Portugal
PRACTICE, plot, connivance
PRACTISE, plot, conspire
PRECISIAN, puritan
PREASE, press, hasten
PREFER, promote
PRESENT(LY), immediate(ly)
PRETENCE, design, intention
PRETEND, intend
PREVENT, anticipate
PROTRACT, delay

QUAINT, artful, cunning
QUICK, alive, living
QUITAL, requital
QUITTANCE, repay

RACE, raze
RACK, drifting vapour, scud; clouds in the upper air driven by the wind
RAMPIER, rampart
RANDOM, act without restraint
RASCAL, base, pertaining to the rabble
REACHING, far-reaching
REAVE, bereave
RECK, heed, care for
RECORD, sing, warble
RECOURSE, flow, flowing into
RECURE, restore
REDE, counsel
REFUSE, reject
REMORSEFUL, compassionate
REPAIR, renew, restore
RESOLVE, decide
RESPECT, consideration, motive

RESTING, (?) continued, unalterable; perhaps wresting, extorting
ROUND, bring round; whisper
ROUNDLY, without circumlocution
RUTH, pity
RUTHFUL, pitiful
SCONCE, fort, bulwark
SCORN, reproach, disgrace
SEAM RENT, ragged
SECRETARY, one to whom secrets are confided, confidant
SECURE(LY), confident(ly), unsuspecting(ly)
SELD, seldom
SENSELESS, void of feeling
SENSIBLE, having power of perceiving by the senses; able to feel
SHEND, protect, defend
SIGHTED, endowed with sight
SILLY, weak, helpless, simple, innocent
SITH, since
SKILLESS, irrational, reckless
SLEIGHT, stratagem
SLIPSHOE, slipper
SOLICIT, advocate, plead for
SOOTHE, flatter; confirm, bear out
SORT, company, multitude
SORT, allot; choose, select
SPOIL, despoil, plunder
STANDING, point of vantage
STATE, "IN —," legally
STAY, restraint, support, condition of permanence
STAY, delay, check
STEAD, assist, befriend
STILL, distill
STRANGE, distant in behaviour
STY, mount, soar
SUFFERANCE, long-suffering, submission, suffering
SURCEASE, cease

TABLES, game, similar to backgammon
TAINT, attaint, convict
TALL, brave

TENDER, cherish, regard with care and esteem
THOUGHTFUL, anxious
TOIL, snare
TOIL, fatigue, wear out
TOWARDNESS, willingness, docility, aptness
TRAIN, treachery
TRICK, deck, adorn
TROLL, circulate, send round
TROTH, truth
TRUSS, tie up for hanging
"TURN OFF," hang
TWINK, twinkle

UNHAP, mischance, misfortune
UNKIND(LY), unnatural
UNRESOLVED, not having come to a decision
UNSKILFUL, lacking judgment and understanding
UNVALUED, invaluable
URE, habit, use

VILD, vile

WAGER, hire for wage
WANT, to be lacking
WARD, guard (in fencing)
WAIST, girdle
WATCHET, pale blue
WEESEL, weasand, windpipe
WHENAS, when
WHETHER, which
WHILOM, formerly
WHIPSTALK, whipstock
WHISTLY, silently
WILL, desire (him)
WIT, know, learn
WITHOUT, beyond
WREAK, avenge
WREAKFUL, avenging
WRITHE(N), twist, contort(ed)
WROKE, from the verb *wreak*
WRY, deviating from justice or truth, perverted

EVERYMAN'S LIBRARY

A Selected List

In each of the thirteen classifications in this list (except BIO-
GRAPHY) the volumes are arranged alphabetically under the authors'
names, but Anthologies, etc., are listed under titles. Where
authors appear in more than one section, a cross-reference is
given. The number at the end of each item is the number of
the volume in the series.

April 1960

EVERYMAN'S LIBRARY

BIOGRAPHY

Baxter (Richard), Autobiography of 868
Blake (William), Life of. By Alexander Gilchrist. Illustrated 971
 (*See also* POETRY AND DRAMA)
Brontë (Charlotte), Life of. By Mrs. Gaskell 318
 (*See also* FICTION)
Burns (Robert), Life of. By J. G. Lockhart 156
 (*See also* POETRY AND DRAMA)
Byron's Letters 931
 (*See also* POETRY AND DRAMA)
Canton's A Child's Book of Saints 61
 (*See also* ESSAYS)
Carlyle's Reminiscences 875
 (*See also* ESSAYS *and* HISTORY)
Cellini's Life 51
Cowper (Wm.), Selected Letters of 774
 (*See also* POETRY AND DRAMA)
Dickens (Charles), Life of. By John Forster. 2 vols. 781–2
 (*See also* FICTION)
Evelyn's Diary. 2 vols. 220–1
Fox (George), Journal of 754
Franklin's Autobiography 316
Goethe, Life of. By G. H. Lewes 269
Hudson (W. H.), Far Away and Long Ago (autobiography of his youth) 956

Johnson (Dr. Samuel), Life of. By James Boswell. 2 vols. 1–2
Johnson's Lives of the Poets. 2 vols. 770–1
 (*See also* TRAVEL)
Keats (John), Life and Letters of. By Lord Houghton 801
 (*See also* POETRY AND DRAMA)
Lamb (Charles), Letters of. 2 vols. 342–3
 (*See also* ESSAYS *and* FOR YOUNG PEOPLE)
Napoleon, Life of. By J. G. Lockhart 3
Nelson, Life of. By Southey 52
Outram (Sir J.), The Bayard of India. By Capt. L. J. Trotter 396
Pepys's Diary. New enlarged edition. 3 vols. 53–5
Plutarch's Lives of Noble Greeks and Romans. Dryden's Translation. 3 vols. 407–9
Rousseau, Confessions of. 2 vols. 859–60
 (*See also* ESSAYS *and* PHILOSOPHY)
Scott, Sir Walter, Life of. By J. G. Lockhart 39
Swift's Journal to Stella. Ed. J. K. Moorhead 757
 (*See also* ESSAYS *and* FICTION)
Walpole (H.), Selected Letters of 775
Wellington, Life of. By G. R. Gleig 341
Woolman's (John) Journal and Other Papers 402

CLASSICAL

Aeschylus' Lyrical Dramas 62
Aristophanes' Comedies. 2 vols. 344, 516
Aristotle's Politics 605
 „ Metaphysics 1000
 (*See also* PHILOSOPHY)
Caesar's War Commentaries 702
Cicero's Essays and Select Letters 345
Epictetus, Moral Discourses, etc. Elizabeth Carter's Translation 404
Euripides' Plays in 2 vols. 63, 271
Herodotus. 2 vols. (Vol. II temporarily out of print) 405–6

Homer's Iliad 453
 „ Odyssey 454
Juvenal's Satires 997
Lucretius: On the Nature of Things 750
Ovid: Selected Works 955
Plato's Republic 64
 „ Socratic Discourses 457
Sophocles' Dramas 114
Thucydides' Peloponnesian War 455
Virgil's Aeneid 161
 „ Eclogues and Georgics 222

ESSAYS AND BELLES-LETTRES

Anthology of English Prose 675
Arnold's (Matthew) Essays 115
 (*See also* POETRY)
Bacon's Essays 10
 (*See also* PHILOSOPHY)
Bagehot's Literary Studies. 2 vols. 520–1

Belloc's Stories, Essays, and Poems 948
Burke's Reflections 460
 (*See also* ORATORY)
Canton's The Invisible Playmate 566
 (*See also* BIOGRAPHY)
Carlyle's Essays. 2 vols. 703–4

Everyman's Library—Essays & Belles-Lettres—Continued

Carlyle's Past and Present 608
"   Sartor Resartus and Heroes and Hero Worship 278
(See also BIOGRAPHY and HISTORY)
Castiglione's The Courtier 807
Century of Essays, A. An Anthology of English Essayists 653
Chesterfield's (Lord) Letters to his Son 823
Coleridge's Biographia Literaria 11
"   Shakespearean Criticism. 2 vols. Nos. 162, 183
(See also POETRY)
De Quincey's (Thomas) Opium-eater 223
De Sévigné's Letters 98
Eckermann's Conversations with Goethe 851
Emerson's Essays. 1st and 2nd Series 12
"   Representative Men 279
Gilfillan's Literary Portraits 348
Hamilton's The Federalist 519
Hazlitt's Lectures on the English Comic Writers 411
"   The Round Table and Shakespear's Characters 65
"   Spirit of the Age and Lectures on English Poets 459
"   Table Talk 321
Holmes's Autocrat of the Breakfast Table 66
Hunt's (Leigh) Selected Essays 829
Johnson (Dr. Samuel), The Rambler 994
Lamb's Essays of Elia 14
(See also BIOGRAPHY and FOR YOUNG PEOPLE)
Landor's Imaginary Conversations and Poems: A selection 890
Locke's Essay on Human Understanding 984
Lynd's (Robert) Essays on Life and Literature 990
Macaulay's Essays. 2 vols. 225–6
"   Miscellaneous Essays 439
(See also HISTORY)

Machiavelli's The Prince 280
Mazzini's Duties of Man 224
Milton's Prose Writings 795
(See also POETRY)
Mitford's Our Village 927
Modern Humour 957
Montaigne's Essays. Florio's translation. 3 vols. (Vol. I T.O.P.) 440–2
Napoleon's Letters 995
Newman's University Education, etc. 723
(See also PHILOSOPHY)
Prelude to Poetry, The. Ed. by Ernest Rhys 789
Quiller-Couch's (Sir Arthur) Cambridge Lectures 974
(See also FICTION)
Rousseau's Émile, or Education 518
(See also BIOGRAPHY and PHILOSOPHY)
Ruskin's Sesame and Lilies, The King of the Golden River, etc. 219
"   Seven Lamps of Architecture 207
Sévigné's Letters 98
Spectator, The. By Addison, Steele, and others. 4 vols. 164–7
Spencer's (Herbert) Essays on Education 504
Steele's Tatler 993
Sterne's Sentimental Journey and Journal and Letters to Eliza 796
(See also FICTION)
Stevenson's Virginibus Puerisque and Familiar Studies of Men and Books 765
(See also FICTION, POETRY, and TRAVEL)
Swift's Tale of a Tub, The Battle of the Books, etc. 347
(See also BIOGRAPHY and FICTION)
Thackeray's (W. M.) The English Humorists and The Four Georges. 610
(See also FICTION)
Thoreau's Walden 281
Trench's On the Study of Words and English Past and Present 788
Tytler's Principles of Translation 168
Walton's Complete Angler 70

FICTION

Ainsworth's Old St. Paul's 522
"   Rookwood 870
"   The Tower of London 400
"   Windsor Castle 709
American Short Stories of the 19th Century 840
Austen's (Jane) Emma 24
"   "   Mansfield Park 23
"   "   Northanger Abbey 25
"   "   Pride and Prejudice 22
"   "   Sense and Sensibility 21
Balzac's (Honoré de) Wild Ass's Skin 26
"   "   Eugénie Grandet 169

Balzac's (Honoré de) Old Goriot 170
"   "   The Cat and Racket, and Other Stories 349
Barbusse's Under Fire 798
Blackmore's (R. D.) Lorna Doone 304
Borrow's Lavengro 119
"   Romany Rye 120
(See also TRAVEL)
Brontë's (Anne) Tenant of Wildfell Hall 685
"   (Charlotte) Jane Eyre 287
"   "   Shirley 288

Everyman's Library—Fiction—Continued

Brontë's (Charlotte) Villette	351
,, ,, The Professor	417
(See also BIOGRAPHY)	
,, (Emily) Wuthering Heights	243
Burney's (Fanny) Evelina	352
Butler's (Samuel) Erewhon and Erewhon Revisited	881
,, ,, The Way of All Flesh	895
Collins's (Wilkie) The Moonstone	979
,, ,, The Woman in White	464
Converse's (Florence) Long Will	328
(See also FOR YOUNG PEOPLE)	
Daudet's Tartarin	423
Defoe's Captain Singleton	74
,, Journal of the Plague Year	289
,, Moll Flanders	837
,, Robinson Crusoe	59
(See also TRAVEL)	
De Rojas's Celestina	100
CHARLES DICKENS'S WORKS:	
Barnaby Rudge	76
Bleak House	236
Christmas Books	239
Christmas Stories	414
David Copperfield	242
Dombey and Son	240
Great Expectations	234
Hard Times	292
Little Dorrit	293
Martin Chuzzlewit	241
Nicholas Nickleby	238
Old Curiosity Shop	173
Oliver Twist	233
Our Mutual Friend	294
Pickwick Papers	235
Tale of Two Cities	102
(See also BIOGRAPHY)	
Disraeli's Coningsby	535
Dostoevsky's (Fyodor) The Brothers Karamazov. 2 vols.	802-3
,, ,, Crime and Punishment	501
,, ,, The Idiot	682
,, ,, Letters from the Underworld and Other Tales	654
,, ,, Poor Folk and the Gambler	711
,, ,, The Possessed. 2 vols.	861-2
Du Maurier's (George) Trilby	863
Dumas's Black Tulip	174
,, The Count of Monte Cristo. 2 vols.	393-4
,, Marguerite de Valois	326
,, The Three Musketeers	81
Edgeworth's Castle Rackrent and The Absentee	410
Eliot's (George) Adam Bede	27
,, ,, Middlemarch. 2 vols.	854-5
Eliot's (George) Mill on the Floss	325
,, ,, Romola	231
,, ,, Silas Marner	121
English Short Stories. Anthology.	743
Fenimore Cooper's The Last of the Mohicans	79
,, ,, The Prairie	172
Fielding's Amelia. 2 vols.	852-3
,, Jonathan Wild and The Journal of a Voyage to Lisbon	877
,, Joseph Andrews	467
,, Tom Jones. 2 vols.	355-6
Flaubert's Madame Bovary	808
,, Salammbo	869
,, Sentimental Education	969
Gaskell's (Mrs.) Cranford	83
Gogol's Dead Souls	726
,, Taras Bulba and Other Tales	740
Goldsmith's Vicar of Wakefield	295
(See also POETRY)	
Goncharov's Oblomov	878
Gorky's Through Russia	741
Grossmith's (George and Weedon) Diary of a Nobody. Illustrated	963
Hawthorne's The House of the Seven Gables	176
,, The Scarlet Letter	122
,, Twice-Told Tales	531
Hugo's (Victor) Les Misérables. 2 vols.	363-4
,, ,, Notre Dame	422
,, ,, Toilers of the Sea	509
Jefferies's (Richard) After London and Amaryllis at the Fair	951
Jerome's Three Men in a Boat and Three Men on the Bummel	118
Kingsley's (Charles) Hereward the Wake	296
,, ,, Westward Ho!	20
(See also POETRY and FOR YOUNG PEOPLE)	
Loti's (Pierre) Iceland Fisherman	920
Lover's Handy Andy	178
Lytton's Last Days of Pompeii	80
Manzoni's The Betrothed	999
Marryat's Mr. Midshipman Easy	82
,, The Settlers in Canada,	370
(See also FOR YOUNG PEOPLE)	
Maupassant's Short Stories	907
Melville's (Herman) Moby Dick	179
,, ,, Typee	180
Meredith's Ordeal of Richard Feverel	916
Mickiewicz's (Adam) Pan Tadeusz	842
Mulock's John Halifax, Gentleman	123
Pater's Marius the Epicurean	903

4

Everyman's Library—Fiction—Continued

Poe's Tales of Mystery and Imagination (*See also* POETRY) 336
Quiller-Couch's (Sir Arthur) Hetty Wesley 864
(*See also* ESSAYS)
Radcliffe's (Ann) Mysteries of Udolpho. 2 vols. 865-6
Reade's (C.) The Cloister and the Hearth 29
Richardson's (Samuel) Clarissa. 4 vols. 882-5
„ „ Pamela. 2 vols. 683-4
Russian Authors, Short Stories by 758
SIR WALTER SCOTT'S WORKS:
Antiquary, The 126
Bride of Lammermoor 129
Guy Mannering 133
Heart of Midlothian, The 134
Ivanhoe. Intro. Ernest Rhys 16
Kenilworth 135
Old Mortality 137
Quentin Durward 140
Redgauntlet 141
Rob Roy 142
Talisman, The 144
Shchedrin's The Golovlyov Family 908
Shelley's (Mary) Frankenstein 616
Shorter Novels, Vol. I. Elizabethan 824
Shorter Novels, Vol. II. Jacobean and Restoration 841
Shorter Novels, Vol. III. 18th Century 856
Sienkiewicz (Henryk), Tales from 871
„ Quo Vadis? 970
Smollett's Humphry Clinker 975
„ Peregrine Pickle. 2 vols. 838-9
„ Roderick Random 790
Somerville and Ross: Experiences of an Irish R.M. 978
Sterne's Tristram Shandy 617
(*See also* ESSAYS)
Stevenson's Dr. Jekyll and Mr. Hyde, The Merry Men and Other Tales 767

Stevenson's The Master of Ballantrae and Weir of Hermiston 764
„ St Ives 904
„ Treasure Island and Kidnapped 763
(*See also* ESSAYS, POETRY, *and* TRAVEL)
Surtees's Jorrocks's Jaunts and Jollities 817
Swift's Gulliver's Travels. Unabridged Edition, with contemporary maps 60
(*See also* ESSAYS *and* BIOGRAPHY)
Thackeray's Esmond 73
„ Newcomes. 2 vols. 465-6
„ Pendennis. 2 vols. 425-6
„ Vanity Fair 298
„ Virginians. 2 vols. 507-8
(*See also* ESSAYS)
Tolstoy's Anna Karenina. 2 vols. 612-13
„ Master and Man, etc. 469
„ War and Peace. 3 vols. 525-7
Trollope's (Anthony) Barchester Towers 30
„ „ Dr. Thorne 360
„ „ Framley Parsonage 181
„ „ The Last Chronicles of Barset. 2 vols. 391-2
„ „ The Small House at Allington 361
„ „ The Warden 182
Turgenev's Fathers and Sons 742
„ Liza, or A Nest of Nobles 677
„ Smoke 988
„ Virgin Soil 528
Twain's (Mark) Tom Sawyer and Huckleberry Finn 976
Verne's (Jules) Twenty Thousand Leagues Under the Sea 319
Voltaire's Candide, etc. 936
Zola's (Émile) Germinal 897

HISTORY

Anglo-Saxon Chronicle 624
Bede's Ecclesiastical History, etc. 479
Carlyle's French Revolution. 2 vols. 31-2
(*See also* BIOGRAPHY *and* ESSAYS)
Chesterton's (Cecil) History of the United States 965
Creasy's Fifteen Decisive Battles of the World 300
Gibbon's Decline and Fall of the Roman Empire. Ed. by Oliphant Smeaton, M.A. 6 vols. 434-6, 474-6
Green's (J. R.) Short History. 2 vols. 727-8
Holinshed's Chronicle as used in Shakespeare's Plays 800

Lützow's Bohemia: An Historical Sketch. Revised edition 432
Macaulay's History of England. 4 vols. 34-7
(*See also* ESSAYS)
Maine's Ancient Law 734
Motley's Dutch Republic. 3 vols. 86-8
Paston Letters, The. 2 vols. 752-3
Prescott's Conquest of Mexico. 2 vols. 397-8
Stanley's Lectures on the Eastern Church 251
Thierry's Norman Conquest. 2 vols. 198-9
Villehardouin and De Joinville's Chronicles of the Crusades 333
Voltaire's Age of Louis XIV 780

5

Everyman's Library

ORATORY

Burke's American Speeches and Letters 340
(*See also* ESSAYS)
Demosthenes' Crown and other orations 546
Fox (Charles James): Speeches (French Revolutionary War Period) 759
Lincoln's Speeches, etc. 206

PHILOSOPHY AND THEOLOGY

A Kempis' Imitation of Christ 484
Aquinas, Thomas: Selected Writings. Ed. by Rev. Fr. D'Arcy 953
Aristotle's Ethics 547
(*See also* CLASSICAL)
Bacon's The Advancement of Learning 719
(*See also* ESSAYS)
Berkeley's (Bishop) New Theory of Vision 483
Browne's Religio Medici, etc. 92
Bunyan's Grace Abounding and Mr. Badman 815
(*See also* ROMANCE)
Chinese Philosophy in Classical Times. Trans. and ed. by E. R. Hughes 973
Descartes' (René), A Discourse on Method 570
Hindu Scriptures 944
Hobbes's Leviathan 691
Hooker's Laws of Ecclesiastical Polity. 2 vols. 201–2
Hume's Treatise of Human Nature. 2 vols. 548–9
James (William): Selected Papers on Philosophy 739
Kant's Critique of Pure Reason 909
King Edward VI. First and Second Prayer Books 448
Koran, The. Rodwell's Translation 380
Law's Serious Call to a Devout and Holy Life 91
Leibniz's Philosophical Writings 905
Locke's Two Treatises 751
Malthus on the Principle of Population. 2 vols. 692–3
Mill's (John Stuart) Utilitarianism, Liberty, Representative Government 482
More's (Sir Thomas) Utopia 461
New Testament 93
Newman's (Cardinal) Apologia pro Vita Sua 636
(*See also* ESSAYS)
Nietzsche's Thus Spake Zarathustra 892
Paine's (Tom) Rights of Man 718
Pascal's Pensées 874
Ramayana and the Mahabharata, The 403
Robinson, Philosophy of Atonement 637
Rousseau's (J. J.) The Social Contract, etc. 660
(*See also* ESSAYS *and* BIOGRAPHY)
St. Augustine's Confessions 200
„ The City of God. 2 vols. 982–3
St. Francis: The Little Flowers, and The Life of St. Francis 485
Spinoza's Ethics, etc. 481
Swedenborg's (Emanuel) The True Christian Religion 893

POETRY AND DRAMA

Anglo-Saxon Poetry. 794
Arnold's (Matthew) Poems 334
(*See also* ESSAYS)
Ballads, A Book of British 572
Beaumont and Fletcher, The Selected Plays of 506
Blake's Poems 792
(*See also* BIOGRAPHY)
Browning's Poems. (Vol. I, 1833–44) 41
„ Poems. (Vol. II, 1844–64) 42
„ Poems and Plays (Vol. IV, 1871–90) 964
Burns's Poems and Songs 94
(*See also* BIOGRAPHY)
Byron's Poetical Works. 3 vols. 486–8
(*See also* BIOGRAPHY)
Chaucer's Canterbury Tales 307
„ Troilus and Criseyde 992
Coleridge, Golden Book of 43
(*See also* ESSAYS)
Cowper (William), Poems of 872
(*See also* BIOGRAPHY)
Dante's Divine Comedy 308
Donne's Poems 867
Dryden's Poems 910
Eighteenth-Century Plays 818
English Galaxy of Shorter Poems 959
Everyman and Medieval Miracle Plays 381
Goethe's Faust 335
Golden Treasury of Longer Poems 746

Everyman's Library—Poetry and Drama—Continued

Goldsmith's Poems and Plays 415	New Golden Treasury, The 695
(*See also* FICTION)	Palgrave's Golden Treasury 96
Gray's Poems and Letters 628	Persian Poems 996
Heine: Prose and Poetry 911	Poe's (Edgar Allan) Poems and Essays 791
Ibsen's A Doll's House, The Wild Duck, and The Lady from the Sea 494	(*See also* FICTION)
	Pope (Alexander): Collected Poems 760
" Ghosts, The Warriors at Helgeland, and An Enemy of the People 552	Restoration Plays 604
	Rossetti's Poems and Translations 627
Ibsen's Peer Gynt 747	Shakespeare's Comedies 153
" The Pretenders, Pillars of Society, and Rosmersholm 659	" Historical Plays, Poems, and Sonnets 154
Ingoldsby Legends, The 185	" Tragedies 155
International Modern Plays 989	Shelley's Poetical Works. 2 vols. 257-8
Jonson's (Ben) Plays. 2 vols. 489-90	Sheridan's Plays 95
Keats's Poems 101	Silver Poets of the 16th Century 985
(*See also* BIOGRAPHY)	Spenser's Faerie Queene. 2 vols. 443-4
Kingsley's (Charles) Poems 793	" Shepherd's Calendar, etc. 879
(*See also* FICTION *and* FOR YOUNG PEOPLE)	Stevenson's Poems 768
La Fontaine's Fables 991	(*See also* ESSAYS, FICTION, *and* TRAVEL)
Langland's (William) Piers Plowman 571	Swinburne's Poems and Prose 961
Lessing's Laocoön, etc. 843	Tchekhov. Plays and Stories 941
Longfellow's Poems 382	Tennyson's Poems, 1829-92. 2 vols. 44, 626
Marlowe's Plays and Poems 383	
Milton's Poems 384	Webster and Ford. Plays 899
(*See also* ESSAYS)	Whitman's (Walt) Leaves of Grass 573
Minor Elizabethan Drama. 2 vols. 491-2	Wilde (Oscar): Plays, Prose Writings, and Poems 858
Minor Poets of the 17th Century 873	Wordsworth's Poems. 3 vols. 203, 311, 998
Molière's Comedies. 2 vols. 830-1	

REFERENCE

The following volumes in this section are now in the special edition of *Everyman's Reference Library*:

Atlas of Ancient & Classical Geography	Dictionary of Shakespeare Quotations
Dictionary of Dates	English Pronouncing Dictionary
Dictionary of Literary Biography	Everyman's English Dictionary.
Dictionary of Music	Smaller Classical Dictionary. (Revised from Sir William Smith)
Dictionary of Non-Classical Mythology	
Dictionary of Quotations and Proverbs	Thesaurus of English Words and Phrases. (Revised from Peter Roget)

ROMANCE

Aucassin and Nicolette, with other Medieval Romances 497	Kalevala. 2 vols. 259-60
Boccaccio's Decameron. (Unabridged.) 2 vols. 845-6	Mabinogion, The 97
	Malory's Le Morte d'Arthur. 2 vols. 45-6
Bunyan's Pilgrim's Progress 204	Marie de France, Lays of 557
(*See also* PHILOSOPHY)	Nibelungs, The Fall of the 312
Burnt Njal, The Story of 558	Rabelais's The Heroic Deeds of Gargantua and Pantagruel. 2 vols. 826-7
Cervantes's Don Quixote. 2 vols. 385-6	
Chrétien de Troyes: Eric and Enid, etc. 698	Sturlason: Norse King Sagas 847

Everyman's Library

SCIENCE

Boyle's The Sceptical Chymist	559
Darwin's The Origin of Species	811
(*See also* TRAVEL)	
Euclid: the Elements of	891
Faraday's (Michael) Experimental Researches in Electricity	576
Harvey's Circulation of the Blood	262
Howard's State of the Prisons	835
Marx's (Karl) Capital. 2 vols.	848–9
Owen's A New View of Society, etc.	799
Pearson's (Karl) The Grammar of Science	939
Ricardo's Principles of Political Economy and Taxation	590
Smith's (Adam) The Wealth of Nations. 2 vols.	412–13
White's Selborne. New edition	48
Wollstonecraft (Mary), The Rights of Woman, with John Stuart Mill's The Subjection of Women	825

TRAVEL AND TOPOGRAPHY

A Book of the 'Bounty'	950
Borrow's (George) The Bible in Spain	151
" " Wild Wales	49
(*See also* FICTION)	
Boswell's Tour to the Hebrides with Dr. Johnson	387
(*See also* BIOGRAPHY)	
Calderón de la Barca's Life in Mexico	664
Cobbett's Rural Rides. 2 vols.	638–9
Cook's Voyages of Discovery	99
Crèvecœur's (H. St. John) Letters from an American Farmer	640
Darwin's Voyage of the 'Beagle'	104
(*See also* SCIENCE)	
Defoe's Tour through England and Wales. 2 vols.	820–1
(*See also* FICTION)	
Kinglake's Eothen	337
Lane's Modern Egyptians	315
Park's Travels	208
Polo's (Marco) Travels	306
Portuguese Voyages, 1498–1663	986
Stevenson's An Inland Voyage, Travels with a Donkey, and Silverado Squatters	766
(*See also* ESSAYS, FICTION, *and* POETRY)	
Stow's Survey of London	589
Wakefield's Letter from Sydney, etc.	828
Waterton's Wanderings in South America	772

FOR YOUNG PEOPLE

Aesop's and Other Fables	657
Alcott's Little Men	512
" Little Women & Good Wives	248
Andersen's Fairy Tales. Illustrated by the Brothers Robinson	4
Ballantyne's Coral Island	245
" Martin Rattler	246
Browne's (Frances) Granny's Wonderful Chair	112
Bulfinch's The Age of Fable	472
Carroll's Alice in Wonderland, Through the Looking-Glass, etc. Illustrated by the Author	836
Collodi's Pinocchio: the Story of a Puppet	538
Converse's (Florence) The House of Prayer	923
(*See also* FICTION)	
Cox's Tales of Ancient Greece	721
Ewing's Jackanapes, etc.	731
Fairy Gold	157
Gatty's Parables from Nature	158
Grimms' Fairy Tales. Illustrated by R. Anning Bell	56
Howard's Rattlin the Reefer	857
Hughes's Tom Brown's Schooldays. Illustrated by T. Robinson	58
Jefferies's (Richard) Bevis, the Story of a Boy	850
(*See also* FICTION)	
Kingsley's Water Babies and Glaucus	277
(*See also* POETRY *and* FICTION)	
Lamb's Tales from Shakespeare. Illustrated by A. Rackham	8
(*See also* BIOGRAPHY *and* ESSAYS)	
Lear: A Book of Nonsense	806
Marryat's Masterman Ready	160
(*See also* FICTION)	
Martineau's Feats on the Fjord	429
Mother Goose's Nursery Rhymes. Illustrated	473
Sewell's (Anna) Black Beauty. Illustrated by Lucy Kemp-Welch	748
Spyri's (Johanna) Heidi	431
Stowe's Uncle Tom's Cabin	371
Wyss's Swiss Family Robinson. Illustrated by Charles Folkard	430